AN INDIAN ATTACHMENT

Sarah Lloyd

WILLIAM MORROW AND COMPANY, INC.
NEW YORK

For Jungli, who couldn't see the point

'What are you writing now?'
'About our life in this hut.'
'What does that bit say then?' (pointing)
'It describes how you took me to see the snake
  in front of Sitaram's shop.'
'Who'd be interested in that?'
'Some people might.'
'Well they'd be off their heads. I've told you before,
  you're just messing up good paper.'

Acknowledgements

I would like to thank my editor Carol O'Brien and my agent Hilary Rubinstein for all their advice and encouragement, and Om Sharma for checking the manuscript.

Contents

Glossary
Prelude   1

PART 1: VILLAGE

1 Arrival   7
2 Dwelling   16
3 Outsider   31
4 Inheritance   43
5 Inheritors   51
6 Nihang   62
7 Outings   73
8 Traditions   81
9 Prisoner   89
10 Travellers   98

Interlude   107

PART 2: DEHRA

1 Expulsion   109
2 Householders   118
3 Neighbours   128
4 Dehra   144
5 Langar   155
6 Pilgrimage   166
7 Wilderness   173
8 Enterprise   181
9 Heat   187
10 Invaders   195
11 Mama   204
12 Removal   214
13 Rains   224
14 Saint   233

Afterword   243

Glossary

Note: The English spelling is a transliteration of the Panjabi (hence, for instance, Panjab is spelt with an 'a'). Panjabi words are not italicized unless they could be confused with an English word of the same spelling. 'Th' is aspirated.

acacia	*A. nilotica* (Panjabi: kikar)
Akhandpath	two-day continuous reading of the *Granth*
allopathic	Western system of medicine
ayurvedic	Indian system of medicine
balta	shallow iron dish employed in carrying earth or rocks on the head
banyan	*Ficus bengalensis*
bhang	cannabis
charpoy	Indian rope bed with wooden frame
chola	tunic worn by Nihangs
dacoit	robber or bandit
dal	curried lentils
dari	woven cotton floor mat
darshan	sight of a holy place or person
dehra	strictly speaking, gurdwara or temple. In the context of this book the term is also used to convey the entire complex of buildings supporting the gurdwara
dhoti	long piece of white cotton ingeniously looped and tied to make a species of baggy trousers
dub	coarse unpalatable grass
dudh wallah	milkman
dupatta	woman's long headscarf or veil
Granth	Guru Granth Sahib or Adi Granth, holy book of the Sikhs
granthi	reader and caretaker of the Sikh holy book in a gurdwara
gurdwara	Sikh temple
hakim	ayurvedic doctor
jaggery	unrefined lump sugar

Jat	landowning caste in Panjab; highest Sikh caste
Jhai (Ji)	name used to address or refer to an older unrelated Hindu woman
kaccha	rustic, indigenous
kachera	long bloomers worn by baptized Sikhs
khes	thick cotton hand-woven sheet
Khalsa	Sikh military brotherhood
khir	sweet rice pudding
kirtan	Sikh hymns
kusra	hermaphrodite, eunuch or transvestite
langar	free kitchen started by the Sikh Gurus
lungi	length of cotton tied round the waist and reaching the ground
Mazbi	person of low caste who has embraced Sikhism
mala	rosary
Mama	mother's brother
mantra	word or words repeated, to bring peace, protection and spiritual power
Mataji	mother (respectful)
mesquite	*Prosopis juliflora* (Panjabi: pahari kikar)
Mul Mantra	Guru's description of God
Nihang	member of the Guru's army
neem	*Azadirachta indica*
pakka	properly made; westernized
pakoras	deep-fried chickpea flour fritters
pandit	Brahmin priest
path	excerpts from the *Granth*
pathi	paid reader of the *Granth*
Persian lilac	*Melia azedarach* (Panjabi: traig)
pipal	*Ficus religiosa*
Pitaji	father (respectful)
prasad	sacred food offered to God and distributed among the congregation
ragi	gurdwara musician
raita	raw or parboiled vegetables in spiced yoghurt
sabzi	raw or curried vegetables
sadhu	Hindu ascetic
salvar-kamiz	Panjabi woman's tunic and baggy trousers (the salvar are the trousers)

sangat	congregation (also means religious gathering)
sat	male gathering place
Satnam	God's name is true
Sat Sri Akal	Sikh greeting (lit. True Lord God, or God is Truth)
seva	voluntary service for the benefit of the community
sharik	rivals in a feud
shisham	Indian rosewood or *Dalbergia sissoo* (Panjabi: tahli)
tabla	small drum
thatch grass	*Saccharum bengalense* (Panjabi: munj)
tonga	pony trap
UP	Uttar Pradesh
Waheguru!	Great Guru! (i.e. God); the communal Sikh mantra

AN INDIAN ATTACHMENT

Prelude

HE SAT CROSS-LEGGED on a brown blanket. It was a powerful face that instantly registered: high forehead, long nose, fine mouth and skin the colour of almonds; but it was a face that suggested sadness. On his head he wore a high dome of blue turbans. Over his aquamarine tunic a length of orange fabric was tied around his waist, and a second piece hung over his left shoulder. In front of him lay a sword.

I had been in a train for three days, crossing northern India from its western extremity in Gujerat to Calcutta in the east. The landscape had been unexciting, and so had the company. I was stuck in a bogieful of tedious people all grumbling about how tedious everyone else was; one little girl had found me so tedious (sitting reading a history of the Sikhs all the way) that she had given me a sharp slap to wake me up. I gave her one back and her father laughed, whereupon we all fell back into collective boredom until the lush watery landscape of Bengal announced the proximity of Calcutta.

It was wonderful to be out of the train and back in the familiar chaos and electric energy of the bazaar street life. It was nice to be welcomed by big smiles from people who knew me at the gurdwara.[1] And there was Jungli sitting on his blanket, with the long black beard of the tenth Sikh Guru and the eyes of Buddha, sweeping up at the corners.

Jungli was a Nihang, a self-elected member of an informal religious army maintained by the Sikhs for the defence of their faith. The clothes he wore, the code he followed and the ideals he lived by had survived unaltered the three hundred years of their existence.

At that time I was going through a being-charitable-to-Nihangs phase. Many were poor and some were homeless; as far as I could tell they were dependent on the generosity of others. They were prepared to forfeit their lives in defending their faith, I thought, yet few ordinary Sikhs showed them either respect or kindness. I bought Jungli milk sweets and fruit.

In the morning, without a word, he handed me a shallow iron

---

[1] Sikh temple

bowl. It was one of the most perfect things I had ever seen. I took it and drank: the tea was grey; it tasted of iron and woodsmoke.

Gurdwaras are open to people of all faiths. For more than four centuries they have offered hospitality free of charge, providing basic sleeping and washing facilities and two simple meals a day. Arriving on the night mail from Assam two months previously, this Calcutta gurdwara had been the first I ever stayed in. I had set off across Howrah Bridge and into the bazaar streets, and every now and then I asked someone, 'Where's the gurdwara?'

Blank look. No English.

'Where's the gurdwara?'

'Excuse me. I am not understanding your English.'

'But it's an Indian word! Gurdwara. Sikh temple.'

'Oh you mean gurdwara! No gurdwara is here.'

Then again, 'Where's the gurdwara?'

'You go straight. Then ask.'

'Where's the gurdwara?'

'It's my idea there's one near Victoria Memorial, next to hospital.'

But other people seemed to think there was one in the bazaar somewhere. I spotted a Sikh taxi driver. He was bound to know.

'Where's the gurdwara?'

Shrug. Not religious. Not interested.

Gradually I tracked it down and the answers became more optimistic: 'Straight on. This side.' But I still missed it, for the street frontage was just a plain white doorway in the crowded bazaar, among shops, stalls and pavement hawkers; deceivingly, for it was in fact a large eight-storey building. I learnt to recognize the doorway afterwards by means of a colossal Gwalior Suiting advertisement on the opposite side of the road. Those Gwalior Suiting signs were all over India, I discovered later; everywhere, that was, except Gwalior, where the rage was something else.

Inside the doorway stood a man in a blue turban holding a long spear. 'Gurdwara?' I asked, and he pointed to a staircase. On the first floor was a big stark room that I took to be the place of worship, and above it was a gallery. On the third floor I found an office, locked. I sat down and waited.

'Have you any rooms?' I asked when a lean man, also in a blue turban, materialized.

No English, but from what I could gather no rooms either.

I sat down again. I had spent all morning looking for this gurdwara. But then a little girl appeared and beckoned to me, and I followed her up three more flights of stairs, past a school and an eating hall, on to the sixth floor.

It was just what I had hoped for, a large communal hall with windows all round and people's washing hanging on strings in front of them. The floor was covered in Panjabi daris.[2] And that was all. Everyone chose a pitch and parked himself in it, his luggage against the wall. There were men sprawled across the daris chatting in groups, while others snored on their bedding or tied their turbans. In the corner was what seemed to be a semi-permanent camp of a young Bengali mother and her children; they were cooking lunch.

As evening fell more and more people turned up. They were still turning up at ten and eleven at night. Most of them were business men with attaché cases (which they used as pillows) coming to the city to buy parts or meet a client. They lay down as they were, fully dressed, having cleared the dust from the patch of dari they fancied by swatting it with their towel. The turban acted as padding against the hard edges of their cases; they placed their shoes neatly beside their feet.

The lights stayed on all night, full on, and at two or three in the morning the first contingent, the most devout, began to get up. They shuffled across the hall to the washing cubicles in the corner (from which loud splashing and singing and gurgling noises were originating) and returned chattering their teeth to start morning prayer. Their mumbling and chanting was punctuated by the snores and basal wind of the business men and accompanied by the next shift in the bathroom. What I had to learn was that Indians could sleep at any hour of day or night and that darkness had no particular significance for them.

Calcutta was, and still is, my favourite Indian city. Every day I wandered along the banks of the river and watched the sun set over Howrah Station. Every day I returned to the gurdwara along the same dark back streets, where every other doorway revealed a small Hindu shrine fairylit by strings of naked bulbs, the deity all but submerged beneath garlands of marigolds and the blue haze of incense. Every day I carried back sweetmeats for Jungli and his friends, Inderjit and Bir.

It was January and cold. Jungli got up at four every morning, took his bath and came back shivering, sat wrapped in his blanket and recited prayers till six. I, meanwhile, would be reading Tagore, or

---

[2] dari or dhurrie: woven cotton floor mat

standing on the roof eight stories above the Mahatma Gandhi Road watching herds of goats clattering down its dark ravine past the sheeted street sleepers towards the Ganges. After tea at six we helped prepare the food for the morning meal, sitting in a circle on the daris, peeling onions, shelling ginger and cutting up potatoes, conversing in signs and nursery school Hindi and laughing at our misunderstandings.

Jungli, Inderjit and Bir had travelled fifteen hundred miles to Calcutta from Amritsar in Panjab, on the tail of Bir's runaway brother; he had escaped with money belonging to his joint family, and was making for the fast life in Bangkok. Several times each day they went to his hotel by Howrah Station and tried to persuade him to return to his home and Inderjit's sister, his wife. But Bir's brother had other ideas.

One morning while we were peeling the vegetables, I noticed Inderjit take something from his pocket, pull off small pieces and hand them round. He gave a lump to me and I swallowed it like everyone else, wondering what it could be but determined to find out. Getting off a tram in Chowringee an hour later my head began to reel, so I entered a mosque and lay down on the floor.

'A white women, an infidel, lying on the floor of the holy mosque! Get up! Get out!'

An infidel intoxicated by opium, no less.

Back in the gurdwara, the ceiling doing strange things above my head, Jungli fed me with pieces of orange.

Our unspoken attachment deepened. I was moved by his tenderness, his simplicity and his beautiful eyes. Beauty is a great robber of my common sense. I tried not to be affected by it; tried to avoid him. I knew it to be outside the bounds of the religion he followed. And I was a traveller.

Another thing was that hair.

Having fought all my life against my own hair being cut, I was sympathetic towards the no-cutting tradition of the Sikhs. And I agreed with them when, in answer to the provocative Hindu/Muslim, 'Why don't you cut your hair?' they replied, 'The question is not why don't we cut our hair, but why do you cut yours?' It was partly because of their long hair that Hindus and Muslims found Sikhs objectionable: the fact that they had to look different. They resented their proud bearing (only they referred to it as arrogance); they disliked their straightforwardness, their determination and their refusal to be put down. That, to them, was aggression.

The Sikhs' hair didn't like being imprisoned in a turban all its life, let out only for washing and daily grooming. Most men didn't have that much of it, but occasionally I had seen a man with really long thick hair. I had come across one several weeks previously, in a crowd of Hindus on the steps of the bathing ghats in Benares. Pilgrims were swarming over the ghats, dunking themselves in the holy Ganges, thumping wet saris on the stones and bounding after runaway children. In their midst sat a Sikh, alone and serene, slowly and deliberately combing an avalanche of black hair. The Hindus wore white and red and pink and green but the Sikh wore black: black trousers, black shirt. He was a Daramaraj, a god of Death, among the gaily chattering living. I was transfixed. I could no more avert my eyes than the enchanted sailors could cease gazing at the mermaid on the rock.

He finished combing his hair and melted, an unreal shadow, into the multitude. I wondered how I was ever going to live without him.

Now again, the same thing.

Every morning after the communal tea, Jungli placed a small mirror on the blanket in front of him and combed his hair. It took him half an hour. I watched surreptitiously as he unwound the five lengths of turban material obligatory to a Nihang, fearing that I was trespassing on some secret and intimate act. He leant forward and loosened his hair, which fell in a torrent to the floor. There was red in its black where it strayed loose as he combed it, and blue in its sheen when it lay in a mass and caught the light. I pretended to read a book. He rubbed it with coconut oil, combed it again in long slow strokes from the back of his neck, twisted it into a rope and tied it in a double knot on top of his head. He took each piece of turban material, stretched it taut along a diagonal axis and rolled the fabric towards the centre. Then, securing the front end between his teeth and jerking his head like a bird so he could see the relevant part in the mirror, he wound it round his head, smoothly and symmetrically, coiling the free end like a slack python after each revolution.

On my fifth day in Calcutta, Jungli, Inderjit and Bir took me sightseeing. We took the tram through Calcutta to Kalighat and walked through narrow dirty lanes to Kali Mandir, a big Hindu temple devoted to the goddess Kali, where I noticed a lot of goats and blood on the floor and wanted to get out. But the others were looking on with interest. When I heard the chop of an axe and the thud of a goat's head hitting the ground, I left without them.

'Why do Hindus sanctify one animal and cut off the head of another?' I tried to ask them when they caught up with me, but my Hindi wasn't up to it and they didn't understand. I spoke no Panjabi and Jungli not a word of English.

'Never mind,' was the gist of what they said when they saw that for some reason I hadn't appreciated the goats. 'We'll go and see something else.'

We went on down the road and up the drive of a very ugly modern building. It looked like a crematorium. 'What's this?' I asked. I understood two words of the answer: 'Electric programme.' It *was* a crematorium.

Hindus and Sikhs burned their dead on big open bonfires: crematoria were a recent innovation in India and not wholly approved of, appearing in the cities as a result of the scarcity of firewood. We were lucky, they said, there was a death ceremony in progress. A decrepit corpse scantily covered with a sheet was being washed with ghee and sprinkled with sandalwood by the snivelling next-of-kin, whose suffering was much worse than the sight of the body. Jungli and Bir had seen crematoria before and remained in the background, but Inderjit and I stood in the front row among the relatives and watched with a morbid fascination.

They had a queer notion of sightseeing, those three.

At the end of a week it was time to leave; I had already stayed too long. Jungli, Inderjit and Bir were returning, defeated, to Amritsar, and I was catching a train to Bangladesh. We went down into the street and headed for the hotel to make a final assault on Bir's recalcitrant brother. Inderjit and Bir walked ahead. In the middle of the crowded Howrah Bridge, trams squealing, structure creaking, cartmasters cursing, rickshaw wallahs shouting, engines stalling, beggars wailing, horns hooting, wheels rattling, feet thundering, Jungli said, 'I love you.'

I looked at him. I didn't know he knew any English. The words sounded unreal. Then he was swallowed up in the crowd.

He came with me next morning to Sealdah Station.

'When are you coming to Amritsar?' he asked again and again as we waited for my train. He had plenty of time in which to do so as we were on the wrong platform.

'In about a month,' I hazarded. I don't follow an itinerary when I'm travelling, and I find that sort of question hard to answer. I told him to love God and forget about me, for just as I was leaving Calcutta I would also leave Amritsar. God, on the other hand, wasn't going anywhere.

When my train eventually left, we didn't even touch hands. I watched him standing on the disappearing platform, a lone figure in blue holding a sword, diminished by the great Victorian canopy of Sealdah Station. Two hours later I was in Bangladesh.

PART 1: VILLAGE

1

Arrival

IN THE MIDDLE OF MARCH I came to Amritsar. I was up and ready to get off the train an hour before it arrived at 5 a.m., and then, instead of waiting for the dawn as I usually did, I took a rickshaw through the dark sleeping streets to the Golden Temple. I took off my shoes and descended the steps. The temple gleamed in the centre of a tank of dark water. I walked round and round while the dawn rose pink over the rooftops; there was an overwhelming sense of peace.

Over the next two days I absorbed the rhythms of the Golden Temple, and slept on the roof of a house nearby. The religious calm of early morning gave way to a colourful throng of Sikh humanity, of untidy sprawls of itinerant Nihangs, of peasant pilgrims, of illustrious city folk on fashionable parade and gaggles of glittery village girls in Sunday plumage. The Golden Temple was an arena and people came, like the Regency promenaders, to be seen and admired. Its black and white marble walkway and cool perimeter arcade, its golden fairytale reflections in the brown-green water and its sense of spaciousness lent them a momentary illusion of elegance and grandeur.

Among the promenaders were the everyday devoted, who circled the perimeter of the tank and bathed in its healing waters, who caressed the dust from other pilgrims' feet and anointed their foreheads with its spiritual balm, who bowed at the entrance of the gold-domed sanctuary and offered obeisance before the holy *Granth*.[1] They sat and listened to their Gurus' hymns, sung to the music of ancient ragas, their faces tranquil and uplifted. They had had darshan[2] of the most sacred temple of the Sikhs.

Suddenly I woke up. I had to find Jungli. Never mind what time it was – it was mid-afternoon and no time to be setting off in search of a

[1] holy book of the Sikhs
[2] sight of a holy place or person

vague and remote address written in a childish hand on a scrap of
torn paper:

> Nam Pritam Singh
> Father Nam Beant Singh
> Amarkot
> District Amritsar

Didn't he say there were ten thousand people living in his village?
Doubtless all with the surname of Singh.

Rattling out of Amritsar in a hot tin bus I wondered idly, though
neither very seriously nor for very long, about the consequences of
my actions. I had no particular plans. My life has always been like
that, the future a glorious blank full of space and possibility, the
forseeable future lasting for about the next fortnight. Work and
places and relationships have happened in finite blocks of time,
beginning and ending cleanly and more or less isolated from each
other. The penultimate chunk of life had consisted of teaching
part-time in three London colleges, sitting on half a dozen commit-
tees, writing the editorial of my professional journal, redesigning
part of a large country park and fighting the local council in a public
inquiry; hard work, good fun, but no time at all to reflect. Travelling
to Jungli's village my present began and ended with the company of
dishevelled Sikhs in the bus and the flat green landscape of unripe
wheat, spindly trees and low mud houses lurching past the windows;
aeons away in space and reality from the old life in London. My
future held Pakistan – possibly – and Kashmir – probably – and a
place miles and days from anywhere, high and remote in the mountains, called Leh. Jungli didn't come into it.

I got off at a small town built around a crossroads and caught a
tonga[3] for the final nine miles. Half a dozen oldish men in white
homespun lungis[4] and turbans clambered in beside me; one man had
a tape recorder and was playing Sikh hymns. Clopping slowly
through the rich green countryside to the accompaniment of these
ancient and solemn ragas, a honey-coloured sun bulging on the
horizon, I was infected by a wave of euphoria, a subconscious
recognition that the elements that made up our journey encapsulated
all I had imagined about the Indian plains.

Four years later I remembered. Something stirred the memory that
had prompted my euphoria, and at last I understood what it was that
had made me travel to India. An image; an incomplete sequence
from a documentary film. The image of a tall figure in white, walking

[3] pony trap
[4] length of cotton tied round the waist and reaching the ground

along a road. A sadhu[5] maybe; a man with unfulfilled eyes. A straight country road in a flat green landscape. Feet disturbing the dust. Music suggesting melancholy; no destination. I had come to India to capture that image.

And here was India; this was India! And the village, when I arrived an hour later, was India too; my first impression of rural life, the real India, the one I had come to find. But I had no eyes for it yet; at that moment it was Jungli I wanted to see.

He wasn't there. His family was at home: Mataji, his mother and Pitaji, his father, and a whole lot of other people who collected from the neighbouring houses. Where was he? Maybe at Inderjit's house on the far side of Amritsar, they told me (an English speaker fetched from the bottom of the alley translated). It's not a place where you should go. Stay the night and Pitaji will look for him in the morning.

Mataji lit a fire and brewed tea. I was surrounded by people. All I knew was I had to find Jungli.

The sun had set and the last bus had gone. You'll have to stay, they said.

I couldn't stay. I returned to the road and flagged down the first thing that came along, which happened to be a scooter; I rode off side-saddle with my bag between my teeth, clutching the spare wheel with both hands. My behaviour would not have been condoned and I felt rather ungracious.

At the crossroads I hitched a lorry into Amritsar and, still too impatient to wait for buses, took a rickshaw to the station where I searched for another to take me to where Inderjit lived in a small gurdwara out in the fields. It was dark by now and none of the rickshaw wallahs were showing any enthusiasm. They didn't know where it was, they said, and anyway it was dangerous out there. It was a long way on unlit roads and we might be attacked. The rickshaw wallah who finally took me insisted on bringing his mate in an empty rickshaw to chaperone him, and I had to pay them both, a once and only extravagance.

Miles we went along pitch black tree-lined roads, and it got late. They really were scared. It seemed crazy to go on as everyone would have gone to bed, but I was enjoying myself. We turned off across the fields on a rutted cart track and I got off and walked. No sign of any lights. Quite mad. But at last a tiny gurdwara shaped like a tower appeared in some trees. A group of people were sitting round a fire and one of them came up to us, a tall young man in an orange tunic with a handsome face and loose beard. 'Sarah Lloyd?' he enquired. So I knew it would be all right.

[5] Hindu ascetic

The man who had greeted me was Inderjit's brother. Neither Jungli, Inderjit nor Bir was there. I couldn't make out where they were, but I had done all I could and it was time I gave in. We sat in the firelight drinking hot milk. I felt I had come home.

But I couldn't sleep. The room I was allocated, shared with Inderjit's wife and sister, was brightly lit and stank of vermin. There were hordes of mosquitoes and my bedding was damp. Rats chased each other along the shelves, clattering beakers and knocking down plates. I went outside and watched the dawn, a smudge of orange over the flat misty fields framed by the grove of shisham[6] trees. In the still dark gurdwara Inderjit's brother was reciting morning prayers, half singing, half speaking, his voice echoing in an unearthly way against the empty walls. The sound belonged to limitless air and space, weightless and pure.

Bir came as the sun rose and led me over the fields to meet his family, a family of brothers and more brothers and their countless wives and children, in a compound shared by cows and hens and buffaloes and straw stacks. Everyone was milking or cooking or building mud walls. Beyond were fields of wheat and clover.

Then came Inderjit, flying over the plain on a bicycle, fresh (as I found out later) from a whorehouse in Amritsar. He and Bir swept me off on a day-long tour of the city's gurdwaras and spare parts workshops. All very enlightening, but where was Jungli? I returned to the house on whose roof I had been staying, telling Inderjit I would come back tomorrow. Maybe someone would have found him by then.

Next day I was taken out to lunch by a tabla[7] player who was doing a comparative study of Christianity and Sikhism. I went, I thought, in order to discuss it with him. But he didn't want to talk about that, oh no; he wanted me to marry him, all the usual old rubbish. I fled to the Golden Temple and was walking round the tank when suddenly Jungli was beside me, showering me with words, half of which I didn't understand. 'Where have you been all this time? I've been searching for you for two days. Two days! I went to the village then back to Amritsar, out to Inderjit's, back to Amritsar, round all the gurdwaras, back to Inderjit's, back to Amritsar, out to the village again and back to Amritsar. Two days I've been looking! Where have you been?' I understood that much.

I smiled. I rather liked the way he didn't bother to greet me after seven weeks. And it was good to see him.

[6] Indian rosewood or *Dalbergia sissoo*, a tall, elm-like tree
[7] small drum

The rest of the day was taken up drinking cups of tea, fetching my luggage and sitting around in the house among the textile mills off the GT[8] Road in which Jungli had been staying: a village-style house with an earth yard and sheds in opposite diagonal corners. Two sisters slept in one shed, their brother, Jungli and I in the other. Half our shed was open to the sky, and an uncovered drain ran along one wall.

In the morning Jungli took me on a tour. I had learnt a few words of Panjabi, but not enough to grasp where we were going. Yet in spite of our lack of words we seemed to talk all day. Language was never a problem: without understanding, we communicated.

We caught a bus out of Amritsar and set off on foot down scented green lanes. The narrow grassy verges and irrigation bunds were sprinkled with flowers, a Flemish tapestry foreground of English wild flowers: mallow, melilot, spurry and nipplewort, knotweed and thistle, sow thistle and fat hen, clovers and vetch and celery-leaved buttercup. And the air was full of birds: larks and rollers, koels and bee-eaters and flocks of migrant rosy pastors. I couldn't believe it, all this freshness and beauty and calm after weeks of crowds and dust and illness and fighting to get on trains. There was nothing I should have enjoyed more. We hitched rides on tractors, bathed in the sacred tanks of the gurdwaras we visited and sat in gardens of cornflowers and marigolds. The holy blues and oranges of the Sikhs; the colours of Jungli's clothes.

The last gurdwara was near Jungli's village. I was awake this time, taking in my surroundings objectively and looking where I was going.

The country through which we passed on our way to the village reminded me of some of the flatter parts of southern England, where a few hedgerow trees have survived but the hedges themselves have disappeared. It was a landscape devoid of refuge, open to the horizon, changing only in detail and uncluttered by landmarks. We passed mud-built villages, set back from the road and presenting low blank walls to the passing traffic, as wanting in prospect as the fields were in refuge. Coming in to Delhi several months previously I had flown over a landscape like this: its villages, almost circular, crusty like lichens on the bark of a smooth tree, were scattered regularly across a cream and green patchwork of fields. It was as if a chessboard had been hit with a mallet and then slightly shaken up, misplacing corners and irregular pieces of the cream and green squares.

[8] Grand Trunk, locally referred to as GT

Then in the distance I recognized the outline of Jungli's village. Built tightly clustered on a small hillock formed by successive cycles of building, falling into ruins and rebuilding on the rubble of the old village, it looked out over the flat farmland on which the existence of most of its inhabitants clearly still depended. From a distance, and especially with the rising or setting sun behind it – as we now saw it – it resembled a cubist painting, or a fortress made up of blocks. The effect was accentuated by the abrupt cessation of fields and by the tight arrangement of two- and three-storey fired brick houses on the top of the hummock, and one-storey mud ones in a flat expanding fringe around the edge. Few trees broke the horizon of stepped rooftops, and there was no indication of the network of alleys linking the small semi-communal spaces within.

We alighted from our tonga on the far side of the village (the road swept round it, separated from it by a strip of cultivation) beside a large expanse of barren land. Several rough tracks led into and

PLAN OF VILLAGE

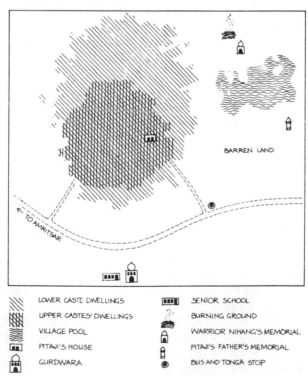

BARREN LAND

← TO AMRITSAR

LOWER CASTE DWELLINGS		SENIOR SCHOOL	
UPPER CASTES' DWELLINGS		BURNING GROUND	
VILLAGE POOL		WARRIOR NIHANG'S MEMORIAL	
PITAJI'S HOUSE		PITAJI'S FATHER'S MEMORIAL	
GURDWARA		BUS AND TONGA STOP	

around the perimeter of the village, supporting a tributary system of narrow alleys bounded by high mud walls. They zigzagged between the adjoining house compounds and came to a dead end towards the centre of the village, its physical and social watershed. Here lived the upper castes, the land-owning Jats, and, a bit sheepishly, I followed Jungli into one of these compounds through the open door.

Mataji was expecting us. She handed me a block of hard yellow soap and I washed our clothes under the hand pump in the yard in the last light of day. Jungli showed me how to hold the end of the garment in my left hand, pump up water and spread on soap with my right, and then churn it loosely beneath both hands and thump out the dirt with a flat-sided stick. By the time I had finished it was dark. Mataji was blowing on the hearth, poking in sticks[9] and chunks of dried dung in preparation for the evening meal. I sat on a plank and watched her, sniffing the frying spices and enjoying the practised economy of her movements.

Mataji was small and round. Her eyes turned up at the corners like Jungli's, only they weren't so good on her, and her long thick grey hair was coiled in a fat bun at the back of her head. Squatting on a board in her cooking enclosure, her knees wide apart and her belly dangling in the space between them, everything she needed was within her reach. Old jars and rusty tins containing ghee, salt, spices, sugar and tea stood in individual rounded recesses in the low mud wall behind her. A heavy stone mortar and wooden pestle leant in a corner. Spread out in front of her were onions, green ginger and thirty or forty cloves of garlic, a pan of water, a mound of dough, a circular board and a rolling pin. Sticks and dried dung were stacked on the far side of the hearth.

Mataji was a good cook, I was to discover; better than most. She had a natural flair for balancing flavours and didn't skimp on ingredients. Not for Mataji the substitution of hot red chillies for the mild aromatic blend of cumin, coriander, pepper and black cardamon, dried on sacks and ground in the mortar, with which she flavoured the eggs and dal[10] – the best dal I had ever tasted – that we had that night.

We ate by the light of a paraffin lamp and slept in a room at the top of the yard. Jungli had said that was where we would sleep, and no-one had protested. He slept on one side of the room, I on the other; Mataji and Pitaji slept in the yard. Mosquitoes hummed,

[9] the dried stalks of *Sesbania sesban*, grown as an annual crop
[10] curried lentils

leaves rustled in the breeze and moonbeams shone through the open door.

I cannot remember coming to Jungli's house as a stranger. Maybe it was because I was never treated as one, was presumed to be accustomed to village ways. Maybe it had to do with being left to fill my own time, wonderful after the fuss and flap and everyone-on-their-toes-digging-out-wedding-albums-and-trying-to-impress-the-foreigner syndrome that I was used to in urban middle-class India. Maybe it was because I was familiar with third world peasant architecture from staying in similar houses in other continents. And maybe it was because the style of building in this part of India was so human, so homely, so Steineresque, with hardly a straight line and never a sharp angle to impair the imperfection of the mud walls. And maybe it had something to do with being Jungli's house, and my assumption that I had something to do with Jungli. And maybe – and most probably – it was due to the conditions of my arrival, the first shambolic arrival when I couldn't see the house for people, didn't stay long enough to look and was intent on finding Jungli, and the second when it was too dark to see.

So on that third morning, waking in a house I had never seen, I was no stranger. I felt at home and at peace with the world. Jungli and I went out in the dawn for a long walk across the pale dewy fields, balancing on the narrow earth bunds that divided the cultivation plots. People were already at work, guiding their ploughs and cursing their bullocks and squatting on clod-crushing beams, that broke the soil into a fine tilth. Everything was so perfect, the clear early morning, the smell of damp wheat, the flowers in the verges and the sky flecked with birds: blue birds, green birds, black birds, white birds, bulbuls, hoopoes, so many kinds of birds. And we were happy in all this newness, in a simple, unconstrained, uncompromised way we never were to feel again.

Respectful of Indian traditions, I was careful to avoid any physical contact with Jungli and did nothing to attract it. At the same time there was something proprietorial about our friendship, even in those first few days, that belonged to relationships of much longer standing. The force of Jungli's feelings made subtle and invisible demands on me. He seemed to have no doubt but that they were returned in like strength, as if love automatically created an equal response in the object of its attention. I was very much attracted by Jungli, but whereas his emotions were blind and unlimited, my feelings for him could be rationalized. And they were finite. I was attracted to Jungli because he seemed different from anyone I had ever known. I was intrigued by the culture he had inherited, and the movement of Nihangs to which he belonged. I was interested in the Sikhs and their faith. I was touched by Jungli's tenderness, his simplicity, his religious devotion, his directness and the sadness in his eyes. These things were all I knew about him. And at the time they were enough; I didn't analyse what was happening to me, I just let it happen.

After a week of being together twenty-four hours a day, the relationship did become physical. It was inevitable. I had tried to prevent it for, quite apart from anything else, Jungli's religion prohibited sex outside marriage. 'You've been baptized,' I reminded him in my faltering, ungrammatical Panjabi. 'It won't do.' I respected the Sikh faith and its moral code. Women were supposed to be treated as sisters.

'Oh one or two won't matter,' he replied offhandedly.

His lightheartedness was deceptive. When he touched my arm, awkwardly, woodenly, as if I were a goddess and above that sort of thing, I realized that this was the first time in his life. I was thirty-one and so, near enough, was he.

2

Dwelling

THE FIRST HINT of homecoming had taken place on my departure at Heathrow Airport, where I had stepped into a planeful of Indians. The effect was instant: I smiled and relaxed. Such a thing could never have happened to me in English society: on the contrary I can go into a pub, or a restaurant, or a supermarket, or even a university and feel an overwhelming desolation and alienation.

A handful of films had been my introduction to India. I knew no Indians; I had read nothing. To arrive in a country with the minimum of preconceived notions is to explore it through the medium of one's own experience.

It was not pure accident that I came to live in a Sikh community. Within a few days of landing in India I had felt drawn towards the Sikhs, and wherever I was it was their company I sought and whenever in trouble it was they who bailed me out. They rarely let me down. They were manly in a country where men lean towards effeminacy, they were proud and dignified, fearless and determined, passionate and warm-hearted, adventurous and enterprising, self-reliant and adaptable: everything I liked and admired and wanted to be. Jungli, to a greater or lesser extent, was all of this, an archetypal Sikh. I came to know him inside out, his character, his moods, his thoughts; he was the soul of my India.

Jungli wasn't his real name. Within families people called one another by affectionate nicknames, not necessarily shorter, but less formal in meaning. Jungli's was Pahari, meaning 'hillman'. But that was Mataji's name for him. I didn't care for his real name, Pritam ('Why not?' he asked, hurt. 'You should do, it means "beloved",'), and since it would not have been proper for me to use it, I invented a new nickname: Jungli; unsophisticated; untamed. I meant it as a compliment.

Mataji was an awesome women. Much as I regarded the good sense, honesty, efficiency and high standards of cleanliness and moral behaviour that I could see she had, I soon learnt to keep out of her way. She had a blunt, patronizing way of talking and a habit of putting other people down. Thinking it would help me to grasp what she was saying she shouted, in the way strangers tend to raise their voices when addressing blind people, and my fear of not understanding and having the same incomprehensible sentence flung with even greater force made me all the more stupid. So Jungli would explain in simpler language. Much of my communication with Mataji during the months I stayed in the village involved him as my interpreter.

Pitaji never offended anyone. He was a gentle and tolerant man in his early seventies whose presence was undemanding. He got on quietly with the things he had to do, with an implicit understanding that everyone else was free to get on with their own lives in their own way. Although it was his house he made no attempt to rule it. I liked and respected him.

Jungli rarely spoke to Pitaji. They seemed to have nothing in common. Pitaji was tall and thin with wispy white hair and a pleasant, though not notable, face. Temperamentally he and Jungli were poles apart, and I wondered at their difference. Pitaji was a shy man and he didn't speak to me. I don't think he would have known what to say. I didn't address him either. It wasn't my place.

In the first few days it was difficult to understand what was going on. I questioned things in my mind – my presence in the house, my status as a friend of Jungli's, the rather curious relationships between various members of the family, the kind of behaviour expected of me – but had to accept that I wouldn't find answers. My Panjabi wasn't good enough to discuss such matters with Jungli, and none of the family spoke any English. But it didn't seem to matter. Jungli was endlessly patient, explaining things over and over and other ways round until I understood.

Before coming to the village I had purchased a book, an *Introductory Course in Spoken Panjabi*, from which I had learnt some basic words and phrases. At first Panjabi seemed fairly straightforward, with many words similar to Hindi and a simpler script. But I changed my mind. Among the chapter headings were, 'Specification and Enumeration', 'Correlation and Recognition', 'Reduplication of Past Happenings' and 'Disability and Suggestion'. The alphabet contained four 'n's, four 'd's and four 't's; one of the 'd's sounded like a 't' when placed at the beginning of a word, making it five and extremely tiresome. Sometimes four verbs were strung together in an apparently simple clause, not only declining but agreeing with the object as well. The words for Panjabi numbers followed no logical progression in their construction and from one to a hundred all seemed to be different. And word-for-word translation just didn't exist. Apart from different dictionaries giving conflicting word equivalents, a single Panjabi term could have several English meanings, and vice versa. The Panjabi word 'bahut' could be used to convey 'very', 'much', 'too much' or 'just about enough', but on the other hand the language had special names for 'wife of the younger brother of the husband's father', 'the part of a carrot where the leaves and root join', and 'thick end of a stick', all needing to be learnt.

Gradually I did learn, but my early experience of the house and village was largely sensory. I saw, I smelt, I touched, I heard, but I lived in a world of my own.

Mataji and Pitaji lived in a small mud house. The yard felt like a crowded version of the children's enclosure at Whipsnade Zoo, housing, beside the family, three hefty buffaloes, a cow, a calf, two dogs, a hen and cockerel and a donkey who slept outside. The cow and calf were a mistake on my part: I unthinkingly said that people didn't drink buffalo's milk in England and then they appeared, soon after I arrived. I was filled with guilt and vowed that in future I would not say that I liked or was used to doing anything that was not immediately available.

Traditional village houses like Pitaji's were built to keep out heat, cold and invaders. Their thick windowless mud brick walls, flat roofs and rounded walltops admirably expressed an organic belonging to the land on which they stood. Like most other Jat-owned dwellings in the village Pitaji's house comprised an irregularly shaped dung-floored yard, with two small rooms, a kitchen and cooking enclosure, a buffalo byre, a chicken house and a dung store ranged around it. In the centre stood a Persian lilac,[1] its deep green foliage throwing a leaf-patterned doily of shade on the pale dung floor beneath. Emerald parakeets swung from its branches.

Jungli was a bit ashamed of his kaccha[2] house. He wanted me to be comfortable and have everything I was accustomed to. He himself preferred kaccha houses and so did Pitaji. So did I, I assured him; I thought it was a lovely house. Lovely soft colours and smooth rounded walls: beautifully simple. As for the life I was used to, whatever that was, it was the last thing I wanted or expected in a Panjabi village. Most villagers who had once seen 'civilization' wanted it for themselves; pakka[3] houses with lots of smart cement, windows with glass in them, built-in cupboards and other senseless, prestigious luxuries that had never been produced, or thought necessary, in the villages.

[1] *Melia azedarach*
[2] rustic, indigenous
[3] properly made; Westernized

Kaccha houses looked the same whether they were two or two hundred years old. There was no immediate way of telling until you looked at the rafters, which went black with age, or the doors, which had formerly been made up of small panels studded with brass nails. Pitaji's house was relatively new. In consultation with his carpenter he had decided where the rooms, the kitchen and the byre should be built, and where the pump was best sited. Two hired builders constructed the thirty-six inch wide house walls from thicknesses of sun-dried mud bricks, and the carpenter made the roof: first beams, then rafters, then a layer of thatch grass[4] stalks and finally a thick coat of mud with a raised mud rim. Pitaji built his own kitchen and byre and Mataji, with the assistance of two Mazbi[5] women, did the plastering and ornamental sculpting of cooking enclosure walls. Not only the mud but all the timber and the thatch grass for the roof came from Pitaji's own land. It was absolutely Pitaji's house; he had grown it.

Built on two levels to accommodate the slope, the lower yard housed the kitchen, the pump and the animals, leaving the upper one free for sleeping. The kitchen was the most decorative place in the compound, with unglazed pottery and polished brass utensils on moulded shelves and in rounded niches, and any food there happened to be – there never was much – in little safes with carved wooden doors. Beside it was the small enclosure where Mataji cooked, separated from the upper yard by a waist-high broad mud wall. On the outside this wall was perforated with almost lace-like patterns using sticks as a framework, reminiscent of Californian screen walling but infinitely nicer. The patterns devised by each household were different, vigorous yet elegant, and often included primitive animal and bird forms, either in relief or free-standing: Mataji had sculpted a strange stylized beast, an emblematic guardian of security and prosperity. In one corner of the cooking enclosure was a small mud hearth, sited so as to be in shadow at cooking times; three more hearths were spaced around the yard in such a way that at least one would always be in the shade.

At the top end of the yard were the sleeping quarters, small unventilated rooms secured from the outside by heavy chains and padlocks. Their smooth walls with slightly rounded corners were washed thinly with pale aquamarine and orange paint, through which the plaster of mud and chopped straw was clearly visible. In one of the two rooms stood a grainstore on legs, mud-built and

---

[4] *Saccharum bengalense*, a tall grass grown along field boundaries and roadsides
[5] person of low caste who has embraced Sikhism

PLAN OF PITAJI'S HOUSE

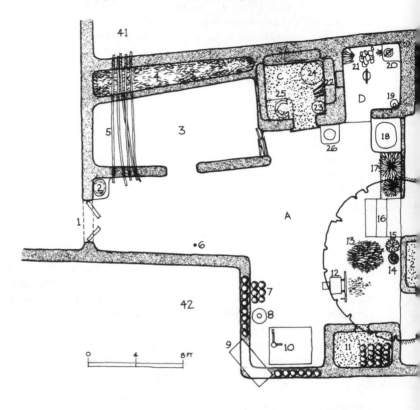

0   4   8 FT

A	LOWER YARD	
B	UPPER YARD	
C	INDOOR KITCHEN	
D	COOKING ENCLOSURE	
E	GUEST ROOM	
F	SLEEPING AND STORAGE ROOM	

1   ARCHED ENTRANCE FROM ALLEY
2   TROUGH TO HOLD VEGETABLE WASTE
    FOR FODDER OR COMPOST
3   BUFFALO BYRE
4   FODDER TROUGH
5   TINJAN STICKS STORED ON ROOF
    FOR SHADE AND LATER FUEL
6   STAKE FOR TYING ANIMALS
    DURING MILKING
7   DRYING DUNG BUNS
8   PORTABLE COOKING HEARTH
9   SPARE CHICKEN HOUSE
10 HAND PUMP
11 DUNG STORE
12 FODDER CHOPPING MACHINE
13 FODDER (TO BE CHOPPED)

14 PERSIAN LILAC
15 LOOFAH MARROW
16 STEPS UP
17 BED CONTAINING TULSI AND
    YOUNG GUAVA
18 ENCLOSED FIRE FOR
    PREPARING YOGHURT
19 PESTLE AND MORTAR
20 COOKING HEARTH
21 DRIED STICKS AND
    BROKEN DUNG BUNS
22 MUD SHELVES AND FOOD SAFES
23 SEALED MUD VESSEL
24 FLOUR DRUM
25 MUD HEARTH
26 MUD HEARTH
27 FILIGREE MUD WALL
28 CHICKEN HOUSE
29 WALL NICHE
30 ROOF GULLEY
31 WALL NICHE WITH SHELVES
32 NAILS FOR HANGING CLOTHES

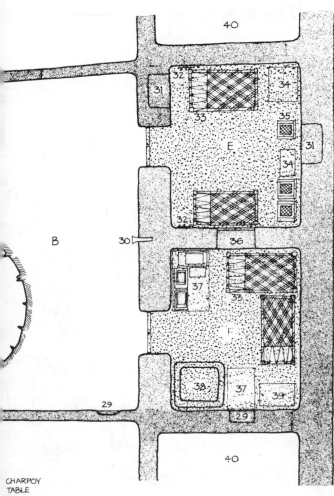

CHARPOY
TABLE
CHAIR
NICHE WITH HATCH DOORS
TRUNKS AND SUITCASES
GRAIN STORE
WOODEN STORAGE SAFE
NEIGHBOUR'S BYRE
FRIENDLY NEIGHBOUR'S YARD
UNFRIENDLY NEIGHBOUR'S YARD

MUD WALLS

COVERED ROOMS OR STORES

AERIAL VIEW OF PITAJI'S HOUSE

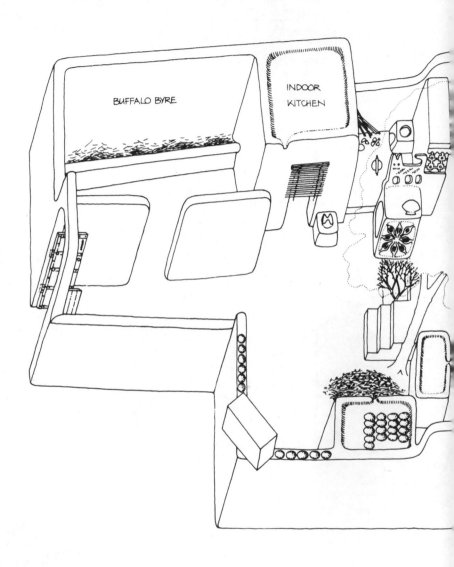

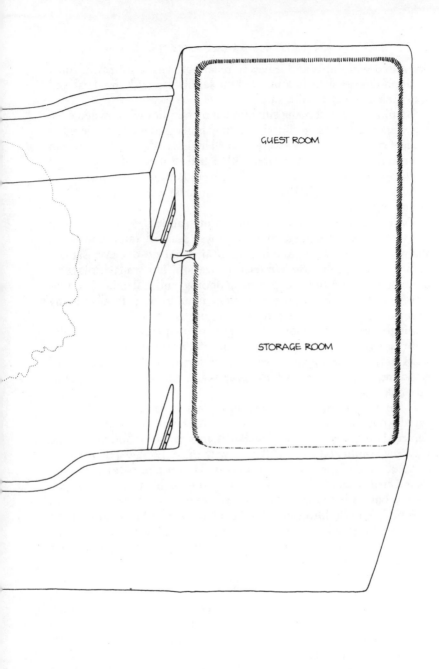

decorated with birds and leaves in relief patterns, a fortress against rats and thieves since it contained the family's wealth in wheat and was their equivalent of a safe.

Owning little, but being surrounded by families who owned even less, almost everything Mataji and Pitaji possessed was considered of value. Locked steel trunks were stacked in descending order of size in the room with the grain store, with a frayed piece of rust-spotted cloth between each. Clothes for best were kept inside, while house clothes hung from nails in the walls. Charpoys[6] were wedged into the remaining space.

The other room, the room in which Jungli and I slept, was reserved for visitors. It contained two charpoys, a small table and some slightly broken plastic cane-backed chairs that no-one ever sat on; items of status; tokens of Western civilization. The walls displayed a permanent exhibition of pictures, photos and calendars, ten to fifteen times as many as there might be in an average English living room of the same size, arranged in vigorous profusion with a dis-armingly childish sense of order. The top row perched on a rail and leant outwards at thirty degrees from the vertical; sparrows built nests in the angles behind. Below were further lines and groups of wedding, school and army photographs and religious prints in paint-box colours.

I counted twenty-three 1979 calendars in that room. No-one cared what day it was, but calendars were cheap and decorative. All depicted religious scenes and included, in a generous and hospitable way, the Hindu god Krishna flirting with the milkmaids, the mosque at Mecca and Christ nailed to the cross. The Sikh pictures portrayed their Gurus and gruesome excerpts from their history: gory battle-scenes, babies being spiked on spears, severed heads and limbs and men boiling in cauldrons of oil or being sawn in half vertically. I tried to pretend the calendars weren't there but Jungli was always draw-ing my attention to one or other horrendous scene, recounting their stoic exploits with pride.

There were more pictures in stand-up steel frames, dangling from nails in the shelf fronts and when all else failed across the door frame. Between and around them plastic flowers with missing leaves shel-tered complacent plastic pigeons, a crop of unused teapots and toys and earthenware kept for best. Medicine and vinegar bottles were tucked in at the sides.

Family photographs were the only things in the house whose role

[6] Indian rope beds with wooden frames

was to be admired. Exquisite family heirlooms held no intrinsic value, their only merit lying in their continued usefulness. I caused much amusement through my appreciation of old doors and rafters, through my habit of going round the house examining everything with minute care, by wanting to run my hands over the hand-beaten bell metal pots, bowls and beakers, for applauding the indigenous crafts like spinning, weaving, potting and embroidery, and by watching in fascination the performing of simple daily tasks. To the villagers a house was a house; a shelter and little more. Because the village houses and everything they contained were almost identical their inhabitants had no interest or pride in them, and with little notion that houses in the West were any different from their own they were pleasantly surprised, though not flattered, by the obvious delight I took in being there. It was a relief to be in a place where neither household objects nor their arrangement was contrived, in a society where the Western mania for home improvements was yet barely apparent.

The most beautiful and in Western terms the most valuable object Mataji and Pitaji possessed lay almost fully submerged in chopped straw in a disintegrating building down the alley and across the communal dung patch. It was a cupboard made of acacia[7] wood, gone black with age, about four feet square and two feet deep, standing on short carved legs. The sides and the door in the centre were constructed of small square indented panels fastened with large brass studs, each of them slightly different. Everything about this cupboard was immensely satisfying: the texture and colour of the wood, its handhewn surface, the irregularity and individuality of each of its parts. I asked how old it was. 'Oh, well over a hundred years' Mataji said dismissively. Most of her neighbours had similar cupboards.

As far as I could gather there was no room for the cupboard in the house, but since it could be used for storing the cotton quilts during the hot weather it hadn't been discarded. By the time the quilts were needed in November, the buffaloes would have consumed most of the straw and access to the cupboard would be regained: it was a beguiling sort of logic. I liked their lack of affectation regarding things of value from their own cultural heritage too – everything was used, even the heavy, ancient, hand-beaten bell metal utensils, even the embroidered bedspreads that were no longer made – but I was stupefied by the respect afforded to cheap and nasty earthenware

[7] A. *nilotica*

plates and imitation cut glasses from mine. They took pride of place in the best room, gathering dust and fly droppings among other cheap and tawdry monuments to modern factory workmanship and bad taste inherited from the West. No-one ever used them; no-one even looked at them: the important thing was that they were there.

Mataji and Pitaji had a servant called Fikan. A servant was expected of a respectable Jat family, and Mataji thought herself very respectable. Fikan was a low caste Hindu boy of twenty who had lived in the house for the past five years. He slept apart from the family, moved about noiselessly and didn't speak unless he had to: I was scarcely aware of his presence.

Four hundred miles away in Uttar Pradesh, Fikan had a wife and child. He sent them most of his monthly income of £9; once a year he went home on leave. His wife, meanwhile, made a rudimentary living by breaking up stone for road repairs. I had often passed groups of such labourers squatting by the roadside hammering rocks into smaller and smaller pieces. They hammered all day and every day, on frosty winter mornings, in torrential rain and exposed to the noonday heat, and they lived in temporary makeshift huts by the roadside, huts made of sacking and bitumen drums.

Fikan's lot was better than his wife's and, according to Jungli, better than most other servants kept by Jat families. Other people didn't buy their servants such nice clothes as Mataji did, nor give them the same food the family ate. Other people only gave them pickles with their chapattis, or watered buttermilk with salt and green chillies. And other people worked their servants hard all day in the fields. Fikan's duties were light – four animals to graze in the daytime and water evening and morning, the night fodder to bring in from the fields and push through the chopping machine, and sundry errands to run. In the afternoon lulls he would squat with his cronies (Hindu boys who worked in other Jat houses), pound cannabis with a pestle and mortar and drink it, watered down, with salt. It was his chief pleasure in life.

Shortly after my arrival in the village the hot weather began. I had been in India for five months and had often felt cold, but never too hot. The heat came with a vengeance. The earth and sky grew pale and huge; vegetation withered; pools dried up and their grey mud cracked and crazed. I could no longer walk barefoot on the dung floor of the yard, or touch the iron pump handle, or put my hand in a bucket of water left out in the sun.

Every day seemed like Sunday. The daily tasks were discharged in a rhythmical and unhurried routine. Each task had its allotted place and its specified hour, and each was performed with the careful thoroughness that custom demanded. Village people were never in a hurry, for time had no price tag on it and there was nowhere to hurry to. Anyway it was too hot.

The family got up in the first light of the sparrow-chirping dawn, roused by the restless shifting of the animals in the byre. Returning from ladies' time at the latrine ground when it was almost day, Mataji lit the hearth and brewed tea. Pitaji followed her out to the fields, and while she scoured last night's pots with yesterday's ash and a handful of straw he bathed under the pump and recited the morning prayer, sitting cross-legged on his charpoy. Fikan milked the buffaloes and led them out to the grazing land and Mataji's sweeper, a dark-skinned Mazbi woman from the poorer fringe of the village (where fifty or sixty people might occupy a house the size of Pitaji's), mixed chopped straw into the night's fresh dung, patted it into nice round flat-bottomed buns and slapped them along the walltops to dry, like a crusting of chocolate drops on thick slices of walnut cake. Mataji set the new milk on a slow fire to make yoghurt and churned the butter in an earthenware jar.

By now the sweeper was moving crab-like across the rooms and yard, brushing underneath remote corners of charpoys with an ineffectual whisk of grass stalks and sorting the proceeds fragment by fragment into fuel, fodder and dust for the compost pile on Pitaji's portion of the communal dung patch. Everything not used for its specific purpose could be employed for another. And Mataji coveted empty cans.

As the sun crept over the tall roofs of the goldsmiths' houses to the east and chased the grey shadows into the walls, Mataji would be starting on the morning meal. This was the time for callers, for settling the day's work in the fields while the vegetables were being chopped, for begging and borrowing, gossiping and peddling. They came every day: friends, neighbours, relations, caste dependents, field labourers, pickle wallahs, fabric wallahs, sadhus and snake charmers, beggars and the village poor. Mataji would dutifully but half-heartedly offer her visitors tea. 'This is like our own home,' they would protest, 'don't disturb yourself.' She wouldn't if she could help it, but custom forced her to repeat the invitation several times, each time with greater force of persuasion.

Food was taken twice a day in Pitaji's house, at about nine in the morning and eight at night, to avoid the midday heat. Both meals consisted of chapattis accompanied by a small bowl of dal, or sabzi[8] if any was available; both if there were guests and maybe even raita.[9] Poor households, like that of Mataji's sweeper, rarely tasted vegetables but existed on chapattis or rice once a day, washed down with buttermilk or very watery dal.

There was no formal sitting down together to a meal. Members of the family ate at different times and in different places, according to when they felt hungry and where they felt most comfortable. Most people's preference was to sit cross-legged on a charpoy with their food balanced on the sheet in front of them, and to eat alone. Conversation or, worse, reading during meals was bad manners and displayed a lack of respect for the food: if one wanted to talk, one had the rest of the day in which to do so.

Guests were served first, followed by the men and elders. Jungli and I ate together, inside, to be out of sight of the neighbours. Mataji, having satisfied her guests and family, her servant and her dogs (one of whom she believed to have been a sadhu in his previous incarnation, since he fasted every Tuesday), ate last, squatting on her low plank in the cooking enclosure or perching aloft on the roof of the henhouse to catch stray wisps of the warm morning breeze.

By the end of the meal the sun was high and the day hot. Mataji and Pitaji sank back on their charpoys with their knees in the air, waiting for the sun to go back down. They lay comatose in the semi-darkness of the room containing the grain store or in the open yard gate, whichever was the cooler, languidly fanning themselves and grumbling about the weather. The alleys were silent: not even children were out playing; not even crows.

I chose this time to take my bath. It was all very well for Jungli, who could bathe in full view of the neighbourhood (he kept on his kachera, the long white bloomers compulsory to baptized Sikhs, exactly three yards wide round the top and drawn up on a string), but I was disadvantaged in having to keep everything except face, feet and forearms out of sight. Having slept through the specified hours of two or three or four in the morning when devotional Sikhs get up and bathe, even in the below-zero temperatures of January and February, I was forced to wait until the men were either asleep or out, or, failing that, drag a couple of charpoys to the pump and stand them on their sides with sheets hung over them to make a screen. The entire operation of undressing, working the pump handle, washing, drying and dressing had to be performed from the squatting posi-

---

[8] raw or curried vegetables
[9] raw or parboiled vegetables in spiced yoghurt

tion, a position which at first I found excruciating. Mataji was the model of discretion: in four months I never noticed her take a bath.

Through the long hot hours of the day Jungli and I sat on our charpoys in the room with the twenty-three calendars. While I read or wrote my diary, or studied Panjabi, or mended my clothes, or sewed up my shoes, Jungli recited the *Mul Mantra*, the Guru's description of God. He recited it over and over in his head, recording the repetitions on his mala.[10] He was always invoking the Gurus, transforming every hiccough, burp or yawn into a melodramatic 'Waheguru!'[11] or a blessing of one of the Gurus. When he was not praying, entertaining guests, or talking to me, he slept.

By mid-afternoon I would be starving, rifling frantically through my rucksack for leftover sweetmeat crumbs or squashed bananas, gloomily aware that I had another five hours to go until the evening meal and that there was nothing, absolutely nothing edible in the entire village in the meantime. Jungli, less famished, would console himself with a leftover chapatti, dry and rock hard and curling up at the edges in staleness, and smeared with lumpy, grainy, rancid butter that looked like lard; a vile concoction that even the dogs wouldn't touch. I have never been one for missing meals, and I found this eleven-hour gap between them sheer torment.

As the sun went down the village came back to life. People and animals filed home across the grazing land with bundles of fodder on their heads and backs. The dust churned up by their feet glinted gold in the low light and blurred their outlines. Mataji hung the yoghurt pot on the washing line in the coolest part of the yard, and while Pitaji recited the evening prayer and Fikan pumped up water for the buffaloes and put the fresh clover through the fodder chopping machine, she started on the evening meal. Jungli and I often helped her, peeling and cutting vegetables (holding them in our hands, never on a board), and I would search for jobs that hadn't been done, like watering the loofah marrow that grew up the Persian lilac, filling the water pitcher, pulling the charpoys into the yard and unfolding the bedding. Mataji laughed at my efforts.

There was a fresh wave of visitors as the sun went down, of the village poor going from house to house, calling a blessing and collecting a chapatti from each, of Pitaji's Mazbi labourers returning to report on their day in the fields, of friends and neighbours picking up the latest gossip. We ate our meal, drank our boiled milk and retired to our charpoys, lulled by the sounds in adjoining yards. The

[10] rosary
[11] Great Guru (i.e. God): the communal Sikh mantra

neighbourhood was now intimate, no longer a cluster of separate compounds divided by walls but a communal open-air dormitory of people settling down for the night in the yards and on the rooftops, calling to each other and monitoring each other's behaviour. From where I lay, I could see Mataji fanning herself a few feet away in our doorway, monitoring me, stationed squarely on her charpoy chatting in a desultory way to Pitaji for hour upon hour until the cool night breezes brought her sleep.

3

Outsider

WE SETTLED DOWN in the village. I didn't think about why I was there, or whether I ought to be there at all, or how long I would stay. There seemed to be no question of my going anywhere else. The yearning to travel and see new places faded into the background beside my desire to be with Jungli. But my conscience pricked me about Mataji. According to Sikh laws of hospitality, no-one asks a guest why he has come, or how long he intends to stay. I mentioned my concern to Jungli.

'This is your house,' he said. 'You can stay a year, two years, ten years or a hundred years.' And he meant it.

Every day it grew hotter. It became too hot to walk during the hours of daylight and we took to going out at dusk or after dark. One evening I went out alone.

The twilight landscape held a special kind of magic, a more tangible quality of India. Shisham trees stood stark against the evening apricot light. Fireflies danced in the marshes beside the pool, and spires of smoke rose from cooking hearths in the village. As it grew darker, sounds and smells came into their own: frogs honked in the dykes, weaver birds chittered in the reedmace, cow bells tinkled as the animals returned home to their byres, distant voices hung suspended in the air and the evening prayer floated over the fields from the gurdwara. I had another of those sensations of total awareness, of this-is-what-India-is and this-is-why-I-came.

Ice. I longed for ice. Blocks of it arrived by tonga late in the morning, having been brought wrapped in dirty sackcloth from the ice factory in the local town. A lump would be hacked off and wrapped in newspaper, to be further bundled in layers of clothing and more layers of sackcloth in the house, as if to keep it warm. On the rare occasion we bought some – it was regarded as an unnecessary extravagance so I usually kept quiet – there was still plenty left by nightfall.

And with the heat came flies. Every morning as the first rays of sunlight touched the yard they swarmed in hundreds, almost thousands, into the room with the twenty-three calendars. Jungli and I were inside.

I detested the flies. They settled on our food, and walked across our mouths as we ate. There was animal dung in the yard and the latrine ground was not far away. Mataji tried to console me. 'Never mind,' she said. It was always 'never mind'; they were the first words I learnt from Jungli. 'Soon there won't be any flies. When the hot weather comes they all die.'

'Hot weather? You mean it's going to get even hotter?' I had been ominously warned by educated Sikhs that white people couldn't tolerate the sort of heat we were about to receive.

'Only a little.' She was adept at telling me what I wanted to hear, of creating illusory comforts. Actually once I got used to it I was no more bothered by the heat than she was; probably I grumbled a lot less.

When the flies became intolerable to him too, Jungli hung a sheet across the open doorway and swirled around the room like a dervish, swatting them with his shoulder cloth. They rose in an angry buzz and dived for the chinks of light, but a few always remained to dance and hum in the hot air and tickle our toes. There were sparrows, my sole emblem of Western familiarity, twittering over our heads in endless aggravating circuits. There were geckos still as stone, like sacred Hindu sculptures on a temple wall. And fearsome yellow wasps droning in hidden shadows and bats swooshing in with the dusk.

I felt little sense of the passing of time. Days were the same: the early walks (if it wasn't too hot), the washing of clothes, the morning meal, the unbroken eight or nine hours in our room behind the fly curtain and finally the brief and relative cool of evening. One day could have been interchanged with another; there was no continuity of purpose, no unfolding of events, and in any case events didn't come my way. I was immunized from the eventful village life I would have liked to have been a part of by the language barrier, by heat, and by Jungli's shielding me from it.

After a month in the village I had learnt very little about Jungli. We could by now hold simple conversations, though our topics of discussion were limited. He still treated me as an honoured guest, mothered me like a helpless infant and tempered any irritation he might feel towards me with awe. But what lay behind? Or beyond? Where had he lived before I came? How had he earned his living? What did he believe in? What did he care for? And whatever did he see in me? For I had come, fair-haired, blue-eyed, a creature from an unknown world, dropping like a genie into his familiar existence. Different habits; different values; different attitudes. But fortunately

for Jungli, he wasn't to know that then. By the time he discovered
how different I was from the Indian girls of his aquaintance, he was
already accustomed to my ways.

I wonder now, looking back, whether our different languages, far
from being a barrier to communication, actually kindled our relationship. Our inability to converse was the one thing we shared. Had
we spoken the same tongue, we might have found our differences too
great. Had I understood what Jungli was saying, the words might
have dimmed his aura of romance. Had there not been the challenge
of learning Panjabi, would there have been sufficient impetus to stay
so long? My curiosity got me into the situation I was in. It held me
engrossed for two years in India. And in the end it was my curiosity
that caused me to leave.

When I wasn't permitted to do something I wanted to know the
reason. There was the case of the village shops. I had never noticed
any commercial premises in our walks round the village, and their
absence seemed remarkable. In England a settlement containing ten
thousand people would be referred to as a town rather than a village,
but here there were no proper shops, no hospital or dispensary, no
offices or factories and no places of entertainment. But Jungli vowed
that there were shops. There was even, he said, a branch of the
Punjab and Sindh Bank in a mud room like the one we lived in.

'Then take me to see them,' I said.

'There's nothing to see,' he replied. 'Just mud houses selling a few
basic commodities like sugar and soap, the same as the shops in
town.'

But I wanted to see for myself. I got it into my head that my life was
incomplete if I couldn't go to the village shops. Jungli couldn't
understand my persistence over a matter so trivial, and would never
take me with him when Mataji sent him out for something. He gave
no reason, so still I asked him.

In the end, and for the first time, he lost patience. 'Go where you
like!' he told me in an exasperated tone. I was rather surprised. 'Only
if people insult you don't come and complain to me.'

I never saw the village shops. It was then Jungli told me what the
villagers thought of foreigners, and why it was, and from what it
was, that he wanted to shield me. He protected and looked after me
with a devotion I found deeply moving, almost sad in its single-
mindedness.

Outsiders, it seemed, were a potential threat to the sanctity of
village life. Visiting government officials and bureaucrats were resented and mistrusted, treated with a superficial respect but glad to

be got rid of. As a representative of the Outside, and probably the first white visitor to the village since the demise of the Raj, I was also a target for suspicion, though the villagers expressed their feelings in a different way. Being a guest of an important Jat family they couldn't interfere directly, but numerous questions were put to Jungli when I wasn't there. During the first week of my stay I had wandered round looking at and photographing the village, for I loved its restrained palette of pastel colours and its plastic architecture – almost sculpture rather than architecture. It was a village of beige mud walls, of spindly black pumps and fodder cutting machines etched against them, of quizzical buffaloes slowly ruminating in lazy yards and camels laden with fodder swinging majestically down the alleys, of men squatting in groups under banyan[1] and pipal[2] trees and women leaning on one forearm in open doorways. It was a village whose visual qualities didn't strike with sudden impact but settled slowly and warmly in the subconscious.

I was followed on my village walks by a shrieking mob of Mazbi women and excited children who chanted 'Photo! Photo!' and stood to attention like soldiers the moment they suspected I was levelling a camera in their direction. The temptation to record images was difficult to resist: I had never been to an Indian village before. But the villagers had never been anywhere else, and it wasn't really surprising that Jungli was questioned. 'Why does she keep taking photographs of nothing at all? Just walls and alleys and yards – what's the use of that? It doesn't help us. All that money, and she could be taking *our* pictures. Tell her to come and take one of me – or shall I come to your house?' By Jungli's reckoning two or three dozen people had expressed similar views and it exasperated him. Others asked, 'Why does she stay so long in the village? A rich educated person doesn't go and live in a backward place by choice. What's she here for? She's always walking about looking around her.' Indian people didn't behave like that, and it worried them.

Much of the present attitude towards foreigners must have stemmed from the time of the Raj. Westerners were still envied for their wealth, education and freedom, and both envied and mistrusted for their power, laxity of morals and lack of faith or adherence to religious ethics. For all their technological advancements and the length of their period in office, village life *per se* had been only superficially affected by the Raj and inner life went on as it had before. That people wore machine-made clothes, moved about, rode

[1] *Ficus bengalensis*
[2] *Ficus religiosa*

bicycles, possessed an odd chair or china plate or steel trunk, did little to alter their inherited beliefs or lifestyle. Post-Raj effects of British rule, such as agricultural security and the infiltration of a monetary economy, had had more powerful effects.

A few villagers totally mistrusted foreigners. One of the rumours being passed around was that I was from the CIA, making a survey to assist the British in regaining control over India: there had been some recent government propaganda to the effect that the CIA was sending agents out to villages and creating trouble. Other villagers were afraid I would go back to England and tell people that Indians were dogs. At least forty people to whom I had never even spoken had said insulting things about me, Jungli told me reproachfully, though I expect he was exaggerating. They believed he had befriended me for my alleged money ('all foreigners are rich'), and in the end he got so bored with it that he ceased even bothering to deny it. 'If that's what they want to think let it be,' he said. Instinct told me they thought more than they dared say, and my suspicions were soon confirmed.

I went out for a walk in the late afternoon. Jungli was engaged in Nihang talk and I was tired of being shut up in the house. I watched a group of dark-skinned roving labourers energetically threshing bundles of wheat on a log while one of Pitaji's relatives – a large man in white homespun – stood over them and boomed out orders. I walked on through the fields and crossed to the road. It had become a corridor walled by tall thickets of flowering thatch grass, its stem leaves angled like the deft brush strokes of a Chinese watercolour. Two men approached. I was a quarter of a mile from the village and there was – most unusually – no-one in sight. Almost as if they had paid them not to be.

'Hey sister, hey sister! Where are you going?'

'To the village.'

'Let's go to our village.' It was in the other direction.

'No. I have to get back.'

'You're coming with us!' There was a dangerous gleam in the man's eye.

'I'm not. Go away.'

They didn't go away. Instead they dragged me to a tractor and trailer I hadn't previously noticed, parked a little way down the road, from which about fifty schoolboys were gazing, open mouthed, at the spectacle.

I appealed to the driver. 'Hey, take these men away!'

He didn't reply, but an older well-dressed Sikh spoke up from the trailer, in English.

'Where do you come from?'

'That village,' pointing.

'Whose house?'

'Beant Singh's.'

'Who's he?'

One of the draggers interceded. 'She's staying with a Nihang.' From the way he said it, it seemed to make a difference; it was what I had been afraid of. But I had had enough of this talk, and most of all I had had enough of being gaped at by fifty schoolboys. I shouted at the well-dressed man, 'These men are drunk, and they dragged me here by force!'

He turned to them. 'She says you're drunk.' Then he addressed himself to me. 'No no,' he said placidly, 'they don't mean any harm. All they want is some sexual enjoyment.' He seemed to take it for granted it could be had for the asking.

I delivered an explosive speech and strode off. Fortunately, for there was still no-one in sight, it was enough to dampen their enthusiasm and they let me go. At home Jungli gave me a further harrowing. 'How many times have I told you not to go out alone? In future take Mataji or Pitaji with you if I'm not here. Did you hear that?' he called to Mataji, and disappeared into the yard to recount the tale to her as she kneaded the dough for the evening's chapattis.

Such experiences chastened my abundant self-will and rebellious-ness, and gradually I discovered the limits of behaviour beyond which my actions embarrassed Jungli's family. Although technically men and women enjoyed equal status, there were many things I as a woman would earn disfavour by doing, like roaming about alone, riding in lorries and sitting on the roof racks of buses when they were full up inside. Men could do all these things, and it took me some time to get used to the fact that I couldn't do them too; it was maddening, for they were invariably things I really enjoyed.

Slowly I adapted my ways. I respected Jungli's few demands on me, and on the whole I liked his family. Nor did I begrudge the villagers their colourful fancies concerning my mission in the village. Their low opinions of British morality were justifiable; their suspi-cions of outsiders understandable. The Panjabi characteristics I did find trying were usually due more to a personal reaction against being treated in ways I had been brought up to think of as uncouth or ill-mannered than to inherent defects in the villagers' personalities. It was quite acceptable for a villager to take advantage of someone better off than himself, to impose upon another's privacy for as long as he chose and to poke his nose into their personal affairs. It was normal for him to stare for as long as he liked at whomsoever he pleased and from as near as he could get, and to push rudely past anyone – child, old man or pregnant woman – who happened to be in his way. Children were the worst elbowers and shovers: they did a kind of breast stroke through crowds, levering people sideways with their arms as if they were made of water. I often felt like putting my foot out and tripping them up, though I never did.

Something else I found disconcerting, because I wasn't accustomed to it, was the villagers' lack of sympathy. They didn't even understand the word. 'What?' said Jungli when I looked it up in the dictionary. I had certainly never heard anyone use it.

If I was ill I would be diligently looked after as far as food was concerned, but what I could really have done with was a bit of sympathy. The stock phrase, whether one was suffering from a slight headache or a burst appendix was, 'Never mind, you'll soon be all right,' spoken in a standard indifferent manner. I would have liked a bit of sympathy when I was jeered at on the latrine ground, and I would have been reassured by it the evening I was assaulted. But it wasn't forthcoming.

When I first met Jungli in Calcutta I had been wearing long skirts and Panjabi shirts in the bright reds and pinks and greens that look so vibrant in the Indian light. In so doing I had drawn attention to myself and become a target to convoys of bottom pinchers. On returning to India from Bangladesh I had gone to stay in the family home of a Sikh friend in Bihar, where I had lamented my fan club.

'Wear the clothes of the Sikhs,' my friend advised, 'and they won't touch you. The Hindus and Muslims are afraid of us.' He bought six yards of fabric and his mother tailored my first salvar-kamiz, blue like the tunics of the Nihangs. After that the incidents ceased.

The salvar-kamiz has remained essentially unchanged since the days of the Moghul empire: no female in the village wore anything else. A fitted mid-thigh length tunic with side slits, the kamiz, is worn over baggy trousers, or salvar. Two yards wide around the top, and gathered up round the stomach with a drawstring, the legs taper to a buckramed baseband on which each tailor creates a personal and intricate pattern of machine stitching. A veil, or dupatta, of chiffon or voille covers the head and chest, the latter to conceal the female shape from the male eye.

From that day forth, and long after I left India, I wore nothing but the salvar-kamiz. Apart from disguising me as a Sikh (I did it properly and knotted my hair in a bun, and covered my head with a veil), the clothes were cool, socially appropriate, and supremely comfortable. As old ones wore out and had to be replaced, the colours I chose became more and more drab, culminating in a sombre midgrey brown, the exact hue of the north Indian dust. I wore unpatterned cotton and a loose-fitting kamiz, which happened to be the style of the older village women. They, too, reflected the Panjabi landscape in the colour of their dress: cream and beige like the house walls, pale sky blue, unripe wheat green, camel and donkey, ripe corn gold and sunset peach.

People would say to Jungli, 'Why doesn't she wear good clothes?' No doubt they found me unaccountably frumpish.

'Because she likes to dress simply,' he would reply. 'It's up to her.' He liked simplicity too.

He himself spent most of his life in vest and kachera, as did most village men when they were at home. He looked a lot less romantic in his underclothes. The women lived in threadbare grimy and torn salvar-kamiz, but to go out they put on their best. There *were* people who wore plain cotton clothes when they didn't have to, who did so for religious reasons, but Jungli was as contemptuous of their motives as he was of those who put on finery they could scarcely afford. 'It's just as much a conceit to go round in cheap cotton clothes as expensive silk ones: you're putting yourself above other people by saying, so to speak, "Look at me! I'm pure! I'm religious!" which is no better than saying "Look at me! I'm rich!"' Of all human failings, conceit was the one Jungli most loathed.

People who were at all fashionable wore synthetic fibres, especially nylon and terycot, boldly patterned in hideous occidental arabesques and bridesmaid's bouquets. Indian women didn't ask the tailor for pockets in the sides of their garments: pockets didn't look nice, and the first consideration was to be attractive. And wearing no ornaments was unthinkable.

'Haven't you got a pierced nose?' they would ask me. Many Sikh women, like Hindus, wore a jewel in their noses called a laung, or clove. 'Why don't you wear bangles?' They all did. 'Don't you like gold?' Not particularly.

For a time I ignored the criticism and went on being mistaken for an old village crone. Until, months later, I found a street cobbler who made me a pair of sandals out of tyres and inner tubes for twelve pence. I was thrilled by this wonderful bargain, but the villagers were deeply shocked that I should have bought a pair of shoes that cost so little. I wasn't permitted to wear them.

*

Pitaji's relatives in the neighbouring houses were no less inquisitive
about the white stranger on stage in their midst than the rest of the
village, and they had the advantage of front row seats. Since the yard
walls were only four feet high, my movements could be effectively
observed by the near neighbours on either side, while villagers
further away had only to ascend to their rooftops for an upper circle
view. Pitaji and Jungli would bellow, 'Is this a cinema show?' but to
no avail: throughout the sub-continent respect for a visitor's feelings
pales into insignificance beside the desire to satiate one's own curiosity.

The next door neighbours on one side of the yard – cousins of
Pitaji's – were on good terms with Mataji and would carry on an
intermittent repartee over the wall. On the other side the neighbours
were of greater interest, for although distant relatives of Pitaji's, not
a word was ever spoken between the two families. They were fine
examples of local vice and generally condemned: the men rented out
their land since greater profits could be made with less effort by
smuggling; their women were wayward; and what was more, they
traded in opium and distilled their own alcohol, much of which they
consumed themselves. Sounds of excessive merrymaking – to Mataji's way of thinking – would float over the yard wall long after all
decent people had gone to bed. And Mataji, stationed behind the
wall and peeping between the dung buns, would purse her lips and
frown a frown of self-righteous disapproval.

If anything found its way into the next door yard by mistake that
miscreant family appropriated it. I was warned by Mataji not to
hang my clothes on the washing line when a north wind was blowing: several things of hers had blown away and woken up in the next
door trunks. And one afternoon a chicken belonging to the neighbours on the respectable side trotted into the forbidden yard. There
were good smells from the cooking pot later that evening but it was
impossible to prove anything.

Throughout the months of my stay the villagers came to see what
Mataji and Pitaji were harbouring in their house. They stared in-
solently and uninhibitedly. When just once I was introduced to a girl
in her early twenties and she hid her face in shyness, my heart went
out to her. Normally my inquisitors would sit in a row on Jungli's
charpoy, eyeing me with undisguised interest, asking questions and
discussing my appearance in detail. I was eternally grateful to my
salvar-kamiz for lowering my entertainment value, but if I neglected
one minor detail of correct Panjabi attire, like rubbing coconut oil
into my hair, it would set off a major debate in which I had no role

other than to sit and look amenable. Pitaji's family were the only people to be impervious to the supposed honour of having a foreigner as a guest. Far from employing me as an exhibit or status symbol, they rarely asked questions and showed no interest in my luggage. I was treated as one of them.

I had already had more than my fill of being stared at before coming to the village. And I had naïvely believed that being with Jungli would put an end to it; that staying in a rural community, hardly going out, with Jungli there to protect me – to explain to people I didn't like it – would, after the initial interest had died down, be a solution to the problem.

It wasn't, of course. The phenomenon had its roots in extreme racial prejudice.

'Isn't she beautiful?' people would say. Beautiful because I was white. Had I been black, Chinese, low caste or of tribal origin, I would have been ignored. And Jungli made no attempt to restrain the viewing; he couldn't see why I minded.

What I wanted was only partially attainable. To be with Jungli, getting to know him through our growing ability to communicate: that I could have. To indulge my nostalgia for English village life fifty years ago, a life arranged not by machines but by nature, where people and animals lived in close contact, where every tool was comprehensible and the earth was held sacrosanct: that, to a lesser extent, I could also have. But to be a part of Jungli's village, living in the style of its inhabitants, absorbing its customs and sharing its labour: that, for the present, was beyond my reach. For as long as I stayed, I was a guest: I remained an outsider.

I liked being in the village. People were less complicated, less competitive, less spoilt by consumerism than most people in the West; in the absence of the media, they occupied their own reality. I was sympathetic to their way of life and disturbed, therefore, that they should find me so peculiar. Their staring alienated, when I was trying to integrate.

Sometimes when visitors came I would be reading: I had joined a library in Amritsar and taken out books on the history and culture of Panjab. Pitaji owned a handful of books, religious ones, locked in the trunks safe from mice and dust, for they had cost good money. Very few villagers read out of choice (if they belonged to the twenty-five per cent, mostly younger Jats, who could read at all): reading was considered a poor substitute for company. I realized our visitors didn't like my reading, for it ruled them out. They would make conversation instead.

'What are you doing?'

'I'm reading.'

'What are you reading?'

'It's a book. An English book,' I added, thinking I'd better make more effort.

And though they couldn't read English they would pick it up and deliberately turn the pages over one by one and scrutinize the cover and hand it on to the next interested party. Jungli didn't mind my reading, though it rather perplexed him, but he felt left out if I laughed at something funny. 'Only an idiot laughs alone,' he warned. When friends of his were present they would laugh with me, to forestall my impending lunacy.

It was a year before I learnt, quite by accident, of the other side of the staring phenomenon. I was staying with a friendly Panjabi family in a village near Simla and the children couldn't take their eyes off me. 'People don't stare like that in England,' I laughed when their parents showed no sign of telling them to stop. People who put me up had a right to stare though, I thought.

'No,' sighed the mother. 'The English don't respect us.'

The English don't respect us! So Indians didn't see their behaviour as bad manners at all, but as a deferential esteem we didn't return! Curiosity about other human beings is, after all, natural and healthy. Then perhaps it is we who are abnormal, taught not to stare, afraid of catching a stranger's eye, our minds so crammed with information we have often ceased to be interested in the real thing. I had, and still have, a lot to unlearn.

An Indian's position in life, his stability and his sense of personal fulfilment were founded on the degree of respect he achieved. Jungli wasn't concerned whether or not people liked him: he cared only that they showed him respect, a different matter altogether. Mataji's attitude might therefore be interpreted as one of conceit: I wasn't worth taking an interest in since there was nothing to be gained by me. She was conceivably even jealous of the attention I received.

Something else I discovered was that individuals didn't count. I was accepted or not accepted, entertained, assisted and generally responded to not as the person I was, but as a specimen of white womanhood. The Western cult of projecting oneself and nurturing 'meaningful relationships' would have astounded the villagers had they known of it. They preferred to toe the line, as if afraid of discovering they might be different.

One day a man came who spoke English. I hadn't spoken any for some time and didn't particularly want to: talking in my own language again somehow distracted me from my purpose, broke through my disguise and reminded me of who I really was. The man was puzzled by my monosyllabic replies and confused as to why I was there. He went away unsatisfied.

4

Inheritance

PITAJI'S WAS THE OLDEST, largest and most highly-respected family in the village. His predecessors may have been its initial colonizers, for the hereditary position of village headman was still held by the oldest in direct line, at present Pitaji's nephew.

While Pitaji's father was alive the family still lived jointly in a single household, but after his death the women quarrelled, each desiring to run the household in her own way. The men sought independence and personal possession of land and property. The brothers split up into individual family units and built a cluster of house compounds abutting the alley leading to Pitaji's house.

Although powerful, they were a simple and unaffected family. They shunned foreign products and luxury goods, wore traditional white homespun clothes, and lived in kaccha dwellings. At one time they had been talked into building pakka houses as befitting men in their position, but they found them too hot and moved back into their old ones. The pakka buildings were left to decay: pipal trees took root in the brickwork; buffaloes ruminated in the front rooms.

Of the five thousand acres pertaining to the village, Pitaji and his brothers held two hundred. Already a series of separate plots while their father was still alive, the land had been further subdivided at his death into widely scattered compartments. Pitaji's fifty acres consisted of seven small plots, some of which were several miles from the village and from each other. 'Eight acres here,' Jungli would say to me, indicating vaguely a sea of ripe wheat extending to the horizon, in which there were no discernible boundaries. Pitaji's Mazbi labourers were squatting at the edge of the golden tide, hacking at it deftly with sickles. 'And another four on the far side of the track.' This contained clover, Lucerne,[1] past its best and peppered with pale flowers.

Jungli was proud of Pitaji's land. A fifth was already his in name, a legal contrivance to avoid its being seized by the government and redistributed among the landless poor. But in spite of his pride he lacked that special relationship with the soil that a lifetime of strug-

[1] *Medicago sativa*

NEIGHBOURHOOD PLAN

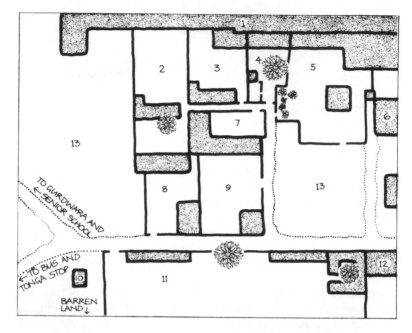

1 GOLDSMITHS' HOUSES
2 PITAJI'S YOUNGER BROTHER
3 PITAJI'S ELDEST BROTHER'S YOUNGER SON
4 PITAJI
5 PITAJI'S SECOND COUSIN
6 PITAJI'S FORMER HOUSE
7 PITAJI'S ELDEST BROTHER'S ELDER SON

8 UNRELATED FAMILY (WATER CARRIERS)
9 PITAJI'S ELDEST BROTHER'S WIDOW
10 PITAJI'S FLOUR MILL
11 GOVERNMENT JUNIOR SCHOOL
12 PITAJI'S COUSIN
13 DUNG HEAPS

gle engendered: that was Pitaji's concern, not Jungli's. Young men
left the village now, and tractors took their place. Those that remained were the less enterprising, the conservative, the unmaterialis-
tic, the cautious and the contented. Pitaji was all these things.

We were limited in our choice of walks as Jungli preferred to stay
on the family land. For some reason he was uneasy about crossing
other people's, and in the end refused to. Our walks began on the
barren land by the tonga stop where Pitaji's buffaloes passed their
days, expressions of puzzlement on their foolish faces as they placidly munched its wiry unimproved grass and wallowed in the pool. We
passed the onion-domed monument to Pitaji's father, its bricks
crumbling like soft biscuits in a heap around its base, its walls half
obscured by a leafless tangle of khaki stems and salmon flowers.[2]

[2] *Capparis decidua*

And beyond were the fields. We tiptoed along the unstable dykes looking at flowers and watching for snakes, but Jungli soon tired of being out in the hot sun, answering questions about nesting habits and the manufacture of mud bricks and other things that he considered of no importance, and longed to return to the protective shade of the house. I, on the other hand, longed to go on, to explore to the horizon; my greatest enjoyment in the village was these walks.

If the landscape gave the villagers pleasure, they didn't express it. Their appreciation would be in the wonder of God manifested through His creation of the land's capacity to fill their stomachs rather than a curiosity about the life it supported or a recognition of its beauty. Nature was just there, it was nothing, it was too familiar, it was a clock: the sun to get up by and the rain to stay in by. I sometimes sneaked out to watch birds just before dusk, and homeward-going villagers would stop and stare at me in wonderment. What was I looking at? All they could see was a bird on a wire.

I in turn was just as incredulous about their attitude. There were such marvellous birds: why could no-one see them? Wild peacocks roosted in ancient banyans and foraged for grain in the fields. Broad-bean-green bee-eaters, resplendent rollers in turquoise and indigo and king-size kingfishers with fierce crimson bills perched on overhead wires. Paddy birds stood dolefully in the marshes, like sad old men hunched up in overcoats and mufflers with their trouser legs rolled up. On my way to the latrine ground I would pass within a few feet of a pair of hoopoes elegantly grubbing for insects in the silt. High above soared eagles and kites and singing larks; in the grass at my feet were quail, partridge and red-wattled lapwing.

Although I didn't stay in the village more than a year, I often went back to its vicinity and was able to observe the land in all its seasonal guises. The speed at which it changed was remarkable: I could return after a fortnight's absence to find the fresh green watercolour scene that I had left transformed into a tarnished brown canvas in oil. Crops rose – some to ten feet and more – turned dry and were gone in what seemed like contracted time. One volume would heighten while another was razed: the interraction of man and nature inadvertently created a dynamic Ben Nicholson landscape expressed in oscillating rectangular planes of green and gold.

It was this constant metamorphosis, the fourth dimension, time, and the little unplanned delights that materialized along its seams and hems that made the Panjabi plain interesting. In itself it wasn't an endearing landscape, composed as it was of imported vegetation and smudged with alien artefacts. With minor variations it stretched monotonously up to the Himalayan foothills, across central Pakistan and southeastwards over Uttar Pradesh and Bihar. But it had its moments, and one of them coincided with my arrival, in the short apple-green spring when the wheat was high and the clover lush and the trees clad in crisp new leaves. It was mid-March, one of the two short periods in the year when it is not too hot, too cold or too wet.

During the next few weeks the flowers disappeared; the trees remained green but the wheat turned the yellow-buff of the mud walls in the village. Mid-April heralded the harvest, and the village turned out and the fields were briefly as animated as English ones must have been in the days of poppies and cornflowers (which had gone, if ever they were there, from Panjab too). By mid-May the fields lay dry and brown: only the straw stacks with their pointed caps – like primitive tribesman's huts in an African desert – in any way compensated for the sense of desecration. The earth baked under a vast, featureless sky.

With the rains in July came an intense greening, of ground that had seemed barren, of trees that had shed their leaves in the long white heat and of crops that burst upwards in triumphant growth. With the rains in July the land that in March had resembled southern England grew lush and tropical: it was at this time that to me it was most beautiful of all. Vegetation burgeoned, soft, sensuous and full-blooded. Villagers in white squelched in the mud beneath black umbrellas, and giant storks and crested cranes fed in the wet earth. Water filled the pits on the barren land and pathways turned to mud.

By the end of September the rains were over and the sorghum was house-high. Weeks of rain had bleached the straw stacks and made them saggy and shapeless like the breasts of old women. Along the roads plumes of thatch grass soared majestically in the whitewashed sky and shone silver in the moonlight. Those few weeks between the rains and the cold weather were a period of heady scent and rapid change: crops crumpled, turned chrome, turned crimson, turned khaki and crackled in the dry air. Then they were gone, and once more the landscape was devastated and once more ploughed in preparation for the winter wheat.

Having left Panjab for Uttar Pradesh at the end of the rains, I returned briefly at the end of November, by bus. Dawn melted into rows of white eucalyptus trunks receding into a thick white mist. As the sun rose the mist went pink and gradually cleared. A wispy carpet of wheat seedlings veiled the pale earth, interrupted here and there by small rugs of lush young clover. In mid-January I again returned, at the coldest time of year when ice thin as a brandy glass lay over dawn puddles and early annuals had greened the fields and verges. In two months the wheat would be knee high and pea green, and it would be spring.

On one of our walks to Pitaji's farthest ownership boundary we came to a line of acacia trees: black-trunked, square-crowned and bristling with white spines, as unproductive-looking a line of trees as one could expect to see. Yet their timber was hard and black, Jungli told me, ready to become furniture and doors, tools and charcoal. Their spines protected them from browsing animals and were still used by the poor as pins. Their thorny branches were cut for temporary crop protection and the yearly prunings for firewood and fodder. Their twigs were used for toothsticks. Their bark was employed for tanning and the distillation of alcohol. Their resin could be extracted for dyeing and printing, for making a cough medicine and a substitute for soap. They represented, in fact, a major component in the peasant's survival kit, and from that day on I viewed them with a new benevolence.

Jungli took a swipe at the outer twigs with his sword. From the fallen pieces he selected a straight section of pencil thickness and broke off two six-inch lengths. We continued our walk chewing one end until it formed a brush (it had a faintly bitter but not unpleasant taste), and we scrubbed our teeth until they shone. They felt strong and were absolutely clean.

Every inch of Pitaji's land was profitably used and it supplied most of his family's needs: mud from the barren land for building and plastering; timber for rafters, furniture, tools and fuel; hemp fibre for charpoys, stools and tethers; thatch grass canes for ceilings, barriers and door chicks;[3] fodder for the milch animals (from whom came milk, buttermilk, curd, butter and ghee, and dung for fuel, floors and compost); and all the staple foods – wheat and rice, sugar cane for jaggery,[4] rape oil for cooking and cosmetic use and a variety of vegetables. A few years previously the land had produced enough cotton for the clothes and bedding, and although Mataji still wove daris, setting up a loom in the room with the grain store, the making of clothes had ceased to be economical. Reliable irrigation methods and the widespread use of new and improved types of grain had caused farming systems to move towards specialization and the growing of cash crops.

[3] screen-blind bound with twine
[4] unrefined lump sugar, often taken after a meal to aid digestion

Pitaji had worn white homespun shirts and lungis like his brothers until Mataji – foolish woman – had manoeuvred him into striped pyjamas and nylon shirts. Poor Pitaji: it was easier to wear them than argue with Mataji. The home-grown, handspun, hand-woven cotton was cheaper, cooler, better quality and more comfortable, and there must have been a sense of pride in having produced it oneself.

Mataji governed the household. Pitaji's duties extended from immediate family responsibility – his land and its farming – through group or extended family obligations and neighbourhood affairs to village government.

Pitaji's elder brother's family were his shariks, or rivals. Almost every family was riven by a feud: it was an accepted fact of rural society. Whatever Pitaji did the brother had to outdo: if Pitaji bought a cow he must have two cows; if Pitaji had a tractor he must acquire a more powerful one; if Pitaji's crops were doing better than his own a few buffaloes accidently let into the fields concerned would soon amend matters. The two families hadn't been on speaking terms since an incident several years before when one of the brother's in-laws had broken into the house to steal Mataji's ornaments and Jungli, rather the worse for drink at the time, had shot him. Not dead, but he was badly wounded. But the feud went back further than that, to the day Pitaji's father died and the land was apportioned between his sons.

It took a lot less than that to trigger off a family feud, which once begun could be expected to last for generations. A careless action or gesture, or the twirling of one's moustache while looking the other fellow in the eye, could be interpreted as a challenge, break into a quarrel and go on developing (with all the members of the extended family congregating around one or other combatant) until the chief parties were cutting each other's throats. Lawyers were said to exploit such feuds and the police to ignore them. Since a decent income depended on crime the police promoted it, extorting bribes and suppressing true cases. Whenever possible they were kept out of village affairs: the villagers preferred their own forms of justice.

As a Jat, Pitaji took no physical part in the cultivation of his fields. He organized his work force and walked miles every day between his plots, checking on their water supply and making sure the crop was still there. We would pass him on the road, a lean elderly figure with an upright, graceful walk. Mataji moved like a buffalo.

Instinctively on guard against danger or threat, men rarely went out unarmed. Even the Mazbis, with nothing to lose but their lives, carried a spear or a battle-axe or at least a long pole. The Jats had to

protect their fields when the crops were ripening, and Jungli and I
were sent out one evening to keep vigil against thieves: for five nights
running someone had been helping himself from Pitaji's clover
patch. I had heard tales of clashes with swords, sickles and knives –
whatever came to hand – caused by the theft of a small bundle of rice
or clover, and Jungli had once put a man in hospital for six months. I
sat silently in the darkness, the machete across my lap, hoping, for
their sakes, that no-one turned up.

In the afternoons Pitaji sometimes went to the sat.[5] The daily male
gatherings on the platform under the big banyan tree were formerly
the focus of neighbourhood community life: ideas were given a
hearing, mulled over and absorbed or discarded, world news was
injected, local gossip disseminated, farming methods chewed over,
repairs and improvements organized and minor punishments meted
out. Serious misdemeanours were referred to the central village
council, the panchayat, an institution as old as the villages and
through which they were still controlled. Pitaji was an elected member of the jury; previously he had been its chairman.

As the villagers came to have more first hand contact with the
outside world, the institution of the sat was gradually collapsing. It
was a symptom of a more general sadness that I sensed in the village:
the loss of cohesion; the erosion of dignity; the retreating into
self-contained family units; the emigration of the more capable to
the far corners of the industrial West, Middle East and Pacific
countries; the pursuit of materialism and factory-made produce and
the consequent disappearance of the village-level self-reliance; the
lessening of dependence of one caste upon another and the breakdown of the system that supported it. Had I been a visitor to the
village thirty years ago (and I wish I had), I would have found the
powerful inter-caste dependence still intact. In those days if a Jat
woman wanted a woollen coat for her husband she wouldn't go and
buy it in the second hand clothes bazaar, as I did for Jungli, but
would have it made to her precise requirements by a long chain of
people of different castes and faiths on all of whom she was dependent, and likewise they on her. The same applied to every necessity of
daily life: if your plough was broken the carpenter mended it; if your
nails needed cutting the barber was sent for. Everyone was paid in
kind; if a harvest was poor the entire village was proportionally
worse off; the good and the bad were divided equally.

Village life was in a state of transition. It was losing its past – the

5 men's meeting place

old caste-system which in spite of its drawbacks had worked and
been accepted – but its present was uncertain and it feared the future.
There was still a sense of timelessness – of days that had passed but
yet held meaning. The ancient village wells were derelict and forlorn;
for centuries they had been a hub of activity, the female counterpart
of the *sat*, resounding with the thumping of wet washing and the
splashing of pails, the groaning of the pulley and the chattering of
women's voices. No longer was the village the lively, noisy, medieval
place it had been in the 1940s or even 50s, with water carriers
shuttling back and forth in the alleys, bullocks turning oil presses,
potters potting under trees and weavers and blacksmiths and goldsmiths and leather workers glimpsed through open doorways,
women grinding corn in the early hours of day and spinning cotton
in the shade of the mud walls at noon. Men worked in the towns
now; there were pumps in the yards and machines ground the corn.
People ate better meals, they were stronger and healthier, and no-one
wore rags.

5

Inheritors

UNAFFECTED BY EXTERNAL CIRCUMSTANCES, my relationship with Jungli had no cause to change. It moved along an easy path, the first bend in which, the first realignment of vision, was out of sight ahead. Expending our energy in trying to communicate, there was no time left for rows.

Having quickly forgotten his initial apprehension, Jungli had become warm and demonstrative. We sat in our room, side by side, hand in hand like teenage lovers, listening for approaching footsteps. Mataji, slopping about in her vulgar, two-tone, plastic flip-flops, could be heard across the yard. But Pitaji, the silent one, sometimes surprised us. When he appeared round the curtain to fetch his shirt from the nails we would spring apart guiltily, and Pitaji would pretend not to notice.

To live in a small house with a family of three and, except in greeting, never to exchange a word with one of its members, might appear unusual in a Western context. In this traditional village household the absence of communication between Pitaji and myself seemed quite natural. An Indian girl does not address her father-in-law unless he speaks first. She keeps her head covered in his presence. Mindful of this, for my status was similar, I kept silent and stayed in the background.

Pitaji, for his part, was uncertain of me. Since the British departed in 1947 (when Pitaji was already approaching forty), he had had no dealings with white men. His memory of the British was as his superiors: where did I fit in? Yet there was no sense of animosity between us. I was fond of Pitaji and believe he, in his way, felt the same.

They were a strange sort of family though. There were tensions in the air that I couldn't quite put my finger on. They lacked solidarity: a recognition of themselves as an integral social unit. On no one occasion, in the months I stayed in the village, were Mataji, Pitaji, Jungli and I all together in one place at one time. In no one instance did we all share an outing, a celebration, a discussion, a meal or even a task of work. Pitaji had his particular duties to perform; Mataji had hers. Jungli and I were there on sufferance.

Instead of responding to each other in a spontaneous way as people or relating to the group as one of its members, internal family relationships followed stereotyped one-to-one patterns rooted in traditional norms of respect and duty: husband and wife, mother and son, host and guest, master and servant. The servant obeyed the master. The son obeyed the mother. The wife obeyed the husband. Everyone humoured the guest, who was second only to God.

This particular kind of emotional isolation was present in other families I visited, but in the case of Jungli's it was more pronounced. Most households comprised people of three or more generations; there was a continuity of purpose about them, of son following father, and stronger emotional bonds. Individualism was ruled out by numbers.

Pitaji's household was unusually small. Jungli played no part in its running, but remained all day with me. His relationship with both parents was strained. He was perpetually on his guard with Mataji and remote in his dealings with Pitaji. There was, in fact, good reason for his behaviour. But it would be almost a year before the truth came out.

Jungli's old widowed aunt, mother of the present village headman, lived alone in a kaccha house at the bottom of the alley. She spread herself between her relatives and was in and out of the house every day, chatting and gossiping with Mataji. Once she didn't come for three days and when she did, Mataji was out.

'Where's Mataji?' she asked Jungli, leaning on her stick and peering about her through thick horn-rimmed spectacles. Like Pitaji and other elderly villagers who remembered the Raj, she was much less aggressive in her attitude towards me than the younger ones, and too respectful to address me directly.

'Well, didn't you know? She's been dead these two days!' He was a terrible tease, though I had yet to be on the receiving end of it. 'Where have you been all this time? We burned her yesterday.'

'No!'

'It's true. You can see she's not here.'

The old aunt chuckled and hobbled off down the alley.

Mataji and Pitaji sometimes disappeared at a moment's notice to a distant village where Pitaji's second cousin's husband's sister, or similar, had just died, and we wouldn't see them for a couple of days. Each time this happened, unfortunately, another widowed sister of Pitaji's had been staying, so we never had the house to ourselves. Mataji tolerated this sister-in-law in a resigned fashion (she drank too much tea and couldn't be trusted to cook a decent meal), but Jungli virtually ignored her. I could see why: she was feeble minded and lazy, and she had an unattractive habit of snuffling through our belongings when we were out, and consuming our reserve rations of food.

Jungli had a younger brother and sister, neither of whom lived in the village. His brother Balwant was two years younger than he was, a rebel who had cut off his hair, a family black sheep whose life consisted of drifting from place to place doing various things he oughtn't. His visits to the village were infrequent, but one day when Jungli and I were returning from Amritsar he was on the same bus. It was the first time I had seen him.

'There's my brother,' announced Jungli indifferently. He hadn't seen him for a long time either.

'Where?' I asked. Half the people on the bus could conceivably have been Jungli's brother.

'Vest and checked lungi. His face is the same as mine.'

Balwant didn't turn his head. He got quickly off the bus and strode ahead across the barren ground. When he came to Pitaji's alley he turned into the house next door.

'Why did he go in there?' It was the house of the opium-trading, liquor-distilling anarchists.

'He has a woman in there. He rarely comes to Pitaji's house.'

'But why didn't he speak to you?'

'He never speaks to me. We haven't spoken to each other for years.'

Later on I discovered why. Five years previously Jungli and Balwant had mortgaged some land they had inherited for 11,000 rupees (£700) to their paternal uncle so that they could buy a tea shop on the GT Road in Amritsar. The business had thrived for several months: they had undercut other people's prices, served better food and ploughed the profits back into the shop. Then one day Balwant absconded with 8000 rupees, and when, soon afterwards, someone stole the utensils as well, Jungli gave up in despair. The 11,000 rupees was still to be paid back, and only then could he claim his land. Meanwhile his uncle was receiving its profits in interest on their capital.

I never met Balwant. I was intrigued and would have liked to. On his next visit to the village it was dark and we were all asleep: he appeared at Pitaji's house sozzled, and talking non-stop. Pitaji, being sensible, took no notice, but Mataji sat on her charpoy, thin-lipped and in stony silence until he collapsed in a stupor. Next morning he had gone, and I had missed him again. In spite of repeated incidents like this, Mataji constantly worried about Balwant and would send Jungli to Amritsar every fortnight or so to see if anyone had news of him. But they never had.

A month later Balwant turned up again. He stole the little paraffin stove on which Jungli and I sometimes cooked in the afternoons when my hunger got the better of me and presented it to his lady friend next door. I was annoyed when I heard, and the family was too, for all three of them went to the police station nine miles away and made a report against him. It wasn't the first time and they were sick of having their possessions depleted by their wayward child. The police came to the village but Balwant had flown and wasn't seen again for several months.

Mataji's youngest child was Rajinder, a pretty girl in her early twenties who wore her hair in a waist-length plait. Of all Jungli's family it was Rajinder I liked most. She was alert and intelligent, friendly and magnanimous; when Rajinder came home the tensions dissolved and the disparate elements of Pitaji's household seemed almost like a family. But she was happy, I was to discover, against all odds.

Few village women understood the principles of colouring or design, but Rajinder had a natural unerring instinct and always looked nice. Village taste was the taste of the child, of heraldic simplicity and shiny surfaces and obvious pictures that told a story. Modern architecture, modern fabrics, modern utensils, modern pottery and modern embroidery were almost universally ugly in India, and the villagers – even the educated ones – liked them like that: few could discriminate between dignified design and vulgarity. The only 'art' they knew was their religious calendars, executed in a kind of quasi-kitsch realism in El Grecoesque colours.

Three years previously Rajinder had been married to a soldier. She and her husband lived near Delhi, where Gurmit was stationed, and sometimes they came home on leave. If Gurmit was around I temporarily lost my status as a visitor, for traditionally the son-in-law must have the best of everything. The family went without in order that he should be well fed and comfortable: charpoys were borrowed from next door and the upper yard took on the appearance of a doss house. Jungli was sent from house to house for eggs, while Mataji squatted dismally on her plank in the cooking enclosure, churning out chapattis and grumbling that she would be there half the night.

Jungli and I were invited to Gurmit's house. His family lived in a flat leafy village to the south of Amritsar, where koels sang at dawn in ascending crescendos. It was an old house, larger than Pitaji's, with beautiful panelled doors and arched recesses in the mud walls. When the afternoon cooled into evening we went out for a walk with a rifle.

I discovered then that Jungli had a passion: hunting.

Jungli and Gurmit's sort of hunting involved asking every peasant in sight if he had seen any pigeons lately and, when they had located some, a lot of standing around with the rifle looking important and gazing up into banyan branches while a bunch of admiring small boys looked on from a respectful distance. I sat in some bushes thinking my own thoughts. In the end there were four or five pigeons and for supper there was pigeon curry. Jungli and Gurmit tucked in like a couple of hyenas, juices dribbling down their chins and scrunching up bones. Rajinder wouldn't come near us: she never ate meat.

Gurmit was a tall young man with a sparse beard and a rubbery sneery face. I had often asked Jungli what he thought of him. I personally found him conceited and overbearing. Jungli was evasive but in the end admitted that he didn't like him.

'Then why do you behave as if you do and spend so much time with him?'

'Out of respect to Rajinder.'

'Does *she* like him?' I repeated this question several times over several months. At last I got the answer. 'No.'

'But she seems happy enough with him.'

'What else can she do? She has no choice but to put up with him. You know how difficult divorce is.'

'What do Mataji and Pitaji think of him?'

'Listen. Liking or disliking him isn't the point. Rajinder is married to him and everyone must make the best of it.'

'The rest of the family seemed pleasant enough,' I remarked. We stayed with them for several days; it was a good place for bird watching.

'The whole family is rotten.'

'But the mother was all over Rajinder, hugging and kissing her.'

'That's just for show. In public she's all sugar and sweetness but she treats Rajinder like a serf when there's no-one to impress: nags her and calls her insulting names.'

Poor Rajinder! She was a nice girl and deserved better.

Sometimes after a marriage one or other party's family would be found not to be all it had been made out to be beforehand. By then it was too late to do anything about it. Superficially the families might remain pleasantly hospitable to each other, but underneath the

surface, as in many apparently affable relationships, there would be
a resigned enmity. Such a situation occurred after Rajinder's marriage. A suitable match had to be found and Mataji's younger sister
suggested Gurmit. 'What a nice young man!' Mataji's sister said, and
she added some more about what a lot of land they had and what a
respectable family they were. After the marriage it was discovered
that they only had two and a half acres to Pitaji's fifty. Hardly
surprising then that the father and five sons were all in the army.

It was the duty of a Sikh to get married and rear a family.
According to Guru Nanak a man should do his work, bring up a
family and be in the world, though not of it. Individuals like Jungli
who had refused to marry ran the risk of being dismissed as characterless, or free and undisciplined, which in Panjabi eyes is the same
thing. Compromise and adjustment were considered good for the
soul.

The villagers tittered at the mention of love marriages, and oddly
enough the victims of these do-it-yourself arrangements that I came
across had mostly become disenchanted. Perhaps it was the lack of
respect for parental control that caused the titters; perhaps they
contained a hint of jealousy; or perhaps they were in fear of a
breakdown in Indian tradition.

Men and women were largely segregated. As their activities and
responsibilities were different, so were their topics of conversation.
While staying in the village I rarely saw a man conversing with the
wife of another. Emancipation made women corrupt, people
thought.

Although the Sikh faith preached the equality of women, it seemed
to me at the time (I was partially to change my opinion later) that in
certain respects they were still subservient. Even an aggressive
woman like Mataji, self-opinionated and with total command in the
house, served her husband diligently as a lord and never uttered his
name. Had Pitaji been a drinker, fighter or philanderer, Mataji could
neither have left him nor witheld his dinner: her place was to look
after him whatever, and to retain the respect of others by being
virtuous herself. She could curse him under her breath and grumble
to the neighbours, but it would be most unlikely that she could
reform him.

Everywhere Jungli and I went we were left to sleep where we
chose. It astonished me. 'Where do you want to sleep?' I would be
asked. 'Inside, out in the yard or on the roof?' And then the rest of the
household would tactfully pull their charpoys away and spread out
their bedding somewhere else.

Why did no-one put up any opposition? Even husbands and wives didn't normally sleep on their own. They occupied separate char-poys which they shared with the younger children, and everyone slept in their clothes. I wondered how they managed – it was hardly the ideal arrangement for wedded bliss – but the answer of course was the same: compromise and adjustment are good for the soul. There must have been moments, I suppose, when the children were all asleep at once, or everyone was out. And if you couldn't wait that long there were always the fields when the crops were high, and the barren ground at night where husband and wife could arrange to meet on tryst.

Had I been an Indian girl our situation could not have arisen. No village man who had a girlfriend would have taken her to his parent's house. *Were* it to happen she would have been absorbed into the family sleeping circle or set apart with the women, as I was when staying on my own in other Panjabi households. It was particularly inexplicable at home, where everyone would have known that Jungli and I occupied the same room (albeit with Mataji on guard by the door) and there was the family's respectability to think of: was Pitaji not criticized for his *laissez-faire* attitude?

I never knew. It might have been that as a foreigner people made allowances both for me and for what they believed my own customs to be. It might have been that as a guest I was given free choice. It could have been that they were afraid of Jungli, had learnt from experience that it wasn't worth crossing him. It could even have been that they wished to encourage our relationship, and took it for granted that it would end in marriage.

Jungli did exactly that.

'We could live in England,' he said. He thought I would be more comfortable there. 'You could do your work and I could stay at home and look after the house and grow vegetables and bring up the children.' Had I wanted to get married it might have been a sensible arrangement. But I did not. I tried to say, as gently as I could, that I wasn't sure if it would work. I was very fond of Jungli and had no wish to leave him. But marriage was another thing.

Jungli was wounded to the core. Hope and faith were essential to him; there was no room in his life for doubt. After this our joy was clouded. I lived for the present – always had done – but Jungli, like the village, feared for his future. He swallowed a large lump of opium and crashed out on his charpoy.

I still had no idea that Jungli was addicted to opium, that he took it every day. He swallowed it when I wasn't looking, and its physical manifestations were not very apparent. For perhaps a year I remained unaware of the depth of Jungli's dependence on the drug; ignorant of its transforming effect on his life.

The villagers were extraordinarily ignorant about sex. Young men would be told what to do on their wedding day by their elder brother's wives, who probably didn't know much either, since (Jungli assured me) many women viewed the sex act as no more than their duty to their husbands: 'his happiness is my happiness', etc. In the circumstances perhaps it wasn't surprising. Both men and women were full of taboos and only straight lovemaking 'as God meant it to be' was permissible. They took the doctors seriously (at least some did) when they warned that twice a month was quite enough for anyone or a man wouldn't have the energy to plough his fields. And unmarried men kept jugs of cold water by their bedsides because 'You'll never be able to satisfy your wife if you do *that*,' they warned. Jungli never had done. The young men listened and were silent.

Rajinder and Gurmit had a daughter of two. While Rajinder completed a domestic science course in Delhi, Kaki came to stay in the village, and fell in love with Pitaji. She stayed on, and Rajinder unselfishly never demanded her right as a mother (or *was* it her right?) to look after the child herself, though I am sure she would have preferred to. Pitaji taught Kaki to sing hymns, and sat her on his lap while he recited his prayers. Whenever he was at home she played by his side, and at night she slept on his charpoy.

But there wasn't much scope for playing in the village, and none at all for curiosity or inventiveness. At two Kaki was helping Mataji (of whom, like a lot of people, she was terrified): fetching and carrying, staying close by in case she was needed. By four she would be pumping water and by six or seven learning to cook, by which time the sons and daughters of poorer families would be supplementing their families' incomes. For children were regarded as miniature adults, inadequate grown-ups: they stayed in the company of their elders and learnt to join in their conversation and talk with equal authority. Having grown accustomed to the adult behaviour of these mature beings of eight or nine it came as a shock to see them blubbing over trivia like babies.

Kaki was a sweet child. I felt sorry for her. I felt sorry for the village children generally, for I believed the traditional mode of upbringing suppressed their childhood. Undoubtedly almost every villager would disagree, contending that the natural buoyancy and creativity in children was not suppressed but rather rechannelled for the mutual benefit of child and community. But to me it was just the first of a series of limitations on natural human behaviour that the villager would have to contend with throughout his life: limitations on personality and self expression, natural talent, sexual energy and freedom of choice.

Children soon learnt to be tough. Kaki was perhaps more fortunate than most: she had Pitaji, who doted on her, and for the present she had Jungli and I. All of us had time on our hands and enjoyed her company and vivacity.

When there was a wind, the children flew coloured paper kites from the rooftops. Kaki loved to watch them soaring bird-like in the sky. Some children had clay tops and others collected pebbles for a Panjabi version of jacks. They improvised games, hiding and chasing each other round the house compounds, and played hopscotch marked out with a piece of broken brick on the yard floor.

But Kaki was more interested in new dresses, necklaces and bangles than she was in toys. Like other little girls of two she wore lipstick, nail varnish and kohl in black rims round her eyes when she went out, and prickly frilly nylon dresses with puffed sleeves. Whenever she had something new she would come barging through the fly curtain to show it off to us.

'*Very* beautiful!' Jungli always said.

Children showed astonishing obedience to their elders. Not just their own parents, but any elders. Women ordered their neighbours' children about as they did their own, slapping them if they were naughty and sending them on errands. Jungli or I could lean out of a bus window if it stopped in a traffic jam to command a boy or youth to fetch water or something to eat and he would go running without a murmur. Jungli showed Mataji the utmost respect. Should he be asleep when she called him, faintly from the other end of the yard, he would leap up as if an alarm clock had rung in his ear. His duty to her weighed heavily upon him.

Gurmit had done extremely well for himself out of Pitaji. Included in Rajinder's dowry had been ten acres of land, money, clothes and household necessities. Pitaji had even thrown in a couple of trees. Gurmit had felled the trees and built himself a new house in the flat leafy village. On its yard door were the stencilled words GURMIT SINGH in huge letters. No-one else wrote their names on their doors like that, but then no-one else had such a highly developed yearning for recognition.

Pitaji wanted Kaki to remain in the village. He offered to bring her up, to pay for her education, to feed and clothe her and, when the

time came, to provide her dowry. Quite possibly he didn't trust
Gurmit as far as he could see him.

When Kaki was a few years older she would attend the village
junior school. From Pitaji's yard door we could see it beyond the big
banyan tree where the buffaloes were tethered in the midday heat. It
had a large walled yard, bare but for one and a half newly-planted
trees and a series of empty barrack-like buildings with heavily barred
windows and mud floors. During lessons long lines of coir matting
were unrolled for the children to sit on; the teacher sat on a chair.

Whenever we passed the junior establishment during school hours
there seemed to be straggles of children hanging about in the track
outside.

'Why aren't they inside being taught?' I asked.

Jungli said the teachers didn't care much for teaching, and
preferred to spend their time chatting and drinking tea. At the
beginning of a lesson the children would be told to open their books
at a certain page and read to themselves. The only other things they
did that I was aware of was learn songs, or rather one song: the Sikh
communal hymn.

I peered through the schoolroom bars. Children were sitting on
the floor in groups, talking and scratching on slates. A teacher was
sitting by himself, aloof, on a chair, reading the newspaper. If a child
needed attention, I thought, he would have to go and interrupt him,
but he wouldn't, being a small child, for the white wall of newspaper
held strategically between himself and the teacher would have been
enough to intimidate even an adult.

If village schools were ineffective in developing capacities for
thought and creativity and in helping a child relate to his environment, most parents were worse. Formerly, with hours of spinning
and corn grinding each day, the women had had no time to instruct
or play with their children. Although time was now available the
habit wasn't there, and the women, themselves uneducated, felt
unsure of their inherited knowledge when confronted with the modern school system. They hesitated to teach their children the simplest
of things, like the names of birds and trees and the writing of the
alphabet. In any case it was not their duty but the role of the teacher,
Mataji said, to instruct the young.

When Kaki had been in the village for two months it was decided
that she should return to Delhi for a while with her parents. Pitaji,
Jungli and I accompanied them to the station to see them off. We
built a camp on the platform with their luggage – a sack of flour, a
bucket of cane sticks, two cloth bags and a tin trunk – and Pitaji sat

in the middle. Kaki nestled in the hollow made by his arms and legs, dolefully tearing the hard outer layer from a stick of sugar cane with her teeth, and clinging to his neck. As the train drew into the platform there was clamour and confusion all about us. But Pitaji and Kaki were silent: they knew the train was going to part them.

6

Nihang

JUNGLI WAS IN CHARGE of the local Nihangs. One of half a dozen Nihangs in the village and thirty or forty in the surrounding villages and hamlets, he was the equivalent of their district officer. As a mark of his leadership he wore a gathered loose end of material emerging from the top of his dome of turbans. He was responsible for contacting the other Nihangs in an emergency and seeing they didn't abuse the movement's numerous rules of etiquette. The work was voluntary and sporadic, but the uniform was mandatory at all times.

As a Nihang Jungli enjoyed certain privileges. Whereas there was a theoretical limit of three days on the time anyone else could put up at a gurdwara, a Nihang could stay, getting all his meals for nothing, virtually as long as he liked. An equally useful advantage was his proclaimed right to travel free on the Indian railways (Jungli had ridden to Calcutta and back, six days' journey in all, for nothing). I am not sure why this was so except that they sometimes needed to travel great distances to the scene of a skirmish but couldn't afford the fare. Nihangs would say it was because no-one dared ask for their ticket: they took great pride in their ability to instil fear into the remainder of the populace. A Nihang had only to say 'Go!' and a crowd of onlookers would turn tail like startled rabbits. I was most envious.

I still harboured romantic notions about Nihangs. Staying in gurdwaras over the months before I met Jungli I had come across plenty of them: proud, individual, extroverted beings who covered themselves with weapons, chains, knife blades and iron bangles to the extent that with the slightest twitch they clanked like medieval knights in chain mail. The weapons they carried would have been more appropriate to the days of King Arthur than the late twentieth century, yet they were the Nihang's most prized possession, his counterpart to the flashy foreign watch. Most Nihangs had swords and knives. Others carried long spears, battleaxes, bows and arrows, rifles, pistols, long-handled machetes and bicycle chains (swung on the end of an iron rod and possibly the most debilitating). Jungli valued his sword and its association with the tenth Sikh Guru, his hero, his mentor, above all.

Although theoretically limited in both style and colour, Nihangs showed remarkable invention in their dress. They stretched the sacred blue and orange to peacock, apricot and turquoise, aquamarine, gold and sky blue, shocking pink, tomato and ultramarine. And they put them together to make them sing; the Nihangs were the real folk artists of the Sikhs.

I knew that many Sikhs considered Nihangs to be disreputable and wouldn't invite them into their homes, but I had refused to listen to their criticisms. It was Jungli himself who changed my mind.

There was one Nihang in particular whom I knew before I met Jungli and whom I subsequently bumped into many times. He was a tall, compelling young man with a mischievous gleam in his eye and a voice as deep as the ocean, who everybody obeyed. That was mainly why I liked him. But, as I found out later, such acquaintances wouldn't do at all.

I first met him in one of the big city gurdwaras where, dressed like a footballer in blue and white striped waistcoat and matching woollen leggings, he and another Nihang, rather fat and plainly dressed, occupied a certain corner of the sleeping hall. If anyone else spread his bedding there it would be unceremoniously rolled to the side, but I was allowed to sleep in the very corner, in their protection. They shared their food with me – it saved me queuing for the langar,[1] and they usually procured raw onions to liven up the dal – taught me Panjabi, kept an eye on my luggage when I went to the bathroom (five minutes walk away), gave me a ring, sided with me against the authorities (who were trying, unsuccessfully, to throw me out, having had many problems with insensitive foreigners) and, best of all, wouldn't allow anybody else near. They accepted me as I was, treated me with respect, and never asked a single question.

After that I was always pleased to see the tall one (the fat one had less sparkle) and he would buy me cups of tea and proudly show me his latest weapon. I even spoke to him in defiance of the system, for I was all too aware of the frowns of censure if I so much as greeted him, and the suspicious looks of those who hung around to monitor our conversations.

It must have been on the fifth or sixth meeting that I came across him in Amritsar, retwisting his hair after a dip in the sacred tank. He was doing the rounds of the five holy tanks in the city, taking a dip in each.

'Don't trust anybody,' he told me. I wondered if what he meant

[1] free kitchen

was 'Don't trust me.' He needn't have worried, for I didn't, but I still enjoyed his company – he was refreshingly different – and as long as we remained in public I couldn't see the harm in it.

Then for the first time I noticed his legs. They were covered in deep weals and scars. There was a gaping wound in his foot, probably only a day or two old, and he had just immersed it in the khaki-coloured tank which people bathed in and drank from and which was fed by the canal.

I winced. 'How did you do that?' I asked innocently.

'I caught it on the end of my machete,' he lied, shrugging as if it was just a minor scratch. But it looked a formidable machete, razor sharp with a hooked tip. It was celebrated among the Nihangs, I discovered later, having decided to ask Jungli if he knew anything about him. He described it to me in perfect detail after I had given him an account of the tall Nihang's appearance and voice, as a means of identification. It seemed I had picked a hardened criminal; the man and his deeds were as notorious as the weapon with which he carried them out.

'He's a very dirty[2] man,' Jungli told me sternly. '*Very* dirty. That deep voice isn't his real voice. He has many voices and many names. He's a renowned thief. He picks pockets at stations and on trains. He takes people into his confidence at the gurdwaras and then dopes them with chloroform and robs them of everything they have. He's a rich man, and always intoxicated.' Jungli paused. 'Yes,' he said on reflection, 'and he's a murderer too. So's the fat one.'

'How do you know?'

'I know,' he said. 'I'm a Nihang too. And I've seen him murder a man with my own eyes. It was at a gurdwara, one of the most important religious sites of the Sikhs, and actually in the courtyard. He and the man concerned had been partners in a robbery, and the other Nihang was demanding his share of the proceeds. The tall one refused to give it to him and when challenged he slit his body open. Like this,' Jungli drew his hand across his chola[3] diagonally from shoulder to waist. 'The tall one couldn't be caught, he was too quick. Only once has he been in jail.'

By the time this conversation took place I had seen enough for myself and I wasn't particularly surprised. Jungli thought only about ten or fifteen per cent of Nihangs were true to their cause, and those one rarely came across, for they would be at home, working in the fields. The constant warnings of people in the early days now made

[2] a direct translation from the Panjabi, meaning no good or wicked
[3] knee-length tunic worn by Nihangs

sense too. It would be, 'Don't go near these men; these are not family men,' or 'Beware of the Nihangs, they will offer you intoxicating substances and then rob you.' Or again, 'Don't be deceived by their religious dress. For many Nihangs it is merely a cloak behind which to conceal their antisocial behaviour.'

They had been right, unfortunately. From then on I took little more notice of them.

Actions, aspirations and interrelationships in the enclosed society of the village were governed by the faith of its overwhelming Sikh majority: the basis of daily life was the word of the Guru. Thus those who could afford to gave to the poor. Thus strangers were treated as sisters and brothers and people surrendered their individuality to the efficient functioning of the group. Thus all effort was devoted to earning a living, raising a family, helping the community and praising God. Thus talents remained undeveloped and nothing was done for its own sake: no music (except religious music); no poetry; no art; and no feeling for the beauty of nature. And thus anger, greed, lust and ego were seen as sinful, and anyone indulging in intoxicating substances did so in private.

Divisions between right and wrong were clearly demarcated, and people seemed to operate in either one or other sphere. To those who feared God, life happened according to His will, in turn determined by their own past acts. To the minority (I could only guess that they were still a minority) who had rejected that belief, the forbidden fruits of 'Western' freedoms were a dangerous temptation. Their unsophisticated minds had neither the knowledge of how to respect them nor adequate self-control to resist them, so reactions to generations of religious oppression could be extreme. I once met an ingenuous-looking youth in a gurdwara and a year later received a letter saying '. . . you will surprise I smoke cigarettes, charas, ganja, take opium, heroin, LSD, etc. (these kinds of drugs). I do not believe in Sikhism. In it there are many restrictions. I will cut my hair.' He was right: I was rather surprised.

Jungli's best friend in the village was a shy young Nihang called Gian Singh, who worshipped Jungli and was as far from the prototype of fierce bad Nihang as anyone could get. I liked Gian Singh; he had a gentle manner and an open face and he worked all day on his family's land. He came to Jungli when his brothers quarrelled, and sometimes accompanied us on our travels.

Jungli rarely went out. He might spend an hour with an acquaintance in the morning or early evening, but the home of Gian Singh, his real friend, was out of bounds. Gian Singh had two unmarried sisters, and if Jungli was seen to be entering his compound he would become the centre of conjectural gossip that grew more fictitious as it was passed from one eager ear to the next. 'That Pritam Singh, Beant Singh's son from the next neighbourhood, I saw him going into Gian Singh's house again – he must have evil designs on one of those girls,' could turn without difficulty into accusations liable to damage the prestige of Pitaji's family. It was better not to go at all.

The only other Nihang in the village that Jungli had any time for was Harbans Singh, an archetypal Nihang who was stoned all day and every day and could never remember to whom he had been talking half an hour earlier, nor a word they had said. He lived by himself out in the fields by the burning ground, tending the memorial of a local warrior Nihang who had died on the spot defending his honour. Out there people were unlikely to poke their noses into his misdoings. Jungli and I sometimes called in on our evening walks and squatted under the old gnarled jand[4] trees that were, for me, the main attraction of the place, gazing out at the columns of smoke rising from funeral pyres fifty yards away, drinking nauseous opium poppy seed tea out of shallow iron bowls and exchanging gossip about absent Nihangs and all too present weapons.

The Sikhs are renowned, among other things, for their penchant for alcohol. 'If you must drink, drink at home,' warned posters in Amritsar. People did just that, which was why the habit was not very obvious to the casual visitor. But I remember walking along the road one evening with Jungli and Mataji. A man was lying on his stomach in the verge, his face in the dust. 'Oh poor man, we must help him,' was my immediate reaction.

'Leave him alone,' said Mataji sharply. 'He's drunk.' She turned her face in the other direction and walked stiffly on.

It seemed that people either took whatever intoxicants they could lay their hands on or strongly condemned them all. Illicit liquor was distilled in oil drums in secret corners of the villagers' yards. Opium was as accessible as alcohol on the local black market, and cannabis grew wild in nettle-like thickets, to be made into a drink the colour of dirty dish-water, called bhang like the plant it came from. It was bhang that kept Fikan the servant boy going during the long afternoons. And Harbans Singh drank a bucketful every day, enough to render most people permanently insensible. (On the one occasion when Jungli had unwittingly drunk a single glassful he had been

4 *Prosopis cineraria*

knocked unconscious and woken to find himself mysteriously without money, watch or sword.)

What the Sikhs didn't do was chew betel or smoke cigarettes, and as far as I was concerned that made up for a lot of booze and bhang. Only once or twice did I ever see a turbanned Sikh with a cigarette in his mouth and that was in a city, though Jungli believed that many more smoked in private.

Harbans Singh appeared at the house one evening looking anxious. There was a ripe bhang patch nearby and he had to harvest it before it dried up in the heat. He borrowed a camel and bore Jungli off at dawn next morning to back him up should anyone make trouble: being Nihangs they could get away with things that any ordinary mortal would be locked up for but they might be obliged to flash their spears a bit. They returned at dusk with the camel piled high and very sore buttocks – the ten-mile journey had taken four hours each way. I was still in a bad mood because I hadn't been allowed to go too. Damn it, I had never ridden on a camel.

Try as I might, I couldn't persuade Jungli to give up opium. He wanted to stop but couldn't, and if I teased him about it I would be teased back. 'Your writing is your intoxication,' he once said to me. 'Aren't I entitled to mine?' I considered this standpoint and realized there was truth in what he said. It was a sobering thought.

Because he took opium he suffered from aching muscles and needed daily massage. I would be summoned to squat beside him on his charpoy and knead and slap and pummel and wrench him as Mataji did her dough, while he groaned in pain and resurrection. I would stand on his back and tread his muscles with my feet, moving from his shoulder blades almost to his knees. Then he would sit up, calm and exhausted, and thoughtfully rub himself down with rape oil.

We talked a lot, Jungli and I. The days were ours to talk in. It was through Jungli rather than my book that I learnt to speak Panjabi, and because of him that I never succeeded in speaking it correctly. He could usually sense what I was trying to say however badly I said it, and in spite of the expressions of blank incomprehension affected by the rest of the family. He liked it like that, and never (unfortunately) attempted to rectify my mistakes. He even adopted them for his own use. He remembered me when I went away, he said, by the funny way I talked.

I would have loved to speak perfect Panjabi. In the *Granth* there are some wonderfully architectural word constructions. I liked the Panjabi habit of repeating certain words with the substitution of one of its letters for another to give it emphasis: 'sap sup' for snake, and 'cha sha' for tea. I liked the romantic word badal, meaning both 'clouds' and 'change'. What I didn't like were the unmentionable anatomical terms and incestuous accusations with which most village men offhandedly salted their conversation; terms and insults that were so often used they had lost practically all meaning beyond that of a basic insult.

Living in a village where one could expect to know almost everyone by sight, it would cramp one's style to stop and gossip with each passing acquaintance. At such times the villagers made use of an abbreviated sign language through which a conversation could be enacted without opening one's mouth or slackening one's steps, in the space of a few seconds:

'Sat Sri Akal.' ('Good day' (literally 'True Lord God').)

'Sat Sri Akal.'

'How are you keeping?'

'Not too bad thanks. And yourself?'

'Fine. Where are you heading?'

'Just going round the corner for a pee.' Nice expressive gesture this. 'Be seeing you.'

Within two or three months I knew enough words to be able to discuss almost anything with Jungli. We talked of philosophy and Sikhism, of the village and the land, of India and Indians, of Nihangs and neighbours, of illness, of money, of food. What we never touched on, not once in two years, were the arts and sciences, huge holes in our communication. But at the time I never noticed.

Much of our conversation consisted of questions and answers. I listened and asked questions: Jungli explained.

'How did people wash before there was soap?'

'They would use a mixture of yoghurt and chickpea flour or the skin off boiled milk, rinsing it off once the fat had been absorbed.'

'Did that make them clean?'

'Very. It leaves the skin soft and smooth.'

'Does anyone still do that?'

'Some of the older people do if there's yoghurt available. They wash their hair in it too. I sometimes use stale yoghurt as a skin conditioner, having washed with soap first.'

'What about clothes?'

'People used to wash them in several days' old buttermilk, or with soda.'

'Soda?'

'Soil soda. It forms in a thin white film on the surface of barren land and has to be scraped off. The Mazbis still use it. Even Mataji uses it for the bedding and daris which she carts three miles to the canal to wash.'

This conversation might have taken an hour once I had puzzled out meanings and looked up words like soda in the dictionary. Jungli was amazing like that. I am an inexorable asker of questions but he really seemed to enjoy it. The only thing he didn't like was questions prefaced with the word 'why'. Being stumped by logic, I was putting him on the spot and giving offence. He rarely asked such questions himself.

I was gradually becoming aware of the enormous gulf between us. I represented the analytical, doubting, educated West; Jungli the innocent, irrational, mystical East. He was possibly unusual for a young Panjabi (in general the most Westernized and outward-looking Indians) in that he showed no interest in England and knew nothing about life there. He disliked Western clothes and pakka houses, and scorned those millions of Indians who adopted Western values. He didn't care where he slept and didn't mind if he got nothing to eat all day; not once in two years did I hear him say 'I'm hungry,' and not once did he go out of his way to get food. He ate when I did, and frequently went without. Like the older village people he was almost wholly untouched by the Raj except for his addictions to tea and terycot (though he had adopted terycot reluctantly when his friends mocked him for wearing the homespun he really preferred). He lived a life of absolute simplicity, preferred to eat and drink from his hands, had no sense of personal territory and owned nothing that wasn't immediately essential.

Although he never asked about my life in England he was quite prepared to listen to whatever I chose to tell him. It wasn't much. I was fully absorbed in being where I was, and at the time was no more interested in the West than he. Usually when I talked he made no comment beyond the occasional scandalized snort at the irregular behaviour of the British, whom he generally dismissed as being crazy and undisciplined. But one day I was reading an early edition of Kenneth Grahame's *The Wind in the Willows*. It was bound in deep green leather and decorated with a small gold tooling depicting the god Pan playing his pipes, while Mole and Rat sat in a little boat listening in enchantment. When I showed it to Jungli (who liked the directness of pictures) and told him about Pan, he listened with an attentiveness I had never known in him before. Who was this Pan? he asked. What sort of music did he play? How big were his pipes? This big? Longer? What was he like? Did people believe in him? What did he do? How could one find him? He, Jungli, would meet him. Pan was the only Western phenomenon he ever showed any enthusiasm for, and in a way I sympathized with his attitude. I wouldn't mind meeting Pan myself.

Not that he was very complimentary about India or things Indian either. Like many of his countrymen he was disparaging about his government, about the low quality of Indian products and the dishonesty in all walks of life; but unlike them he didn't object if I was the one who made the criticisms.

Corruption *was* everywhere: I knew that. It permeated every aspect of the bureaucratic machinery from the directors to the peons, and was thought by some to have become a necessary ingredient for its efficient running. In spite of Guru Nanak and modern legislation the villagers were still the victims of money lenders, mortgaging land, home and possessions and paying back the ever-increasing loans at interests of twenty or thirty per cent. It was the poor man, like Jungli, with little experience of forms and government institutions, who always came off worst. An Indian passport cost two or three pounds. With the agent's fee a man could expect a total bill of six or seven pounds. Jungli's passport cost him seventy-five pounds. He chose the wrong agent (who held out for more and more money), he wasn't familiar with the short cuts, and he didn't know the right people. Otherwise a tough and fairly aggressive person, he was helpless against the system. I still fume about it.

Jungli was like a cat, a sleek black cat. He could sleep all day and night if there was nothing better to do, and work all day and night if there was. He never complained of being bored though, so far as I could tell, his mind was often unoccupied. He showed displeasure like a cat and instinctively lashed out when threatened or insulted. Like a cat (and like other villagers) he showed a disarming aptitude for insincere flattery to get something he wanted. And like a cat he was oblivious of his own nature, and of mine. He believed in me, trusted me, never criticized me and never spoke ill of me to others. My past didn't concern him, for it was outside his experience and therefore meaningless, and he made no attempt to understand what I did or said. He was unable to sense my feelings, except when I was hungry – he knew when I was hungry all right. He never used me in a mercenary way and had no shame in doing women's work: if I was ill he did everything for me. All he knew about me, he said, was that I was his friend.

He hadn't trusted me at first. A combination of credulity and suspicion, I think he had maybe never met anyone on whom he could absolutely rely to tell the truth. And I never lied to him. Whatever he asked I told him, even if I thought he would explode or sulk for days in consequence. Curiously he did neither, so amazed was he that I wasn't afraid to tell the truth. In return, and though he lied to others – almost everybody lied – he never, I don't think, lied to me.

One day he asked, 'What kind of man am I?'

I replied, 'Do you really want to know?'

'Yes, tell me.'

'You might not like it.'

'Never mind.'

I thought for a moment. He probably expected me to say good, not bad or very dirty, which is the villager's way of assessing character. Instead I replied, 'Full of suppressed anger and inclined towards violence. Efficient, ingenious and intelligent. Strong-willed and physically courageous but weak-minded. Unselfish, adaptable, straightforward, faithful, instinctive, compassionate and soft-hearted. Wounding but easily wounded, mistrustful, self-pitying, non-analytical and pessimistic. Tidy, high-moralled and religious. A procrastinator and an unrelenting tease.' It took me some time to think of it all.

It went in one ear and out the other. I might as well have been discussing Indira Gandhi. Anyway he never asked again.

Jungli knew what he needed to know and didn't clutter his head with what didn't concern him. I asked him who the Prime Minister of India was – they kept changing them at the time – but he had even less idea than I had. He didn't know what Asia was, but had a vague feeling it was the same thing as India. Europe he had never heard of. Nor Karl Marx. 'How far is London from England?' he once asked me, and he took some convincing that the question was unanswerable. 'It's *in* England,' I said. 'It's the capital. Like Delhi is in India.' He had long forgotten what he had learnt in school: his maths was atrocious, and once he asked me how to write $\frac{3}{4}$. Neither did he have a sense of geography, of direction. If I referred to places in terms of compass points he would look at me blankly, his incomprehension only dissolving when I altered my description to 'Calcutta side' or 'onwards from Amritsar'.

But he knew every bird and every tree. He could identify the origin of every piece of timber, stick or twig broom. He knew how to farm and how to keep house. He knew the Sikh scriptures inside out and could quote long passages, especially from the writings of Guru

Gobind Singh. But characteristically he had no talent for description, and if I wanted to know something about a place or event, I had to find out for myself.

'What's Bombay like?'

'All right. There's a big gurdwara near Dadar Station.'

'What's Cochin like?'

'Quite nice.'

'What happens at Diwali?'

'Not much.'

It irritated me at first.

Unlike many villagers of his caste, Jungli didn't stratify people into grades of worthiness based on their birth. He neither talked down to nor degraded people of lower castes than himself: he had several Mazbi friends whom he regarded as equals.

He came home one afternoon from the house of a Mazbi. 'I've got a new kind of toffee,' he told me proudly. 'You can chew it and chew it and it doesn't go away.' At that moment I experienced one of those revelations people sometimes have in India: Indians don't chew gum! What Jungli had been given wasn't mere chewing gum either, but pedigree pink bubble gum. To demonstrate its potential I chewed it till it was soft – something I hadn't done for over twenty years – and blew vulgar pink bubbles at him. He laughed, delighted, like a child.

I liked him like that. It suited him. Whereas many of his peers were acutely conscious of their manhood, spending an unhealthy length of time in front of mirrors getting their moustaches right and preening their beards and tweaking their turbans, Jungli was totally un-affected by his looks. Tourists would come up to him at the Golden Temple and ask if they could take his photograph, but it never occurred to him that it might be on account of his striking face. He said no-one had ever mentioned such a thing before.

Although he didn't tell me until we had left the village, Jungli kept a pistol hidden in his pillow. He knew I disliked weapons, but as he quite reasonably pointed out, 'Look we are a fighting people; it's in our blood. What sort of man is he that can't defend his home, his woman and his children when they are attacked? The Sikhs are proud; they will die fighting rather than see their women abducted, their belongings looted and their honour sacrificed.' I knew they were not just words.

7

Outings

EVERY NOW AND THEN Jungli and I went to Amritsar. Jungli strode ahead with his sword and I followed through the crowded streets, running to keep up and getting pushed out of the way by rickshaws and bicycles and people and carts. Our days in the city were an antidote to our torpid existence with the twenty-three calendars behind the fly curtain.

The trouble with going anywhere was that people stared. In the presence of an English-speaking Indian or Westerner or when absorbed in something else I had usually managed to ignore it, but travelling in a bus with Jungli, eroded by heat and sometimes illness, with the language and the loss of my independence to cope with as well, the staring faces were more than my nerves could stand. I detested them more and more; became paranoid about them. I pulled my veil across my face and turned away.

'You make it worse,' Jungli told me, unable to understand, but trying to help.

It did make it worse: I was succumbing to them. And they went on staring, greedily and disapprovingly. Men, at least, had the excuse of sex, but women gazed upon me as an outcaste, a freak. I was haunted by their avid eyes.

Getting to any destination from that remote village was time-consuming as well as temper and energy sapping. It took over an hour just to get to the local town. At the crossroads, the hub of its activity, there were teashops and sweetmeat shops, fruit and vegetable stalls, beggars crouching in the eddying dust, long haphazard bus queues that everyone ignored as they flung themselves at the first braking vehicle, and traffic jams of tongas, cycles, pedestrians, bullock carts, buses and plodding pad-footed camels. Above, among the tram-line grid of wires, flew the colourful banners of drying turbans. Jungli and I spent many hours waiting at this crossroads – or rather Jungli waited while I was put away inside somewhere, safe from prospecting eyes. We would get in and out of stationary tongas and buses several times with our bundles of luggage before finally settling on whatever Jungli thought was going to get there first.

The journey from the local town to Amritsar took a further hour

and a half, maybe two hours. A three hour journey in 110° just to buy
fruit and vegetables or post my mail. From Amritsar to visit relatives
in a village on the far side took another two, three hours. Total: six
hours. Fare: eighteen pence. Distance covered: about twenty-five
miles as the crow flies.

On our trips away from the village, even if of two or three days'
duration, the only luggage Jungli carried was his sword, which he
frequently mislaid. Everything he needed was contained in the two
breast pockets of his chola. He drank when water was available. He
washed his clothes, waited for them to dry and put them back on
again. The length of orange cloth he carried over his shoulder served
as sheet, towel, belt, lungi, basket, shawl, spare turban or rope, as the
need arose. His independence from what I considered to be necessities was enviable. I, on the other hand, was permanently weighed
down by a heavy shoulder bag containing water bottle, camera,
clean clothes, notebook, fan, books and numerous small objects,
none of which I thought I could do without.

City people looked at us suspiciously and made no effort to hide
their disapproval. I was evidently one of those 'free foreign girls' that
Indian men seem to know so much about, and Jungli an irresponsible
opportunist making the most of it. Sometimes a respectable shop-
keeper would draw me aside and ask, 'Is this man known to you?' In
his eyes there would be another question, 'Just what is a decent
Englishwoman doing in the company of a Nihang?'

They were quite wrong as it happened, and their stereotyped
assumptions irritated me. Jungli was infinitely courteous and respectful, always looking after my needs and ignoring his own.
Although naturally warm and affectionate, a man reassured by
physical contact, he would have been prepared to remain in my
company indefinitely with no physical relationship at all.

The degree of pride or embarrassment that Jungli's relations
attached to their houses was in direct inverse proportion to how
much I liked them. We paid a courtesy call on Mataji's brother, a
well-to-do banker who lived in a new cement house in a rising
middle-class colony on the outskirts of Amritsar. It had a neo-forties
exterior, and resembled all such houses in all such colonies throughout the third world. In contrast to Jungli's village house with its sense
of fitness and grace, its harmony with the environment and culture to
which it belonged and its gradual evolution towards a constantly
improving ideal, these modern houses were designed overnight,
made from alien materials and belonged nowhere. Inside everything
was new and ugly, with mock timber veneers and terrazzo floors and

machine-rounded corners. A brand-new fridge occupied the place of honour in the living room.

They were terribly proud of it all of course and terribly ashamed of their backward village relations who lived in a mud house with no electricity or flush loo, and especially of Jungli for being a Nihang. He was letting the side down and casting a cloud over the family's prestige. 'Why did you become a Nihang?' his uncle and aunt used to interrogate him, and, 'Why don't you live at home more?' Jungli, remembering, perched awkwardly on the edge of a chair (they didn't have charpoys) and avoided the eyes of his aunt curled coyly, film-star style, in hers, in a crease-resistent orange salvar-kamiz. He disliked her patronizing manner and the show of expensive Western things around him. And as soon as he reasonably could, it was, 'Chalo, chaliye,'[1] to me and we were off to the bus stand and back to the homely mud house in the village.

Most villagers did what little shopping they had to do in the local town. But Mataji went shopping in Amritsar. She was city bred and liked good quality; accustomed to having a large selection she was more particular about her purchases and snooty about those of her neighbours who weren't. It put her out when I chose to go to Pakistan for the day to buy the things I needed. 'What do you want to go *there* for?' she asked disdainfully, not being able to go herself. 'They all come over here; there are much better fabrics in Amritsar.' Nevertheless she gave me a shopping list of everything that was half price in Pakistan, and when I came back the customs officer looked very suspiciously at the small brown lump of asafoetida in my luggage. I hoped he wouldn't ask what it was for, for I wouldn't have been able to tell him.

The purpose of outings, so far as Jungli was concerned, was to visit relations or have darshan at the important monuments of the Sikhs. Knowing how much I liked to travel he conducted me throughout Panjab, a state the size of Scotland, visiting the historical gurdwaras. My strongest memories of these trips are of steaming hour after hour in dilapidated buses, waiting from them to depart, and padding along sweltering country roads when they broke down. Often the gurdwaras were in remote rural areas, and I enjoyed seeing the new landscapes and staying in strange villages. Jungli enjoyed the trips too, though he loathed the journeys far more than I; he showed me round each gurdwara in a proprietorial way and told me long and

[1] 'Let's go'

involved tales about the Gurus associated with them, all of which he knew by heart.

The equivalent of the altar as the centre of worship in a gurdwara is the *Granth*, placed on a low platform and kept wrapped in exotic cloths when not in use. Before it all who enter must kneel in humility and respect, their foreheads touching the floor. Many Sikhs actually kiss the floor and rub their foreheads with the dust from other Sikhs' feet, orthodox and proper behaviour encouraging appropriate feelings of self-abasement in the presence of God and His holy congregation. Heads must be covered and feet bare.

As architecture all but the older gurdwaras fail. Being a comparatively modern faith, its temples are often still in the process of construction and suffer the same fate as the middle-class suburbs. Eclectic or unimaginative externally, they are plainer still inside and prosaic in the extreme. A few cheaply-framed prints of the Gurus on the walls, a small vase of plastic flowers and an off-red border around the faded blue daris on the floor: most gurdwaras are more like school gyms than temples, and the most austere places of worship I have ever set eyes on. The call of Guru and God stands alone, undisguised and unadorned. Attracted as I am by decoration, I could see the strength of this viewpoint. To the Sikh, presumably not too concerned with architectural integrity, beauty lies in Truth, Truth is God, and embellishment is irrelevant. I began to enjoy the spartan spaces.

Before I met Jungli my life in India centred on the gurdwaras. I saw them as a means of getting to know people and an opportunity to share fragments of their lives. Throughout northern India I slept on the floor in communal halls and woke to the sounds of people reciting *path*[2] and making swiss rolls of their bedding. The occupants of gurdwaras were always doing things which were new to me, like making new quills for their arrows or rolling their beards in those frightful narrow hairnets Sikh businessmen wear to look smart.

But much as I was interested in them they were far more curious about me. One by one my audience would come and squat beside me and ask, very politely, about a hundred and twenty questions, always the same questions, as if there were a questionnaire for foreigners implanted in their brains. And like filling out a questionnaire I had to produce answers, 'Yes', 'No', or 'Don't know'; to say any more would have been to break the rules and interrupt their flow, and I soon found people weren't interested in opinions, only facts.

[2] excerpts from the *Granth*

The first question would always be, 'From which country?'
'England.' Sometimes I said Iceland.
Then, 'Where in England?'
'London.'
'Proper London?'
I was already defeated: I had no idea whether I came from proper London, whatever that was, or some masquerading suburb outside.

To be fair I found the questions of Western travellers equally fatuous. Their, 'Where are you going?' and 'Where have you been?', 'How long have you been in India?' and 'How much longer are you staying?', 'Where do you come from?' and 'What do you do?', and sometimes an extra one, 'Are you keen on photography?' also lacked imagination and could be tedious if one didn't progress beyond that level. Long before I met Jungli and for the duration of my stay in the East I avoided other Westerners, there being plenty of them at home. Although fully aware of how hard it was to achieve a mutual understanding with most Indians, and how effortless, once over the first hurdles, with those from one's own background, I wanted to be immersed in India. I wanted to penetrate the oriental mind.

Then I met Jungli, a man untouched by the West. Jungli didn't ask one personal question, ever.

I trusted the people staying in gurdwaras. I innocently thought that anyone staying in a religious place was bound to be honest. I would leave my luggage lying around (in spite of repeatedly being warned not to), or in the care of some vagabond Nihang. I would go out leaving my washing drying on the public lines. And I would talk to anybody I felt like talking to.

I never came to any harm but my behaviour got me into trouble. It wasn't done for single women to be friendly. 'Remain aloof,' people sometimes advised me. 'Sleep apart from other people. Talk to them by all means, but be reserved in your speech and facial expressions. And whatever you do, don't allow yourself to be touched. It may be all right in your own country but it's unthinkable here.'

Travelling with Jungli the situation was altogether different. I learnt to behave like an Indian woman. But it wasn't any fun. I wore a stern expression on my face, followed submissively in Jungli's wake, and was careful not to look at men. Jungli made the decisions and Jungli did all the talking. He stood between me and the world.

The festival of Baisakhi was the anniversary of the creation of the Khalsa[3] movement. Jungli, Gian Singh and I celebrated it in

---

[3] military Sikh brotherhood set up by the tenth Guru

Anandpur, a small town in the Himalayan foothills; its birthplace. Tens of thousands of pilgrims were sleeping on the open ground, and setting up camp on balconies and in the backs of lorries.

In the morning we set off on a day-long tour. The town and its environs were packed with devout Sikhs washing away their sins at each gurdwara and sacred site. One of the bathing tanks contained leeches and frogs; another was green and scummy. But if there was a tank or bathroom we were meant to take a bath in it, however feeble the trickle of water, however little we felt like it and (this applied to me) however much we minded a collection of brown ladies gazing in awe at our white back premises. I envied the Sikhs their stalwart undiscerning souls.

Jungli and Gian Singh thoroughly enjoyed themselves. We climbed to hilltops in the noonday heat ('Do we have to go all the way up there?' I pleaded. 'Yes,' said Jungli firmly, 'it's obligatory,') and we climbed down to the bottom of a deep well, to be splashed with the holy water by the man whose job it was to splash it. We took a bus into the foothills to the site Guru Gobind Singh had chosen for his wedding, and another to Kiratpur on the banks of the Sutlej, where bone fragments of cremated Sikhs are cast into the river. In all we visited over a dozen gurdwaras, placing a small offering, receiving prasad,[4] and getting hotter in each. Jungli and Gian Singh were content: they had done their sacred duty.

Wherever we went we ate in the langars, or gurdwara kitchens. The institution of the langar was set up by Guru Nanak for the purpose of preaching equality, destroying Hindu untouchability, and spreading the doctrine of Sikhism. A langar's status is equal to that of the gurdwara itself, for in it the congregation partakes of holy food first offered to God.

Gurdwaras of pilgrimage like that at Anandpur had barn-sized langars catering for hundreds and sometimes thousands of people a day. We would arrive to find the langar full and a man keeping order with a stick. When our turn came we assembled in rows along the lines of coir matting, left knees up, right legs tucked underneath and elbows closed to our sides. A disc of dried leaves[5] was laid in front of each of us, followed by a leaf bowl and metal beaker. Into the beaker went water from a watering can. Into the bowl went dal from a bucket, and into our open palms fell two or three chapattis, gone

---

[4] sacred food offered to God and distributed among the congregation: usually a mixture of flour, sugar, ghee and water, but sometimes puffed rice or donated fruit or sweetmeats

[5] usually *Butea monosperma* leaves, pegged together with short twigs

cold from having been prepared several hours before. But that wasn't the point and complaining about langar food was insupportable, even to the most irreligious of Sikhs.

When we had finished we threw our leaves in a pile for the cows and rinsed our beakers under a tap, scrubbed them with ash, rinsed them again and stacked them on the pile to be handed out, wet and gritty, to the next shift.

The langar system illustrates the Sikh's belief in sharing what he has and being of service to others, a kind of voluntary communism. It was all the more impressive in a country where I had sadly learnt that many of the apparently holy are holy out of duty, out of habit, out of laziness, out of fear or out of greed. Some of the participants in a langar meal will have donated money towards the cost of the ingredients. Many will have helped prepare the food and others will have served it and cleaned up afterwards. Taking part in any of these operations gave someone like me the sense (however illusory) of belonging to an Indian community. Until I began staying in gurdwaras I had been merely a spectator of other people's lives.

It was fun helping in langars, cutting vegetables and rolling chapattis to a chorus of people saying, 'No, you don't do it like that!' There would be a series of women, each trying to convert me to her personal method of chapatti making, and fire stokers shouting across the yard, 'You're making them too big!' or, 'Don't put flour on the board!' I was slow too, but they didn't blame me for that.

It seemed I couldn't even cut vegetables properly, in spite of fifteen years experience. 'Cut it smaller,' someone would say. 'Cut it lengthwise!' 'Don't throw that bit away!' 'Peel it thicker!' 'That's a bad one!' 'Cut that piece out!' 'Hold it the other way round!' 'Try another knife!' Cauliflowers weren't to be cut at all, but torn, and the peeled stalks were thrown in too. My hands were stained indigo from onions and khaki from carrots, but I had found my milieu: a society of people more bossy than I.

Sometimes I did other seva[6] too, sweeping courtyards with minute bundles of grass stalks, cleaning bathing cubicles, folding floor sheets and dusting in the gurdwara. I even swept latrines. But what neither Jungli nor I ever did was carry mud on our heads. And Sikhs were always carrying mud on their heads, helping in the building of a gurdwara or cleaning out the sacred, silted-up, bathing tanks. To employ a building contractor or suction pump and do the work in two or three days would be to deny thousands of willing Sikhs the

[6] voluntary service for the benefit of the community

opportunity of doing service for their Gurus. This was real and thoroughly organized public participation. I watched several hundred volunteers, low caste Sikhs from villages and towns up to fifty miles away, standing knee deep in black slime at the bottom of a drained tank. They worked in four chains, passing baltas[7] of mud from person to person and up the steps and over the wall. Mud trickled down their headgear, bespattered their clothes and coated their legs and feet, but they didn't mind: on the contrary, in lives such as theirs it made a rare and enjoyable day out.

In most of the gurdwaras where Jungli and I stayed we came across whole families living, cooking and sleeping in single small rooms in a barracks off the yard, queuing at a communal pump for water, using unswept latrines and keeping their belongings in metal trunks. The families who lived in them accepted their situation and seemed as contented as people elsewhere. But I couldn't accept it. Time and time again I wondered, 'How can people live like that?' Later on I got my answer, for I lived like that for almost a year.

---

[7] shallow iron dish employed in carrying earth or rocks on the head

8

Traditions

WHEN A BOY CHILD WAS BORN, people rejoiced. If a girl came they weren't so pleased, but nobody wanted to be childless. Childlessness was a stigma.

Forty days after the birth the child's tongue would be touched with the tip of a holy knife moistened with sugared water. And around this time a group of strangers could be expected to present themselves at the house, to sing and dance in honour of the new baby. I once happened to be in a house where they were performing. There was something odd about them. 'Who are they?' I asked my companion, who spoke English. It was in another village and Jungli wasn't there.

'These are kusras.'

'What's a kusra?'

'In English you would say hermaphrodite.' You wouldn't actually: you might say eunuch, but that wouldn't be strictly true either.

'What do you mean, hermaphrodite?'

'They are neither man nor woman.'

'That's impossible! They must be one or the other.'

'No. They are neither. It's true.'

'How do you know it's true?'

'Some friends and I once paid one to prove it. We took it to a hut where it took off its clothes and there was nothing there. Only a tiny hole.'

I looked at the dancer in disbelief. It was dressed in a sari and doing a sensuous feminine dance. It looked back at me, wiggled its hips and laughed, delighted to be the object of my attention.

'I am not man. I am not woman,' it said to me in English. 'This is golden chance for you.'

It was right: I was absolutely fascinated. There was certainly something masculine about it, but something feminine too.

Kusras, it seemed, lived together in small bands. They were legally recognized by the Indian Constitution and had a right to make a living by performing at houses of recent childbirth. During the performance they would inspect the baby, and if it was a boy or a girl you were all right: you could keep it. But if it was neither they took it away and brought it up to sing and dance in their troupe. How sensible, I thought. Indian society has even a place for hermaphrodites. They have a livelihood and no reason to feel inferior. And people who aren't quite all there can adopt religious robes and get away with that too. Better by far than being put away in the dusty drawers of a mental institution.

Jungli confirmed my story of the kusras, and had even had a similar experience of giving one a rupee to prove itself. 'It may not have had any sex organs, but it wasn't averse to more devious forms of entertainment,' he said, or words to that effect. It had made improper suggestions to Jungli, and he had chased it out of the village.

The aspect of Indian village life requiring the most radical change of outlook for the average Westerner was the business of making one's arrangements. 'Making other arrangements' was how my mother referred to her toilet facilities in the hot summer of 1976 when her well dried up and we couldn't use the loo. What her 'other arrangements' were my brother and I never found out: he and I, lacking her upbringing, dug holes in the garden. Which at least gave me a bit of practice.

Urination was simple enough so long as no-one was looking: we peed in the open drain in the yard or beside a hole in the property wall facing downhill. But our other arrangements were made in the fields. This was where the fun started.

The arrangements area for our side of the village was the large expanse of barren land, laced with pits and ephemeral pools, beside the bus and tonga stop. One had a panoramic view of the barren land on one's arrival or homecoming: strewn with old menstrual rags torn from cast-off clothing, it wasn't the most welcoming of sights.

It was the custom for women to make their arrangements before dawn and men at sunrise. The daily excursion to the barren ground was regarded as a social event and an opportunity for a private gossip. For a few days Mataji woke me at half past five to accompany her. But my system wasn't geared to such timetables. Instead I found myself making the quarter-mile pilgrimage at far less suitable moments. It might be midday under a burning colourless sun with virtually no shade to take refuge in. It could be morning when children bored with school would follow on behind to see the show, for there could be no mistaking my mission when I passed with my pitcher of water. Or it might be dusk when streams of villagers were straggling past, cursing their buffaloes and twisting their tails to hurry them home.

Fortunately, since there was no means of not being in full view of anyone who happened to be passing, privacy at such times wasn't a thing that worried me particularly. Only once, when a strange girl in another village guided me to a suitable spot and gazed at me throughout from a distance of some eight feet, was I really daunted.

Sometimes people passing between their fields and the village would stop and stare with no consideration for what I was doing. 'Go away!' I would shout baldly in the local fashion. This was regarded as the highest comedy: there would be shrieks of laughter and they would advance closer for more. Sometimes women and girls would come and squat down beside me, the better to observe my activities as they got on with theirs.

On one occasion at midday, thinking everyone would be asleep and I would have the place to myself, I settled down comfortably in a slither of shade behind a wall. I was retying my salvar string when I noticed a group of figures bearing down on me and already embarrassingly close. A man waved an aerogramme under my nose.

'Excuse me, but are you knowing this address?' He spoke in English. The place was somewhere in Leigh on Sea.

'I've heard of it, but I've never been there.'

'Then could you be taking some articles there for me?'

I tried to explain that I had no intention of returning to England for several months, that my baggage was already overweight, and anyway I lived nowhere near Leigh on Sea. Wherever it was. He was put out, and apologized, as people were apt to do when they couldn't think of anything else to say. I felt rather mean: the poor man was probably only wanting to establish contact (I later heard he was distantly related to Jungli) or exercise his English.

Though sometimes I accompanied Jungli at eight or nine at night (we would squat companionably, facing each other, about fifty yards apart), I usually made my arrangements alone. This gave certain villagers an opportunity to goad me in ways they never dared when Jungli was around. Jungli's cousins, sisters-in-law of the man he had once shot, would walk right up to me no matter how much I veered off in another direction, and then laugh in my face. Children threw stones and ran round me in circles. I came to dread my visits to the barren ground. It may have been that people disapproved of the circumstances of my being in the village; it may have been that they saw me as fair game for the release of their pent-up emotions; it may have been an indirect attack on Jungli; it may even have been a way of getting their own back on the British (for as far as most villagers were concerned, all white people were British). When I asked why it was, the family just said, 'These people are not educated,' which was all very well but didn't solve the problem. Jungli remained silent: I felt he knew more than he cared to disclose.

When a man has lived in a village all his life and moves to the city, he either has to adapt or take a very long walk each day to find a field. Jungli and I stayed with such a family when we went to Amritsar. There was a loo of sorts that the women made use of, but the men disappeared for extended periods each day, sometimes on foot, sometimes on a bicycle. One day I accompanied them, to see where they went.

It was more like an expedition in search of the Holy Grail than a simple matter of getting rid of one's waste products. We went down the lane away from the GT Road, past loom shuttles clattering in workshops. We crossed more lanes and traversed a piece of waste ground between house compounds on a diagonal trodden path. We picked our way over a railway line, avoiding the cat's cradle of low, death-trap wires, and set off down another road until it joined a busy street. Turning right we walked a further few hundred yards along it and arrived at a second railway. We turned left along the line, stepping gingerly on the steeply shelving clinker, for a quarter of a mile, until the houses gave way to open fields, dykes and lagoons. A man was squatting timelessly in the middle of a ploughed field, smoking. The Lahore train rumbled past. A hot air balloon rose orange in the grey dusk sky. I realized the air was cool.

'Look!' they said in explanation, for they could see I was amused. 'This is a nice place, open and clean. It's cool and there's a fresh breeze blowing.'

I had to agree, but I knew that unless I could lose my consciousness of the value of time I could never follow their example on a daily basis. For a Sikh or Hindu time doesn't travel in a straight line to terminate in death but moves in a circle, ever recommencing at succeeding births. It is therefore of no value, for it will always come again.

The excursion had taken over an hour.

Instead of recycling human waste (for God knows there was enough of it) to build up soil fertility, it was left to desiccate on the barren land. But the ground was remarkably unsoiled considering the number of people who used it. Sometimes I would see a pharaoh's chicken, a dirty white vulture with a yellow head, rummaging about for his unmentionable dinner, but it couldn't account for all of it. On being informed that a good deal more was eaten by sheep, apparently in preference to grass, I got into an argument. Mataji and Jungli had been appalled enough by Western people's lack of respect for cow flesh, but to consume an animal that ate faeces seemed almost worse.

'But sheep in England only eat grass.'

'Why should they eat grass when they prefer faeces?' Jungli wanted to know.

'There aren't any faeces: everyone has lavatories in their houses. Anyway there's beautiful grass in England. It's not like the stuff here.'

'If there were any faeces: they would be bound to eat them in preference.'

Like other discussions about comparative lifestyles in East and West the argument remained unsolved. Rather it opened up the further question of loos inside houses, another sordid obsession of the Western world.

Mataji's attitudes were rooted firmly in tradition. Having cooked all her life on sticks and dung she was decidedly contemptuous of those in the world who taint their victuals with gas or electric stoves. 'How can such food possibly be any good?' Mataji would say in a manner that shut out all argument, wrinkling up her nose. 'It would have no taste.' Mataji, like most villagers, wouldn't dream of eating anything outside her dietary experience, and if I happened to cook even south Indian food no-one but Jungli would touch it.

Nor did she believe in electric light: she had shunned its use from the day her eldest brother died from an electric shock while attempting to wire his house. Pitaji wrote it off – with transistor radios, fridges and furniture, gas and telephones – as a superfluous Western invention, or superfluous at least as far as he was concerned. The warm soft light generated by paraffin lamps, they both believed, was perfectly adequate for illuminating what little needed to be done after dark.

I thought so too. Electric light would have been as much out of place in that immemorial mud house as double glazing or a porcelain bath. But Jungli thought otherwise: he decided I was just being polite. In one of his making-me-comfortable campaigns that I had no say in he cadged a piece of wire off a neighbour and attached it illegally to the overhead government cable at the bottom of the alley. He acquired a bulb and a lampholder and slung the wire over a hook in the ceiling, much to Mataji and Pitaji's disgust. But they said nothing, at least in front of me, and I looked on helplessly as Jungli had his way.

Every few months the house needed replastering. When the cracking, crazing and disintegration of its surface showed signs of going beyond the limits of propriety, Mataji held a mud-smearing session. She took no part in the operation herself, apart from slinging an occasional order and hovering about more than she need have: the real work was done by her Mazbi sweeper. Thin, dark, glistening with sweat but cheerful in the cast-off clothes of a larger Jat, she collected dry mud from the barren land, ground it up and mixed it with water. Then she smeared it over the walls, like a cake being iced, till the hollows and cracks were invisible beneath a smooth new veneer. She finished the house front in two tasteful shades of pale yellow-brown mud, framing the doors with the deeper colour used round the base and sealing the floors with light khaki dung.

Swallowing what prejudices I might have had, my curiosity being too much for me, I squatted beside the squelchy heap of watered-down dung and, holding my palm very flat, spread it in sweeping sixty degree arcs as I had seen the sweeper do. She squatted beside me giggling, chirruping and shouting a commentary to Mataji, cloistered in the cooking enclosure picking grit out of the dal.

All this squatting and sitting cross-legged had inspired a new relationship between me and my feet. The villagers were obsessive about having clean feet. I would see them lovingly washing them at the pump, removing hard skin and ingrained dirt with pieces of broken brick. I had previously regarded my feet as rather remote objects that I wasn't altogether responsible for, but the necessary adoption of different habits made me almost as fanatical as they were.

The young men of the village were full of Big Ideas: they were going to do this one minute and something else the next, but little ever came of it. The most versed Big Idea was to go to England. 'I am going to England,' they would announce with a conceit Jungli found nauseating. 'They just say that to boost their egos,' he said as soon as they were out of earshot. 'They haven't two paise[1] in their pockets.' Besides which, having clamped down on immigration, England was what many Indians called 'closed'.

Such casual acquaintances with hardly two paise in their own pockets were in the habit of making frequent, and I thought a trifle unreasonable, demands on mine. 'Take me to England!' they would

---

[1] one paisa is one hundredth of a rupee

command offhandedly and quite out of the blue. I sensed that my negative replies and protestations of impracticality were a serious transgression, and that I was guilty of inflicting deep emotional wounds. I later learnt that no-one ever flatly denied a request, however outrageous. But I couldn't bring myself to make promises I knew I would be forced to break.

One of the things that had begun to concern me about Jungli was his lack of enthusiasm for life. Unlike the other young men with their Big Ideas, Jungli had no ambition, no interest. It disturbed me to see him sleeping all day and I asked him why he did so.

'It passes the time. What else is there to do?'

Having never in my life done anything merely for the sake of passing the time, I was profoundly shocked. Jungli was often to speak in terms of passing the time, and I was never quite easy with it. Each time I lost a particle of respect for him.

The older generation of villagers were more deeply religious than the young, and they had an ability to be at peace with the world: in India faith and happiness were often synonymous. Religion was the chief escape route from the confusion of daily life, but belief was disappearing as fast as Western values were being inculcated and adopted. It took me some time to realize that most people weren't happy, for they certainly weren't glum. There was a superficial contentedness about the restful rhythms of their daily tasks and the constant chattering between neighbours which belied the bitterness and resignation often smouldering beneath. And somehow the conversation within families – and not just Jungli's family – seemed to lack the real friendship and understanding that is not uncommon in the supposedly arid family life in the West. Not once did I witness positive abandoned joy: it was as if there were wires straining at their hearts.

Months after we first met, I asked Jungli why he had been attracted towards me in Calcutta; for him it had been a first sight thing.

He replied, 'I saw a girl, all alone. No mother; no father; no friend; no relative. She was thousands of miles from her homeland. Yet she wasn't afraid. She looked happy.'

I have heard it said that people fall in love not with a person, but with a quality they lack but would like to possess. My initial attraction to Jungli had been precisely that: among the things I admired about him, living by instinct and supreme generosity came high on the list.

Through being so different in these respects we gradually

weakened what we loved in the other. Jungli began to think things out, and I absorbed his sorrow.

What Jungli said was true: I had been happy in Calcutta. It was my happiness he fell for, the happiness that had eluded him, and might continue to elude him, for the rest of his days.

9

Prisoner

JUNGLI'S LIFE had not been easy. Even by Western standards his personal history was unique: by Indian ones, where boy children are little gods, where family life forms the nucleus of society, where distance and tradition inhibit travel and where the majority still spend their lives in the occupation dictated by their birth, it was exceptional. His story was presented to me as a broken jigsaw with pieces missing, supplied bit by bit over the months as Jungli's trust in me grew and as the information became relevant. It was a whole year before I finally fitted it together. He never asked anything about my background and I rarely mentioned it, for I had been as privileged as he had been deprived. And whereas I wanted to understand why he did and said the things he did, he accepted me totally as I was.

Mataji grew up in a large Delhi family who later moved to a village in Panjab. She was married in her late teens to a sub-inspector of police who had thirty-seven acres of land, and went to live in the small town of Kharanpur. Jungli was the eldest of their three children. No-one knew the date of his birth except that it was sometime during the hot weather. Mataji was even more vague about the year.

When Jungli told me the story of his early childhood, a year after I first met him, the final pieces in the puzzle fell into place. That Pitaji was not Jungli's father made sense at last of their differences, and of the strange remoteness in their relationship.

Jungli's real father, Balbir Singh, was a respected member of his community. He was a religious man and spent much of his time in prayer. But when Jungli was six, Balwant four and Rajinder two, Balbir Singh died. Thirty of the thirty-seven acres had been sold to keep the family going and pay for medicine during his illness, and his death was the end of the family's stability. Mataji was left in her mid-twenties without income and with three small children to bring up. She took them back to her parents' home where they stayed six months until their future had been settled: Mataji was to be married again, to a man fifteen years her senior.

Pitaji already had a wife of his own age. They had been married for twenty years and were happy in each other's company, but she had borne him no children. In such circumstances it was the custom for a man to marry again, for to whom was Pitaji to leave his inheritance? He belonged to a wealthier family than Balbir Singh with more than enough land to support four extra people. His first wife, a kind and deeply religious woman, moved out to make way for Mataji. She was still supported by Pitaji but she lived independently in the house across the dung patch where the straw was now kept, and spent her time reading *path*. She welcomed Mataji and the children, never begrudged their usurping her position, and apparently lived happily until a year before I met Jungli, when she died.

Physically and temperamentally Pitaji had nothing in common with his new wife. Pitaji was silent and serious; when he spoke it meant he had something to say. Mataji was loud-voiced and volatile; she got cross over nothing and grew smug at having moved up in the world. But she bore him no children: on the contrary, she got rid of those she already had.

Keeping the two-year-old Rajinder she had taken Jungli and Balwant to an orphanage in Amritsar. 'These children have no mother or father,' she said to the people in charge. 'I can't be responsible for them. I'm handing them over to you.' Jungli was seven and Balwant five.

The orphanage was free, kept going by donations from wealthy people. For eight years they lived there, Balwant longer. Mataji rarely visited her children, but they went to their 'aunt' in the village for school holidays and stayed for as long as she could stand their wild natures, or they her scoldings. Rajinder, on the other hand, was always well looked after, and was still welcomed to the village after her marriage, given money and allowed to stay as long as she liked. Although Jungli liked her he didn't quite trust her: she had had too much.

Jungli and Balwant were sent to a school outside the orphanage. There Jungli met a girl from Pitaji's village who stayed with relatives in Amritsar during term times and went home, as he did, in the holidays. They became close friends, though she was three years older, and loved each other in a platonic way right through their schooldays. Jungli stayed until the final year, jumping two years since he was brighter than most, and the girl left and became a teacher. She was beautiful he said, and clever and kind.

When Jungli left school he returned to the village to help Pitaji on the family land.

'Would you not have liked to go to college?' I asked him.

'I wanted to go but Mataji wouldn't give me an allowance. In order to concentrate you must eat properly, and to keep up face in front of the other students you need good clothes.'

But on another occasion when we were discussing education, the answer Jungli gave was a different one: 'What's the use of going to college? Look at my cousin, the one next door, it didn't get him very far.' He was an unassuming young man who had decided to take Sikhism seriously and grow his hair long. Jungli was teaching him to tie a turban. 'He has a BA in history and politics, but he can't find a job. He's been back in the village for two and a half years.'

'What does he do all day?'

'What is there to do? All he has to do is sleep and eat.'

'Can't he do anything in the village?'

'His father works as a police inspector in Jullundur, so they rent out their land. Other manual work would be beneath his caste, education and dignity. Even were he to find a proper job, say as a teacher, it would cost one or two years' salary in bribes to secure it. His family haven't got that money. All jobs have a price on them in India.'

'Do most of the villagers think like you?'

'Of course. People especially dislike girls going to college when they are going to spend the rest of their lives bringing up children and doing housework. You don't need a BA to do that! They are afraid for their daughters too. College girls are so free.'

Whatever the reason why Jungli didn't go to college, Mataji pretended it was he who was refusing to go. She beat him for his disobedience.

Jungli still saw the girl he loved, though not so often, for she was working in Amritsar twenty-five miles away. They knew they could never marry: marriage between two people living in the same village was forbidden. But when she died suddenly, of an undiagnosed illness, part of him died with her. He was still only fifteen.

Soon after her death there was a family row and Jungli left the house with a double sorrow to bear and neither money nor place to go. Many of his contemporaries were involved in smuggling, for the Pakistan border wasn't far away and the work was lucrative, high taxes being levied on imported goods by the Indian government. Having no alternative Jungli joined a band of seven or eight, and in 1965 he went to Pakistan.

For three years they smuggled opium, gold and weapons. Two of the band remained in India in charge of distribution. Two Muslims were responsible for the buying in Pakistan and the rest smuggled the goods across the border. They all wore their hair short and shaved their beards in order to pass as either Muslims or Hindus. Once or twice a month on a cloudy or moonless night Jungli crossed the border with a load of contraband. He would walk along the road from Lahore and cut across the fields shortly before the border to rejoin it on the far side. He delivered the goods in the village, buried his share of the proceeds in a secret place on Pitaji's land, slept in a derelict house by day and returned to Lahore the next night.

He led me across the fields to the derelict house. It had once been the home of a saint. It was here, up the narrow disintegrating staircase where you could no longer determine individual steps and along the top of a wide-cracked wall into a little room with cream and blue flaking walls, that he had slept during those lawless days, a gun by his side and his head pillowed on the crook of his arm.

While Jungli was a smuggler he lived in Lahore and had a relatively well-paid job in the Indian Intelligence Bureau. He lived with Muslims, as a Muslim, and to keep up the image had to do as they did: live on halal meat, smoke tobacco and take opium, all forbidden by his own religion and distasteful to him. The only thing he didn't do, and it wasn't for lack of encouragement, was visit whorehouses. After the girl died he vowed never to marry and never to love again; if a woman so much as came near him he would move away. For fifteen years he kept his vow, but he prayed to God for a good woman all the same.

In 1968 he was arrested crossing the border and given a four-year sentence. The police wanted to know the names of his confederates but he wouldn't tell. They strung him up by his ankles and beat him with sticks and straps and the butt of a rifle till the blood streamed down his back and he fell unconscious, but still he wouldn't tell. He was moved fron one jail to another in various districts of Pakistan and set to work, as all prisoners were, on the traditional village crafts. He wove daris for the floor and khes[1] for bedding; he twisted fibre into ropes for charpoys and spun cotton. In one prison he prepared the food for 150 people. Thus he learnt to cook, to mend and wash his clothes, to spin, to weave and to make things out of nothing. My sense of usefulness was severely threatened by Jungli's ability to do all these things better than I could. Women dream of such husbands: I'm not so sure.

A fight Jungli started when someone insulted him brought him a year's solitary confinement. He slept and worked in his tiny cell and

---

[1] thick cotton hand-woven sheet

was let out for half an hour each morning and evening to visit the latrine, bathe and take exercise. For the remaining three years he was kept with other people, usually three men to a cell six feet square.

His only solace was religion. He had not previously been a religious person; Mataji wasn't interested and neither, presumably, were his fellow smugglers. But he began to pray and read *path*, and through his daily hours of devotion he developed total faith.

Sikhism was formulated barely five hundred years ago, at a time of social and religious turbulence. Its creator, a gentle saint called Guru Nanak, bridged the conflicting ideals of Hinduism and Islam; his disciples were called Sikhs, meaning followers. His work was continued by a further nine Gurus, the last of which, Guru Gobind Singh, gave the faith a new strength and final consolidation by formation of the Khalsa, the military Sikh brotherhood. It is to this tenth Guru, saint, scholar, soldier and leader, that Sikhism owes its outward symbols of identification.

At his death Guru Gobind Singh conferred guruship on the Sikh holy book. From then on the *Granth*, composed by six of the Gurus and other Sikh, Hindu and Muslim mystics, was respected as the visible form of the invisible Guru. It is written with exceptional economy of words in a poetic and powerful style, and consists mainly of songs in praise of God. It also describes the way for the Sikh to cross the world ocean, as the Gurus called it, to obtain salvation and merge with Him on the far side.

In September 1971 Jungli was released from prison. He returned to India, was baptized into the Sikh brotherhood and gave up everything that wasn't sanctioned by his faith: the cutting of hair, the eating of an animal not killed by one stroke, sexual relations outside marriage and the use of intoxicants. He adopted the five 'K's, the mandatory symbols of the brotherhood: the kirpan or knife (worn on the left hip in a holster hung from the right shoulder) representing spiritual defence, power and dignity; the kangha or wooden comb fixed in the hair knot for bodily cleanliness and tidiness; the kara or iron bangle kept on the right wrist for purity of action and constraint; the kachera for modesty and freedom of movement and the kes, the uncut hair, for holiness, derived from the ancient association between long hair and saints. The only complication of Jungli's baptism was the necessary renunciation of opium. He was ill for a month, unable to sleep, eat or work, his limbs heavy and aching. Someone would have to massage his body with oil three times a day. But he stuck to it, and for two years lived the strictly disciplined life of a true Sikh. He rose several hours before dawn,

took a cold bath, and recited five long prayers. He strove to follow
the basic principles of Sikhism – the oneness of God, His love as a
means to salvation, repetition of the Name, daily prayer and
congregational worship, the practice of truthful living, the reading
and understanding of the *Granth*, the development of a disciplined
character, selfless service to the community, and equality, democracy and tolerance. He spent many hours each day reciting God's
Name and the Mul Mantra, the Guru's description of God:

Ik Onkar
Satnam
Karta purakh
Nirbhau
Nirvair
Akal murat
Ajuni
Saibhang
Gurprasad

There is one God
His Name is Truth
He is the Creator
He is without fear and without enmity
He was not born
Nor does he die to be born again
He is self-existent
Through the grace of the Guru shalt thou obtain Him.

He repeated them a thousand times daily, counting by an ingenious
method using the tips of his thumbs and the joints of his fingers in
blocks of fifteen, the position of his hands automatically recording
the number he had reached. Jungli didn't understand Sikhism: he
accepted it, and he sought salvation through self-surrender and
devotion.

Shortly afterwards he became a Nihang.

Over the next eight years Jungli roamed, living a few months here,
a few months there, sometimes working, sometimes not, and
sometimes working for nothing. During one of those years he ran the
teashop with Balwant. Another was spent working as a clerk in a
transport company in Aligargh, sometimes accompanying one of the
drivers to Kerala, Madras, Bombay or Bangalore. Two more of those
eight years were spent doing voluntary service for a saint in south

Panjab in exchange for food and a place to sleep, but no money or clothes. Jungli didn't yearn for much but he wanted, like Tagore, to see God face to face. And a living saint, he said, is the nearest thing on earth to God.

Through years of prayer, meditation and living in pursuit of Truth, religiously devoted people developed spiritual power, or sixth sense. One manifestation of this power was a pre-knowledge of the time of one's death. Five years previously Mataji's father had been an elderly though still healthy man. Jungli happened to be staying with him when he made his announcement that in three days he was going to die, so his relations should come and take their leave. Knowing how fit he was they laughed and didn't come; thought the old chap had gone a bit bonkers. And three days later he died, his head resting on Jungli's arm.

But Jungli had had mystical experiences of his own. After years of repeating the Mul Mantra and God's name for several hours each day he had suffered splitting headaches and the sensation that blood was pouring out of his nose. But in the end he saw a light that half blinded him, bringing the power to call the Gurus to his side.

During those eight years Jungli became seriously ill. He was in hospital for seven months, unknown to Mataji and Pitaji, while the doctors tried to establish what was wrong with him; their fees gradually consumed his buried store of money. When he came out, his thick, thigh-long hair again cut short (the doctors had said it was too heavy), he was once more homeless, jobless and penniless. He wandered, sometimes in the company of other Nihangs and sometimes alone, staying in gurdwaras and at the houses of acquaintances. Sometimes he went back to the village, but it always ended the same way, for his brother as well as for himself. 'Why do you come here and scrounge off us?' Mataji would shrill, sharp as a razor. 'This isn't your house! Go and do your own work!'

It was never Pitaji who scolded them. He treated them as if they were his own children. Mataji was the one who got cross, who domineered and bossed and made their lives difficult.

Except when engaged in the smuggling trade, Jungli had never had much money. If he bought anything nice, like an old weapon, it wouldn't be in his possession for long. Someone would beg, borrow or pinch it, and nearly always that someone would be one who had declared himself a friend. Jungli, understanding suffering, couldn't bear to see anyone in distress. If a friend came sobbing that his wife was ill and he had no money to buy medicine, or that he was out of work and if only he had a bit of capital etc., if Jungli had money he would give it to him. The man would thank him and touch his feet, promising to give it back soon. But Jungli was cheated every time: nothing was ever returned to him.

It was the same with his few belongings. All Jungli owned when I met him was two cholas, a sword, five pieces of turban cloth, a vest, a small book of *path*, a tiny notebook, a pen with a broken nib, an iron bowl, a pair of hand-made Panjabi shoes, a small bag, two pairs of kachera, a mala and a brown blanket.

And one other thing: a curious piece of blue plastic, pencil length and width but thin and flexible.

'Whatever is it?'

'A tongue cleaner.' I thought he was having me on.

'Tongues don't get dirty,' I scoffed. 'In all the countries I've travelled I've never known people clean their tongues.'

'Show me your tongue then,' he commanded. I stuck it out. 'Ttt ttt ttt. Look at all that filthy white rough stuff! Why don't you clean it?'

What Jungli did have though, or used to have until he mortgaged it to his paternal uncle, was the three and a half acres of land left to him by his father in Kharanpur. In desperation he could always sell a bit. He did, unknown to me, when I first went to stay in the village. At that time I never thought to ask where his money came from, misled by the ease with which he spent it, the family's neat appearance and Pitaji's fifty acres of land, into assuming that day to day expenses, local bus fares and fruit and vegetables towards the housekeeping were no problem. Moreover, it would have been indelicate to ask. If Jungli had money in his pocket it would be gone in an instant, mostly on generous gestures to other people.

Money had become a bone of contention between us. However tight a budget I was living on I clearly had more than Jungli did and could have been rich had that been my ambition. I had discovered that he had been paying Mataji for our keep, in addition to the food we bought her and in spite of the fact that almost everything we ate was produced on Pitaji's land. It occurred to me later, though Jungli would never have admitted it, that the money was a bribe to keep her quiet, to forestall our eviction from the house. She had turned him out repeatedly in the past: what was preventing her now?

I tried to stop Jungli spending his money, the money from the land he had sold. I tried to give him mine. Yet he would rarely take any from me. I coaxed and pleaded, would put notes in his chola pocket when he wasn't looking and buy new clothes for him when he wasn't there. Then he wept out of helplessness at not being able to provide for me.

Jungli was still a prisoner: a prisoner of his convictions, his nature and his circumstances. He believed I held the key in my hands. I hovered outside, just out of reach, and watched him fretfully through the bars.

10

Travellers

TWENTY MILES across the fields lay Pakistan. It beckoned enticingly, and after ten weeks in the village I succumbed. Jungli couldn't accompany me for at the time he had no passport, and I felt guilty about leaving him behind, if only for a few days. In ten weeks we had not been apart for more than a few hours.

I missed him. I missed him partly because I was fond of him and had grown dependent on his protective presence, but partly also because Pakistan gave me a tough innings. I could find no food; men leered; the streets were hot; the trains were packed; and there was nowhere to sleep. My sole consolation was that Pakistan felt foreign, which India no longer did one bit.

Poor Pakistan, only three days my elder: I didn't give her a chance. My time was short, I scarcely left the well-trodden freak run, and a bad time in Algeria several years before had tainted my vision of Muslims, though I hope not for ever.

Five days later I recrossed the border into India, drew back the veil from my face (I had spent five days behind it), and was welcomed heartily by the Sikhs in Customs, one of whom came from Jungli's village. I caught myself grinning foolishly, like a buffalo gloating in a muddy pool. Everywhere there seemed to be smiling people: in the buses, in Amritsar, at the house of my first hosts where I called to take the children some sweetmeats and at the tailors on my way back to the village. Everywhere – except at home. Mataji and Kaki were in Delhi; Pitaji was reciting the evening prayer and scarcely paused to look up; Jungli was asleep. I'd been longing to see him. He emerged bleary-eyed and drawn looking. He had been ill since I left, with fever. Only, he said, because I wasn't there. Every hour had seemed like a year, he told me, and he had moved from charpoy to charpoy, unable to sleep and holding my soul close to his heart.

A couple of days after my return I began to suffer from amoebic dysentery. Jungli and I set out on the back of someone's tractor to the local town and the family doctor, who gave me a book on the philosophy of Guru Nanak's teachings and introduced me to his son while a long line of sick Indians sat waiting in the surgery. Finally he asked why we had come and prescribed some evil-looking pills which said, 'Warning. Not for minor cases,' and, 'Blood tests must be taken first.' I enquired about the blood tests but he shrugged his shoulders. 'Not necessary,' he said, adding as a quiet aside to me, 'Come and see me at breeding time.' I tried to look knowing and said I would.

In spite of his casualness and ineffective pills, I respected this doctor. On a previous visit he had correctly diagnosed scabies in about five seconds. What's more he never charged us. The only thing I had against him was a large framed photograph on his surgery wall of half a corpse being further dismantled by a group of students. It unavoidably faced those next in line for examination.

It wasn't just me: the villagers were always ill too. We could hardly go into a house where there wasn't someone suffering on a charpoy or humping off to the latrine ground (though sometimes it was hard to tell: people lay around, fully dressed and looking dispirited on their charpoys, whether in the best of health or approaching death). Snatches of conversation picked up on buses, if not about what things cost these days, were most often about illness: who had what, how bad they had got it, when they went down with it, which system of medicine they were using and whether it was working. Poor standards of hygiene, an uncompromising climate and contaminated water made illness inescapable.

Mataji kept a selection of herbs, spices, dried fruits and bark in her trunk for treating minor ailments. When I had a cold she ground up a palmful of opium poppy pods and brewed them with milk and sugar to make a potion totally unlike Harbans Singh's vile brew and barely discernible from best Darjeeling which demolished my symptoms in half an hour. Opium itself had curative powers, which Jungli used as an excuse when I tried to persuade him to give it up. Paraffin was daubed on wasp stings, wasp nest tea was drunk for vomiting, and a minute piece of asafoetida buried in a sultana was swallowed as a cure for something, but they wouldn't say what.

Early morning. Jungli was watching me. I must have been scratching my head absentmindedly.

'Let's have a look at your hair.'

'Uh?'

He didn't wait for me to catch on, but started going over my scalp, mumbling in a predatory way to himself. I sat there patiently.

'There's one! Look!'

A speck, like a flake of skin.

'That's dandruff.'

He shook his head. 'It's a louse.'

'It can't be!' Oh no, not that too!

He crushed it between his thumb nails and it popped. My hair was full of louse eggs, some almost hatched, Jungli told me with relish. One by one he hunted them down.

But the dysentery wasn't so easily got rid of. Thinking a cool climate might be the answer, Jungli and I went to Kashmir and spent our days walking in the watery, willowy landscape of the Kashmir Valley. To the Muslim Kashmiris a full-bearded man carrying a sword was even more of a novelty than a Westerner, and each time we paused to rest a crowd would gather. It drove us crazy. Jungli told them to go away but instead of dispersing, as they would have in Panjab, they stayed and swore at us. In Kashmir a Nihang has no status as a fearsome legendary person to be taken seriously; Jungli had lost his authority and it subdued him.

Being an unpopular minority, the Sikhs tend to hang together. Being a proud people, it disturbs them when others don't share their high opinion of themselves, and it makes them more objectionable to those who are already biased against them. Travelling in Sikh or Hindu territory Jungli had a natural advantage; he bagged seats by throwing his sword through a window, for then even if others got on before us, no-one would have the nerve to sit there. He was strong too, and a good barger. I wasn't bad either, and could hold my own against most men.

But the Muslims were a match for both of us: they were downright belligerent. Every evening in Kashmir we caught a bus out to the gurdwara. In the battle to get on the Kashmiris pushed with every ounce of their strength; they scratched and elbowed and tore at each other's clothes, and grabbed little boys by the scruffs of their necks and hurled them out of the way. Even when Jungli reached the door first, he wouldn't be able to get a foot inside until the Muslim mainstream was seated. I would still be out on the tarmac, stepping into puddles, getting flattened between the door and the bus, and being flung here and there; other women weren't even bothering to try. When at last I levered a triumphant toe on to the bottom step the men behind me, whom I had defeated, took their revenge by pinching my bottom. Mad with fury I stabbed the air behind me with my elbows, and the crowd backed away, momentarily cowed.

From Kashmir we went on to Ladakh.

The seats of our bus were hard and it had been built for people with no thighs. We sat crumpled on our bench, stuffed up with colds and scratching our bed bug bites, while the men in the bus (in spite of 'No Smoking' notices in Hindi, Urdu and English) chain smoked, and because it was cold the windows were kept shut. Cigarette smoke was anathema to Jungli, who sat swathed from head to foot in his orange turban like a Benares corpse. Two days later, cold, stiff and filthy, we reached Leh, the capital of Ladakh.

In Ladakh I vacillated between three worlds. It was the only thing that ruffled my peace in that promised land of lush green valleys, high clear air and bare snow-capped mountains. Wanting, while I was there, to be a part of Ladakh, I was pulled on the one hand by the Western travellers in our guest house to whom I owed my attitudes, and on the other by Jungli, who was out of his depth in this wholly un-Indian environment – stranger to him than anything he had ever seen – and to whom I owed my loyalty. For the first time Jungli was dependent on me. I was as much at home in Ladakh as I had been in Calcutta or Panjab, if anything more so, but Jungli suffered severe headaches because of the altitude and withdrawal symptoms when he couldn't get a cup of tea. He didn't want to be out all day as I did and would have been happier in the company of his own people, eating familiar food and speaking his own language. Jungli had lived in other men's lands only through necessity: I, on the other hand, was a born interloper.

But Ladakh had its positive side for him too. He seemed suddenly to discover the childhood he had never had: whether it was the escape from his homeland, the rarified air or the unfamiliar natural phenomena that liberated it I don't know, but he would play for hours with his new-found toys, manufacturing sparks of static electricity in the blankets, throwing stones at ice on puddles and scrunching through them in his sandals. He would imitate the high-pitched Ladakhi language and squeak gibberish to bemused old ladies and delighted children whom we met in the mud lanes. He loved that.

Six months later and two thousand miles away, in Kerala, I met an American who had been staying at our guest house in Leh. He told me that he and other Westerners had been fascinated by Jungli, by this strange man in those strange clothes who didn't speak a word (he had been shy in their free-talking, free-mixing, laughing, self-possessed company; I had never known him so quiet). They thought he looked compassionate and were struck by the strong presence he emanated: they decided he must be a holy man.

I felt proud of Jungli then. This was the only comment about Jungli I ever heard; in two years neither his family nor his friends ever mentioned him.

One evening, in the main bazaar street in Leh, we saw something that jabbed like a knife at my complacency. A Sikh soldier was out shopping with his wife. He was young, tall and smart. She was dressed in the clothes he would have wanted her to wear, a patterned nylon salvar-kamiz, the salvar cut narrow in the city fashion with a tight-fitting waist-length jersey and a flimsy scarf draped over her chest and shoulders. But she wasn't a Panjabi girl: her skin was white, the skin of an American or northern European.

My instant reaction, appalling though it might sound, was just like most Indians'. I, too, jumped to the conclusion that the soldier was using the girl for sex and to increase his status.

She was a slim and pretty girl who would have looked nice in almost anything, but dressed like that she looked awful. She must live a life of hell, I thought, in that spiritual and cultural graveyard of a military camp four miles outside Leh. By then I had experienced enough to know what kind of existence hers must be: no music, few books, no home or garden and poor company – for women would be few and uneducated and other men inaccessible for conversation. She mightn't be allowed out except with her husband, who would be working most of the time, and in his few free hours there would be nowhere to go. Winters in Leh last seven months.

Was that all there was to it, though? Could my horror at the sight of this captive girl have been produced by guilt? Guilt that until that moment I didn't know was there; guilt about my lack of commitment, a suspicion that I was just play acting? Or romanticizing? Or was it a genuine sympathy for her plight? Whatever it was, the incident brought home to me, absolutely and finally, that just as I had reacted to the soldier and the white girl, so the rest of the world probably saw *us*, and that it was no use pretending to be invisible because it just didn't fool people.

'How terrible!' I said to Jungli, my thoughts back on the military camp. 'How can she live in such a place?' I thought she must be off her head. She didn't *have* to live there. Or maybe she did?

'There's no difficulty about it at all,' he answered aggrievedly, for it reflected on our own future. 'Lots of people do it. Look at the rickshaw wallah who married the American tourist and went with her to America.'

'He came back,' I said. 'You told me.'

How could Jungli know just how much a European or North American, coming from an educated, liberal and cultured background, has to lose? To commit a Westerner to traditional Indian society for life is like caging a wild bird. That girl had given her soul away.

It all happened in a few seconds. We walked on pretending we hadn't seen them, and they did the same. But looking back now I realize it was a turning point in our relationship. I could see it in perspective for the first time; could see that my own attitudes, and Jungli's, were not remotely compatible.

We travelled back down to Srinagar. Our bench beside the back door was half the width of the other seats in the bus, and the floor had dissolved into stairs. My travelling companions were thirty-five men, Hindus, Sikhs, Muslims and Buddhists. I scowled at the prospect of spending two days standing on the steps.

'She's always like this,' Jungli said mischievously to the gang of Muslim youths next to him. His distress over the soldier and the white girl was forgotten. 'In the six months I've known her she's only smiled once.'

'Really?' they said.

But we were recompensed by the appearance of our driver, a middle-aged baptized Sikh. You could see just to look at him he wasn't going to stand for any nonsense. Before we set off he delivered a lecture on behaviour: no noise, no standing up in seats to look out of the window, no wandering off at meal stops, and, 'I don't allow any smoking,' he warned. 'It's a disgusting habit.'

Jungli and I were delighted. A few miles down the road he stopped at a gurdwara and ordered everyone out of the bus. Inside was a rock bearing the hollow impression of a seated figure. It looked natural, but there was no telling. 'Guru Nanak came here on his travels,' he announced in Panjabi to the assembly of Buddhist lamas and uninterested Hindus and Muslims, many of whom wouldn't have been able to understand him, 'and rested by this rock. Afterwards it bore his image.'

Back on the road when he caught a surreptitious whiff of nicotine he brought the bus to a standstill and switched off the engine. 'Someone's smoking', he said theatrically.

There was dead silence and the offender guiltily stubbed out his cigarette. Wonderful, we thought. We resumed our journey and in the two days only one other person had the insolence to light up inside. Yet again he stopped. 'Do you want to go to Srinagar or would you rather get out here?' Very few Hindus would have had the authority to control such a busload; maybe even Muslims. Jungli and I got out at the gurdwara and the driver gave us a generous donation for the offerings box.

Few Indians, even plainsmen, were much interested in the scenery on these journeys. They snoozed, smoked, munched, chatted and were sick out of the window; the landscape they by and large ignored. In between whiles they must have pondered idly on what it was that foreigners found so absorbing. I, for one, could gaze at unfolding landscapes for days and maybe weeks on end, though even I had been dumbfounded by the lone Japanese on the way up to Leh, who didn't speak a word of anything except probably Japanese. Each time the bus stopped to mend a tyre, fill the radiator in a river, refuel, or allow the incontinent foreigners to relieve themselves, this mad Japanese bounded out with a purposeful look and an expensive camera and took half a dozen snaps of whatever happened to be around. It was generally not much – a bare mountain slope, a military encampment, a border post, the road ahead. . . . He boarded the bus only to spring out once more, this time with a cine camera with which he made a replica of his stills. If the bus didn't stop he filmed anyway, through the dirty windscreen.

Indians travelled because they had to get somewhere, and they didn't seem to enjoy it unless they could sing noisy songs or unless there was an accident (the one thing I didn't want to see), when they all leapt up in their seats and craned their necks forward in case they could spot any corpses. Like Albert's family on the beach:

> They didn't think much to the ocean:
> The waves they was fiddlin' and small,
> There was no wrecks and nobody drownded
> Fact, nothing to laugh at at all.[1]

Very secondary attractions were snowy peaks and waterfalls. There would be a few mild exclamations, but after the first half dozen sightings their charisma would have evaporated. But an accident never failed to impress.

We reached Amritsar after a three-day journey and caught a bus out to the village at dawn. A heavy dew lay on the cabbage fields, silver in the early light. Buffalo carts were plodding into the city, their high sagging loads of chopped straw supported by frail pregnant structures of sticks and bits of sackcloth. Immigrant women were hammering stones.

But after a day back in the heat, my dysentery returned. When I couldn't get rid of it we decided I should go to England until after the rains, paying for the return flight by selling the rugs I had bought for that purpose in Kashmir. We fixed a date for a fortnight's time.

'She won't come back,' the neighbours told Jungli. 'These foreigners are selfish.' But Jungli believed I would.

[1] from *The Lion and Albert* by Marriott Edgar

In those last two weeks, when both of us were feeling frail and unsure of our future, Jungli developed a distressing trait. Out of the blue he would thump me with his fist, usually when the previous moment he had been at his most gentle and loving.

'What are you doing? Why are you doing that?' Each time it shocked and hurt me.

But Jungli would walk off without a word.

This continued, with variations, several times a day, and I doggedly persisted in trying to discover the cause. Until finally, the day before I left, Jungli gave in. 'I didn't mean to tell you but you go on and on. What can I do? I hit you so that when you remembered me, instead of being sad, you would say to yourself "Pritam Singh is a bad man. He was always hitting me." Then you would forget and be happy. I don't want you to suffer in England, worrying about me all the time.'

I had still not fathomed the depths of Jungli's unselfishness.

We had to go to Delhi for the day to book my flight, a ten-hour journey each way on the night train. A second class berth in a train cost an extra thirty pence, an unentertainable sum for Jungli and most other Indians, to whom that amount represented a couple of days' food. I normally went second class unreserved anyway, because of my habit of departing on impulse, when the reserved compartments would be full. I must have travelled between eight and ten thousand miles in these unreserved carriages, with thirty or more people packed into an area where there was reasonably room for ten, not to mention their trunks, boxes, sacks, baskets, buckets, bags and bedding.

We waited on the platform at Amritsar, a gentle ebb and flow of several thousand people along a fractured cliff of mountainous luggage, and as the train approached we rose in a crest and surged towards it, breaking against its sides and pouring through doors and windows. It was fairly full already, and its occupants were going through their expected pantomime of fluffing themselves up to look as fat as possible, lolling on the seats with their legs up and conserving extra space with their luggage (which they swore was for absent members of their party who had gone out to fetch water or food, but who never materialized). In this way they defended their sleeping territory, and there would be dramatic ructions if an outsider threatened to diminish it.

Jungli and I ingratiated ourselves with a large family from Lahore who looked like gypsies. An elderly matron was obviously in command; she rattled away in Urdu all night, God knows what about, except that once I heard her address a remark in my direction. 'Look at her!' she said haughtily. 'They said they only wanted a corner to sit on and she's sprawled herself over half the bench.' Draping her ample bosom over the hams of the ugly shaven-headed young men in her charge, she continued to regale them with her monologue, while they wriggled their unspeakably dirty feet on the bench beside me, effectively forestalling any further expansionist manoeuvres I might be brewing.

When I finally left we were better organized. I stayed on the platform guarding my luggage while Jungli disappeared with his sword to locate the train in the sidings and appropriate a luggage rack.

It was June and stifling. Our bodies were soaked in sweat. We lay head to foot on the wooden rack, my luggage stacked beneath our heads. On the opposite rack, legs dangling in mid-air, sat four burly Mohammedans whom Jungli was addressing politely as 'Khan Sahib' since they outnumbered him. Their numerous women and offspring were concertinaed on the seats below. Any possibility of sleep was finally ruled out by the battles raging at every station between the passengers already in the train and would-be passengers outside. Since the doors were locked they heaved their luggage through the windows and swung themselves in head first behind it. The women by the window tried to push them back onto the platform, while unrelated men suspended on luggage racks added to the confusion with cries of, 'Throw their baggage out!' But by that time they were usually in, and those in the aisle, with martyred looks, were inching themselves sideways to make room.

We were both upset, I as much for Jungli's sake as my own, since for him it was worse. I had the option of returning; he had no option in anything. I went to England and met old friends. Jungli remained in Delhi, bereft, and drank himself into a stupor to forget his sorrows.

Interlude

I FLEW TO ENGLAND when the hot weather was at its hottest and Jungli's and my clothes were marked with the salt of our sweat, like the line of foam at the edge of the tide.

Jungli and I wrote letters. I had never actually had to write anything more complicated than shopping lists in the Panjabi script before, and the first letter took three hours.

There would be letters from Jungli lying under the doormat when I returned to the cottage in the evenings, pale blue aerogrammes, two, sometimes three at a time, each, it seemed, addressed in a different hand. For Jungli couldn't cope with the Roman script and wasn't much better at Panjabi: his handwriting was untidy, he was an abominable speller and he frequently threw in words neither I nor the dictionary had heard of. But worst of all was his total omission of punctuation. Not even a full stop; not even a space! I had to guess where they came and fill them in before I could start the laborious process of translation and the almost greater one of replying. But with practice I gathered speed, and I caught on to various time-saving ruses like filling up half the space with drawings of insects and elephants, which anyway, I suspect, Jungli preferred to a lot of misspelt words that he in turn would feel obliged to decipher.

While my letters grew weekly more pictorial, each one of Jungli's looked identical to the last. The top line would be large and straight, but each succeeding line would be more squashed, more slanting and less disciplined than the one before, until there came a line only two or three words long, so tiny I needed a magnifying glass to read it, tipping at an imprecise angle of forty-five degrees in the bottom right hand corner of the page.

During this time I began writing about Panjabi village life, not at first as a conscious endeavour to produce a book, but as a psychological means of reducing the gap between Jungli and myself as I recovered from dysentery in the freezing Herefordshire June. I wrote compulsively and a book had emerged almost before I was aware of writing one, a book that has since been submerged in the present one and of which only fragments still remain.

After the rains (which that year never came) I flew back to Delhi.

Jungli was working somewhere near Ramnagri, – his letters hadn't revealed at what, or where – and I had a week to myself before the date we had arranged to meet in the village. I felt grateful suddenly for this time to myself, and on the spur of the moment caught a train to Hardwar at the foot of the Himalayas. There I discovered a party of a thousand Sikhs about to set off on a week-long pilgrimage to Hemkund, an icy lake at 15,500 feet, where the tenth Guru, Guru Gobind Singh, was said to have meditated for a thousand years in a previous incarnation.

I joined that pilgrimage to Hemkund. We drove through the Himalayas almost to the Chinese border and climbed the mountain, through primeval forests and meadows of flowers and butterflies, to the icy lake amid bare snowy peaks. It was a time of happiness, of total absorption in the immediate present, of mind and body functioning in unison and stretched to their limits. It was a time of sharing, of being equal to the Sikhs whose pilgrimage I had joined, where no-one was host and no-one was guest. It was a time of release, when I could relax and be myself and could talk and laugh with strangers without being thwarted by the social restrictions of settled Panjabi society. And it was a time of recognition of the freedom and independence I had lost. I scarcely thought of Jungli at all.

Ahead of me lay the discipline of life on Indian terms. I relegated my doubts to the back of my mind, for there was much still to learn, much that was positive and dignified about Panjabi village society, and my friendship with Jungli was still young. Though I knew deep down that it must end someday, like everything in life it had to run its course.

Back at Hardwar I caught the night train to Amritsar. I had been away three months.

Jungli

Buffaloes are taken out to graze soon after dawn. Thatch grass lines the irrigation ditch on the right and the trees are regularly shaved for firewood. Ripe wheat covers the plain in April.

Mazbi house compounds at the edge of the village. Dung buns (left) are piled in conical stacks and plastered with mud to protect them. They will be used during the hot weather when the buffaloes produce less dung.

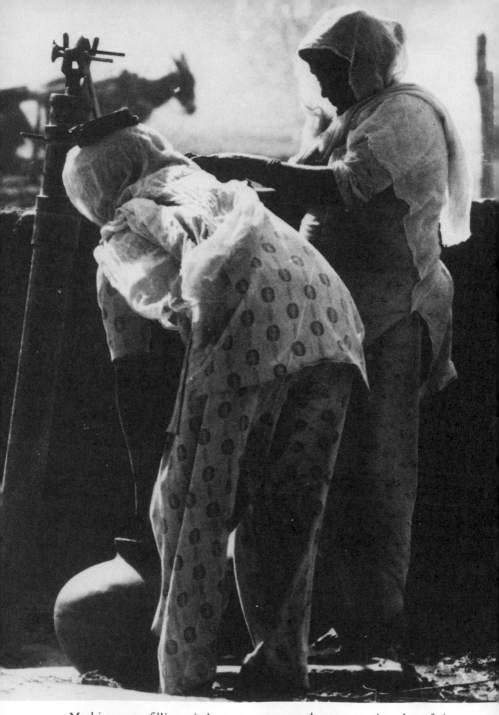

Mazbi women filling pitchers at a communal pump on the edge of the
village.

Mataji churns butter each morning from one-day-old yoghurt. It will be just enough for the day's vegetables or lentils. The remaining liquid — buttermilk — is drunk with meals or given away to the poor.

Jungli stirs vegetables in the cooking enclosure. The mud animal and moulded mud walls were sculpted by Mataji. Yoghurt is made on a slow dung fire in the alcove below the mud animal.

Women preparing chapattis at the Dholpur dehra. It is January and the temperature is near freezing, but shoes are not allowed in langars.

Kaki seeks protection from Mataji's scoldings in Pitaji's arms. Jungli's lazy aunt squats on the charpoy on the right. Rubbish is thrown on the ground throughout the day to be cleared by Mataji's sweeper each morning.

Pitaji and Kaki. Pitaji shells garlic for the evening meal: he is wearing kachera, the baggy white pants compulsory to baptized male sikhs. Kaki wears lipstick, kohl round the eyes and nail varnish.

PART 2: DEHRA

1

Expulsion

THE WAY WAS FAMILIAR. In an overladen bus that rattled and shook and whose engine heaved like the belly of a woman in labour, we circumnavigated the walls of the old city and swung off into its outskirts. We passed the urban rubbish dump, its desolate hummocks of filth picked over by innumerable scavenging hands and abandoned to the crows and vultures, and emerged into open farmland.

Everything was that hot yellow-green of late summer: checkerboard prairies of near-ripe rice, lime green, gold green and bronze green, fodder crops in mid-growth and exuberant weeds in damp borrow[1] pits. Here and there I detected the coarse crochet of a plot newly ploughed: in one, a square of damp chocolate, a flock of cranes was feeding; in another a bare-footed man was broadcasting clover seed, scooping handfuls from a sling and scattering it over the soil in a single graceful movement.

I travelled the last few miles in a minibus. Through its dust-smudged windows and between veiled and turbanned heads I caught glimpses of the land I had come to know but not quite love: the decomposing edges of the metalled road tailing off into the dust, the colonies of weaver birds' nests in patches of high reedmace, the loofah plants scrambling over rain-bleached straw stacks and the timeless group of bicycle repairers squatting by the canal bridge.

I got off the bus and crossed the barren ground. Where the dirt track entered the village and joined the main perimeter pathway I was greeted by a group of men who offered to carry my luggage. Next door's children were playing in the alley and rushed off to tell Mataji I was coming

Negotiating the buffaloes at the entrance of the yard, the first thing I caught sight of was Fikan, lying on a charpoy and looking very

---

[1] irregular depressions often seen alongside Indian roads from which earth has been dug to build up or repair them

dusty. Mataji was squatting on her plank in the cooking enclosure stirring spices into the vegetables. Pitaji laid his hand on my head.

'What's the matter with Fikan?' I asked Mataji. 'Is he ill?' He didn't look quite right.

'He's drunk!' she said, and roared with laughter. She had never been the sort to take other people's feelings into consideration.

Fikan turned the other way. He made no acknowledgement of my arrival and continued sulking dustily on his charpoy. This time Mataji had gone too far; the following day he packed his bundle and left without a word to seek new employment

There was no sign of Jungli. He knew I was coming and I had expected him to be there. I kept quiet until evening, when I could contain myself no longer. I said to Mataji, 'Where is he?'

'How should I know?' she replied. 'I don't ask my children where they are and what they do. It's none of my business. He's probably in Delhi.'

Early next morning Mataji and I were sitting on a charpoy scraping the last of the little loofah marrows for the nine o'clock meal. Mataji, being sharper than I, first noticed Jungli coming up the alley, an older, thinner Jungli than the one I remembered, and dressed all in white. Someone had stolen his sword on a train. His old turbans had fallen apart. Where was his blue chola? The cow had eaten it. We greeted in the Indian manner of distant friends who aren't particularly pleased to see each other, and I unpacked the presents I had brought for the family.

What they really liked were the colour photographs. Neighbours came flocking in to croon over them. 'That's me, that's Kaki, there's cousin Harbhajan cutting clover, that's Mataji making chapattis. . .' repeated Jungli as each new neighbour appeared. '*Very* beautiful,' they agreed.

I had brought some old photographs of my own family to show Jungli. I ranged them along the snapshot shelf in between one of Mataji in her youth, Rajinder and Gurmit at their wedding, Mataji's successful banker brother and several of Kaki looking sullen. In each case the sitters wore their best clothes and the photographer had done some fiddling in the dark room to make their skin white and flawless. My photographs weren't like that. There was one of my father sitting in a deckchair on the lawn in his bedroom slippers reading *The Sunday Times*. There was one of my grandmother and great aunt striding over the mountains of their Welsh homeland. And another of us children on a pebbly beach in Devon. They leant in relaxed fashion against the edges of the stiff Panjabi portraits taken in stuffy photo studios.

But Mataji liked the studio portraits: they were how photographs were supposed to be, for they portrayed her family at more than its best. Jungli's old widowed aunt from the bottom of the alley wouldn't let me anywhere near her with a camera, though she was the most photogenic of the family – what was the use, she said, she was old and ugly – and others were embarrassed at being photographed in their torn house clothes.

I had taken pictures of people half lit by the evening sun coming through open doorways and they came out almost as abstracts in stark black and white. Nice, I thought. But, 'What a hopeless photo studio!' exclaimed Mataji. 'Why can't they print them properly? You'd never know who it was.'

Alone in our room at last, Jungli remarked that I 'seemed' beautiful. I had thrown off my sallow complexion in England and returned to India with rosy cheeks.

Jungli found them wonderful. Lest their rosiness should fade he sucked them every day to make them glow. But he was fighting a losing battle: by the time I left, a year later, my skin was grey.

A month after my return to the village came Diwali, festival of lights. The local town disappeared behind firework stands and temporary sweetmeat stalls, soaring high on stepped planks lined with pink paper and shielded beneath scarlet canopies. There was row upon row of candle-lit crystalline sweets, silver-coated milk sweets, rose-water balls, crispy jalebi, gulab jamon and ladu, specially made and nicer than usual. It was like Christmas; the air was full of anticipation.

In the village the houses were mud-smeared in preparation, each dwelling in a slightly different combination of the available local muds. The few Hindu houses were painted with the white lace doily patterns traditionally applied to propitiate Lakshmi, goddess of wealth.

On the morning of Diwali, Jungli announced, 'I'm going back to work. I'm leaving tomorrow.'

Previously he had had no work for two years. I had encouraged him to find a job, and while I was in England he had spent weeks searching for work, going from place to place and sometimes returning to the same place, asking and asking. He went five times to a gurdwara in Uttar Pradesh where a cousin of his was working before the saint it belonged to finally took him in. Having been there for two months working as a pathi² he had taken time off to meet me in the village (a relative had been detailed to send a crafty telegram worded GRANDMOTHER EXPIRED REACH SOON), and hadn't mentioned anything about going back. We had no particular plans other than to stay in the village for a while and then travel together. At least, that was what I had in mind, and Jungli hadn't suggested any alternative. I was going to pay for both of us but I hadn't reckoned on Jungli's pride. Neither of us had reckoned on Mataji.

'What's happened?' I asked.

'Nothing's happened. If I don't go back to work I'll lose my job, that's all. I have no choice.'

'But you said you weren't going back. And I haven't finished my research.' For some time I had been studying Panjabi history and village traditions. The more I discovered the more fascinating it became and the more I wanted to fill the gaps in my knowledge that the research had opened up.

'You don't have to leave. You can come with me or stay here, as you wish.'

I didn't want to stay in the village at the mercy of Mataji. Neither did I want to go to this place in Uttar Pradesh where, according to Jungli, the water was salty and he would be at work all day.

'I can't stay on my own. Can't you hang on a bit longer?'

I was being unreasonable and Jungli was already worked up.

'It's all very well for you! You can work in England and make lots of money and go wherever you like. I am a poor man and I must work if I want to eat. If I lose this job I won't be able to get another one.'

It turned out that Mataji, with the half-hearted support of Pitaji, had told Jungli to get out of the house. 'What business have you got here?' she had demanded in her usual fashion. 'Go and do your own work.'

She was right in a way, though her reasons for complaining seemed uncharacteristic. She couldn't be bothered to cook extra chapattis, and unlike most mothers she didn't care for her son and didn't want him around. That was what Jungli told me anyway. But I believed there was more to it than that. I had often wondered why Mataji and Pitaji had accepted our unorthodox relationship, and it can only have been that Mataji thought I would marry Jungli and take him to England, in which case it was worth putting up with us for a while. She would then not only be rid of him for good but would be able to boast that she had a son in Britain, married to an English

² paid reader of the *Granth*

girl. She would be sent money and presents and her status would soar.

Maybe Jungli had told her I didn't want to marry, that I Had never wanted to marry anyone. If so, what was I doing there? Jungli was wasting his time, and she hers. We could go.

Diwali is a day of happiness, but it certainly wasn't in our house. Jungli was in a black mood. He and his cousin from next door set about a bottle of rough liquor, alternating slugs of alcohol with chunks of curried goat that Mataji had prepared for Diwali. It frightened me when Jungli drank, for he didn't know when to stop. I felt like going out. I had never enjoyed being closeted in the house all day, and in the company of two men getting steadily drunk on rough spirit I liked it even less. Jungli said he absolutely wasn't going out and I wasn't to either as I might get shot. People drank all day at Diwali and there were always fights.

The alcohol loosened Jungli's cousin's tongue. For the first time he and I held a conversation – being younger than Jungli he hadn't been able to approach me unless I addressed him first. We spoke in English. He said his one ambition was to go 'foreign', and that only I could help him. I advised him to go to the relevant embassies in Delhi and enquire about immigration restrictions. His answer was that I could marry him if I liked. If I liked? I told him to tell Jungli in Panjabi what he had just asked me. I thought he had a bloody nerve but that it was Jungli's business to tell him so, not mine. But Jungli was silent. He continued to drink, and every now and then he threw a sinister look in my direction. When I tried to defuse the tension by slapping him playfully on the arm he got up and hit me full force across the face. He had said he would never hit me. I tried to laugh it off, but it made him worse; he was a mercurial person and lost all sense of reason once roused. He picked up the framed pictures we had had taken of ourselves in a photo studio in Amritsar and hurled them on the ground, grinding the glass under his heel when he noticed it hadn't smashed very satisfactorily on the soft dung floor, and tearing the paper into small fragments. His cousin tried vaguely to restrain him, but he was scared too and Jungli looked about to smash everything in the room. There was a lot of 'Go on, go, I can't stop you, go wherever you like!' talk that I could make no sense of either.

Thinking anywhere would be preferable to the atmosphere in that room I went outside and hid on the roof: I didn't fancy going out and getting shot. But Jungli's aunt spotted me and called me down. I sat in her little mud kitchen watching her push batter through a perforated ladle into a pan of smoking oil. Then Jungli's face appeared over the yard wall beckoning me to come back. I went warily, not trusting him, and his cousin returned home.

The cousin had told Jungli that I had agreed to marry him if Jungli also gave his permission. No wonder Jungli was mad! Had the cousin misunderstood, or had he been trying to cause trouble? I never found out. I tried to explain what had really happened but Jungli went off into a drunken slumber muttering, 'I don't love you at all – I don't love you at all . . .'

By evening things had calmed down and Jungli was still sleeping it off. The villagers filled little clay lamps with ghee, twisted cotton wool into wicks and positioned them around the yards. Pitaji put one on the dung heap. Then the fireworks started, unreliable things that went off in a volley of gunfire the instant they were touched by a match. There wasn't much to look at. The animals shifted uneasily in their straw and a buffalo bellowed in the next yard. Bats flew into the room in terror, and Mataji and Pitaji sat on their charpoys eating their dinner as if nothing had happened. Jungli missed it all: he woke up when the celebrations were over, a nicer man. He smiled at me and I lit sparklers.

He said, 'I was awful, wasn't I?'

'Yes,' I said. 'You hit me.'

'Oh no, I could never hit you.'

'You did. And you smashed our photos. Look at the pieces.'

He looked at the fragments of glass and paper in genuine surprise. That stuff they drink must be strong.

It was long past the time when people in the village usually slept. There was no moon but the hurricane lamp swung dimly from the Persian lilac. By its light I could see Pitaji lying peacefully under his mosquito net. Mataji was sitting bolt upright on her charpoy, menacingly crunching walnut shells between her teeth. The animals were still restive and Pitaji got up and went to reassure them while Mataji held the lantern, her beshawled head and melon belly dark in silhouette against the lamp-lit wall.

That wasn't the end of it though. Next day the arguments continued. The neighbours crowded in so as not to miss the entertainment, and their children scampered round the yard. I sat reading on my charpoy while Mataji, perched on the corner of Jungli's, screeched and wept and threatened insanity and Jungli snarled and roared and told her that if she went on the way she was going a mental institution would be the best place for her. The argument went round in circles, with neighbours tugging at Jungli's elbow and Jungli shaking them off, Mataji getting redder and redder, and me sitting on the far side of the room catching snippets of invective between sentences of my book. Jungli's eyes flashed like swords and it scared me to look at him.

He drank again in the evening to forget. The neighbours had believed his cousin's story and were busy telling each other how worthless I was and entreating Jungli to leave me.

'She agreed to marry your cousin,' they told him. 'These foreigners aren't to be trusted. And she said you were boring.' How they twisted everything! I never said anything of the kind.

Jungli didn't know who to believe. It was a case of my word against that of his community. For several days he wavered, alternately repentant and coldly aggressive. I wondered if our friendship might end, and if it did, whether I minded. Though I loved him too much to instigate our separation myself, the experience at Diwali had chastened me, and the pilgrimage to Hemkund stirred up regrets at my loss of the world outside.

There were, I think, four pivot points in my relationship with Jungli. The first was when I declined to marry him, thus destroying his faith in our alliance. The second was when I saw my image in the guise of the girl at Leh, thus destroying my own. Hemkund was the third, and the fourth, though not the last of its kind, was the incident at Diwali. It was not so much that I minded being hit, but that he had broken the bonds of our mutual respect. My trust in Jungli was never again quite whole.

We went for walks in order to find privacy, and sat in the shade of a pipal tree. It was only then that Jungli told me that Pitaji was not his real father, and that Mataji had placed Balwant and himself in an orphanage. I realized how insecure he was, and how much he needed to believe in me: I felt desperately sorry for him and made up my mind to stay.

Since Jungli was determined to earn his living and we had nowhere else to go, I resigned myself to the idea of the gurdwara in Uttar Pradesh.

'What's it like there?' I asked.

'It's all right; it's an open place.'

'Is there a village?'

'No, it's *jungal*. You might like it.' Jungle!

'Is there somewhere for us to live?'

'My cousin has a house.' Ghar in Panjabi can mean house or shack or rented portion of hovel. I took him to mean house.

'But where would *we* live?'

'There's room.' I couldn't get any further on the subject of accommodation, so I turned to water supply.

'What about the water? You said it was salty and undrinkable and it made your hair fall out.'

'There's sweet water at the gurdwara.'

'How far's that?'

'As far as from here to the big banyan.' That was about a hundred yards.

'You mean we'll have to fetch all our water from a hundred yards away?'

'For drinking, yes. I can fetch it. To me it's nothing.'

'Is there somewhere to wash?'

'There's a place at the dehra.[3] You can go there.'

I thought about it. It didn't sound too bad. I had a mental picture of lots of nice trees and a two-storey house with a courtyard where we would live. So I asked, 'Who's this saint?' There was a framed photo of him on the wall, a rather beautiful young man in white with a long black beard. 'Is he really a saint?'

'He's a saint', he said unconvincingly. 'His power is considerable.'

'And the other people there?'

'There are good people; they have been kind to me and shown me a lot of respect.'

'Sikh?'

'Everything – Sikh, Muslim, Hindu . . .'

Being in the house in the presence of Mataji had become intolerable. We spent most of the next few days away from it, in Amritsar, in the local town, and sitting under the pipal tree on the edge of the barren ground. But we couldn't leave. I had no clothes to put on. My old clothes were torn and patched and the tailor was making me some new ones.

We held out for five days. Mataji screamed her grievances at each new visitor who entered the yard. She resented my being there, resented having to feed me, resented my interest in her village and family. It was worse for Jungli and he bemoaned his helplessness. 'If only I could start a small business! I would pay back the mortgage on my land in Kharanpur and grow dal and maize and potatoes. The land is fertile there. It's a good place to live and there's a large gurdwara where you can listen to music and *path*, and shops which sell eggs and vegetables if relatives come to stay. This village has

3 strictly speaking gurdwara or temple. In the context of this book the term is also used to convey the entire complex of buildings supporting the gurdwara

nothing.' Only when something threatened his inner security did Jungli long for an outer one. I rarely heard him talk like that.

Then we packed our belongings and left.

Pitaji was out. Mataji was squatting in the byre making dung buns, her face scarlet with anger. She was madder than ever, the more so, I would think, because all the time I had shown no emotion, no sorrow or repentance. I had hardly felt any. Their reaction was justifiable; how could they possibly have understood why I couldn't marry Jungli? From their standpoint my conduct had been unforgivable.

We hailed a tonga and made our way to Amritsar. Jungli vowed he would never return.

2

Householders

JUNGLI WENT AHEAD while I waited in Amritsar for the tailor to finish my clothes. On the evening of the third day, I caught the Delhi train. I changed at Ramnagri at dawn, and again onto the number nine bus at Chandinagar. Chandinagar felt good: there was such a colourful mixture of people – UP (Uttar Pradesh) people, Rajasthanis, Haryanis, Panjabis, Muslim ladies in purdah, hill people, Southerners – and the atmosphere was different. Panjab has a distinctness about it, a prosperity, a Panjabness, that divorces it from the states surrounding it; in Chandinagar I was back in India.

The number nine bus shuffled out through the scruffy suburbs, turning the corner at the bullock shoers, past bulldozer repairers and VD clinics, past a colony of Rajput blacksmiths encamped beneath their brass-buttoned wagons, past teashops and stone yards and stockists of the 'Guranted Clutchplate', and past the rickshaw graveyard where an acre of dead rickshaws, forlorn and rusty, lay kicking their wheels in the air. Beyond there was farmland, bleak and fallow: it wasn't the sort of place where you'd expect to find any jungle. Then the fields gave way to a barren plain where there was nothing but a short scrub grass, treeless almost to the horizon. Here and there plots had been sold as building sites to middle-class city escapists: unrelated to either road, landscape or each other, the ugly flat-roofed houses only emphasized the loneliness of the place.

Our journey ended where the open landscape came to an abrupt halt against a wall of modern industrial buildings belonging to an old Muslim village on a low hill beyond. Out in the scrub, half a mile from the road, was a structure that looked like a gurdwara. There was nothing attractive about any of it – except for the village, which from that point couldn't be seen – neither the landscape, nor the buildings, nor the dusty corner where everyone got off and dispersed along pathless tracks through the scrub. People at the dehra called it Number Nine, I found out afterwards, because it was where the bus stopped; it had no other use for them. There were timber yards, a couple of shacks selling tea, and sundry streethawkers and anonymous huts that appeared and disappeared from one day to the next – they could be erected in a day and would burn down in an hour at night. Later, when prohibition was lifted in UP, several more shops appeared selling illicit liquor and Number Nine became a notorious place. If ever I returned from Delhi after dusk I would find Jungli waiting there grumpily to escort me home through the darkness.

This was all later. That first time I didn't get beyond thinking 'What a dreadful place! I couldn't possibly live here!' as I picked a route between tufts of dub[1] and small thorny bushes, jumping across forgotten foundation trenches when they got in the way, to the half-built gurdwara and the makeshift settlement supporting it that was to be my home. Apart from the dehra itself, a three-storey shell with the statutory cupolas, balconies and arched doorways, its raw cement basketed in spindly wooden scaffolding, the buildings were low and temporary looking: too small to form any proper enclosure. They crouched, unrooted, in the open plain. Groups of men in white and orange squatted in doorways drying their turbans. A hundred yards away, across an empty space pitted with excavations, was a row of huts: flat-roofed, windowless, characterless little brick boxes. Of my two-storey courtyard house there was no sign.

Having taken in that much, and feeling pretty silly standing there with my rucksack, I saw Jungli (my husband as far as everyone at the dehra was concerned) in his white turban and chola walking towards me from the line of huts. I think it was at this point that my senses half lost consciousness – to have remained wholly awake any longer would have been too much for them – and I followed silently to the tiny room in one of the huts that was his cousin Khazan's house. I saw my luggage hanging from metal rods high up the walls and Jungli's clothes mixed up with theirs and slung across pieces of string. I ate the food that was put in front of me, while the other hut people gathered in the doorway for the customary inspection; one monster with many eyes, as Henry Miller once put it.

Moved by a subconscious need to find something of beauty in order to begin to identify with the place – for it's not easy to belong somewhere when you have no positive feelings about it – I wandered out into the scrub. I needed to be on my own. How anyone could stand living in such a place I couldn't imagine, but what alarmed me most was the total lack of privacy. But I had resolved to stay; it didn't occur to me that I didn't really have to. To have run away at that point would have been to let Jungli down, to have wounded his pride, and to have shattered what little faith in humanity he still held.

---

[1] coarse unpalatable grass

I came across a scummy pool and a small mesquite[2] tree whose form suggested a butterfly alighting on a flower. The water was black and smelly, but across its surface a spidery white film, like the most delicate hand-made lace, stretched and dwindled, broke apart and reformed. It was enough: I put down my first tentative root.

They thought I was mad. After all that pool was their waste water system, fed by a wonky channel that wove between the dub tufts from the pump. I could hear them laughing as they sat on their charpoys in front of the huts and watched. To give myself time to adjust, I crossed the empty space back to the dehra and took a bath. At least that was familiar; the small cubicle open to the sky, with a cold tap, lots of mud and a door that didn't lock. By the time I'd washed, Jungli had gone on *path*-reading duty in the adjoining room, so I sat and watched him mouthing the words and turning the big floppy pages of the *Granth*. He was still deeply affected by the incident at Diwali, and there was patching up to be done to our relationship before he would trust me again. I was in no mood to face the interrogation of a lot of strangers on my own, or, for that matter, to face the practical details of our future. Back in the hut, two hours later, I went to sleep. I had had enough. I didn't want to know any more.

Hours afterwards Jungli woke me and led me to what was to be our home. We went round to the back of the hut row and through an opening into a tiny windowless room, almost a pure cube. It was the only room whose entrance looked westwards across the open plain; everyone else looked eastwards towards the dehra.

'OK?' Jungli was watching me.

'OK,' I said. I instantly felt happier. The room was dark; safe; a refuge from prying eyes and the omnipresent ugliness. And it represented the freedom at last to live in India as I liked – or so I then thought.

The rent for our new accommodation was a little under £3 a month; expensive, we thought, for a space 8'6'' by 7'6'' by 8' high (visually most unsatisfactory proportions). It constituted one quarter of the hut owned and occupied by a Hindu family from Rawalpindi who were to be our landlords. They had built it themselves, as had all the hut people; it was so basic I think even I could have managed it. Our room was more like a rustic potting shed than a human habitation, I noticed as my eyes grew accustomed to the gloom, with its blank walls of soft orange brick, handmade, all of

---

[2] *Prosopis juliflora*

a slightly different shape and with bits missing at the corners; rejects from the brickworks we could see across the plain. Individually the bricks were attractive, but they were put together in so slapdash a manner, with not even a hint at bonding, that the effect was diabolical. And their coarse texture and deep colour made the room appear even smaller than it actually was.

Mud mortar of the consistency of raw cake mix oozed carelessly out of most of the joints. In others there were gaps. I could see what had happened: they had put mud (very unevenly) in the horizontal joints but hadn't got round to the vertical ones. Instead they had close-butted the bricks (which by their very nature – the rounded corners and irregularities – were impossible to close-butt) and the mortar had trickled down into the wider cracks and spread like lava over the chipped corners. It had also washed down the wall in streaks; clearly it had rained before they got the roof on.

I looked at the splashed mud and the oozing mortar, the holes in the walls and the idiosyncratic bricks.

'Do people in England live in houses like these?' they asked.

Not exactly, no.

The numerous vertical gaps meant that we could be observed from the Hindu's kitchen in the adjacent quarter of the hut, and each time on the first day (and on many subsequent occasions) when I peeped through the wall to see if we were being watched, there would be Kamala's brown eye, cow-like and unashamed, staring straight back at me. Much later on – it was one of the things we took ages to get round to – we blocked up the gaps with screws of used school copy books that shopkeepers get hold of to make paper bags with. But little mice would thieve the paper to line their nests, and the eyes would be there again. There were several bricks missing altogether to let in light and air, and through the two in the party wall the Hindu children passed us cups of tea.

Their father, a clean-shaven middle-aged man with a summing-up look and a small moustache, was laying a floor; our room had never been used. He tapped bricks into a thick bed of silt which his sons were excavating from a pit outside, laying them unevenly and in no particular pattern. By the time he had brushed more dry silt into the joints and sprinkled the floor with water, we had an attractive and more or less level walking surface. We had a nice ceiling too, of orange sandstone slabs over metal girders. All we needed now was a door.

Between our entrance at the back and the Hindus' at the front was a passage off which the rooms opened, blocked down the middle with a pile of the sort of rubbish that might come in useful one day and covered with a heap of viciously thorny acacia branches, enough to thwart any potential burglar. From the rubbish we salvaged some old planks with nails that couldn't be got out of them, and balanced them on bricks and metal rods which for some reason were sticking out of the walls. The room was ours to do what we liked with. Jungli had bought a charpoy the day before: like all charpoys it was too short, and for a year we slept with our feet and ankles hanging over the end and our bodies overlapping the wooden frame each side.

Karam Chand, our landlord, went to Chandinagar to buy a door. He returned after dark with it balanced on a rickshaw, a frail, splintery, biscuit-coloured double door with the odd eye-sized hole where once there had been a knot. There was neither lock nor catch and I could have pulled it apart with my hands. By then it was too late to fit it, so when Jungli went on night duty he laid his sword on the pillow.

I dreamt I saw a hand coming round the place where the door should have been, with a Muslim behind it. Coming to get me. He wore a turquoise shirt, khaki shorts and an opaque skull cap. I beat him over the head with the sword but it made no impression, and the sword got smaller and smaller. Then I woke up. Jungli was still at the dehra and I sat on the charpoy, a tribe of mosquitoes for company, until he returned at half past three.

In the morning, there still being no door, we borrowed shopping bags made of second-hand sacks and, leaving one of Karam Chand's boys on guard, caught the number nine bus to Chandinagar to equip ourselves with a kitchen. We bought a chapatti board and rolling pin, a heavy iron chapatti pan, a flour sieve made of lager cans, a knife, a spice box and spices, a one and a half inch-high plank seat, two saucepans, a plastic bowl, a jug, a tea strainer, four glasses, a bolt for the door, four plastic food containers, a padlock, a plastic bucket, a ladle, washing soap and clothes soap, two plates, four teaspoons, matches, tea, sugar, ghee, flour, pulses, jaggery and fruit and vegetables (the latter food items, together with milk and milk products, were what we lived on for a year). Our shopping cost a little over £5, and was basically all we needed: someone had lent us a small primus stove such as everyone cooked on, we borrowed a broom when we needed it (we bought our own later), and we fetched candles from the dehra. Candles gave us our light.

That day I stopped being a guest of India and became a host: I was responsible for my own dwelling. Doing everything for myself when previously I had only watched others, or at the most helped, gave me a different outlook. For instance I could now sympathize with the village women who replaced the traditional brass and iron kitchen utensils with cheap and nasty plastic and metal alloys. I was buying them myself because, like the villagers, we couldn't afford the traditional things. Too bad if they broke after a month: at 6p we could always buy another.

Break they did, too. Very few cheap Indian machine-made products seemed to function properly or survive for more than a week or two. I once searched for a plastic water bottle through a whole street of household utensil shops: not one actually held water. Of our new kitchen utensils the heavy metal ladle snapped in half after a few weeks while stirring a pot of rice; our saucepan lids didn't fit and their metal handles were untouchable; the plastic jug tore along the handle; the board split in half; the lids wouldn't screw on the storage jars; the holes in our grater (a later purchase) hadn't been punched through and small discs of metal fell into the cooking; the broom fell apart; the knife handle came loose and later the blade broke in two; the stove had to be repaired several times a day; matches were manufactured all in different shapes, half so thin they broke on striking, others with saltpetre running down the sides so you burnt your fingers, and still more with no saltpetre at all.

Coming back from Chandinagar on that second day with an entire kitchen wrapped in Jungli's turban cloths, we were in for a bout of visitors. They peered in from the open doorway, drank polite cups of tea while Jungli was there and descended like flies the moment he went on duty. I managed to escape to Karam Chand's front yard, where the children were amusing themselves by letting off home-made bombs.

It wasn't just that people were inquisitive. 'Poor thing, she's all on her own,' they must have thought, and it was kind of them. 'We'll go and keep her company.' To most Indians it is inconceivable that anyone should enjoy being alone, as I did, very much.

Next morning we were besieged before I had even got up. Karam Chand's children were standing over Jungli watching him chop up fenugreek leaves. I said leave it and let me do it. It was my business, as a woman, to do the cooking; he was infringing on my duty. It annoyed me too that he should start cooking at seven in the morning, making me look foolish. Suddenly there were another six people in the room, poking at our stove and summing up our possessions. I fled to the dehra to have my bath and found there was no water. It was too much. I returned to the hut and sat on a plank in the desert in front of it, watching a herd of buffaloes nibbling at the dry dub. All I wanted was a bit of privacy, and as yet we hadn't been left alone for a single minute. I wasn't even going to be allowed to sit out in the scrub. People gathered, demanding to know what was the matter. There had to be something: no-one chose to sit out in the scrub on their own.

Karam Chand's wife Jhai[3] marched into the hut. She was to patch up many minor ructions that arose through our misunderstandings. 'What are you doing?' she demanded of Jungli. 'Cooking is women's work. Let her prepare the food.'

Cooking Panjabi food on a broken primus was a slow enough process without a succession of nosy people coming to ask what I was doing or wanting to know the time. Kicking off their shoes at the door, they planted themselves round me on the charpoy so that it was impossible to continue even a simple thing like peeling ginger. They waltzed in and out of the hut, unannounced, as if it were their own, staying on to watch the spectacle of whatever we were doing. They came in the middle of the night when we were asleep and the door was shut, and bashed on it and shouted until we opened it. Sometimes they would be hungry and Jungli would give them the food I had put by for breakfast. They came at six in the morning and stood placidly watching as I brushed my hair, did my teeth and went for a pee, things I'd much rather do in private. Jungli was on duty most of the time, and backwards and forwards to the dehra all night; up at 10.15pm, back at 1.15, up at two and back at three, up again at six to return at nine. He was gone much of the day too, and when he came back he needed to sleep, or there would be others with him talking dehra business too fast for me to be able to understand. He, of course, was the one person I wanted to talk to, but I couldn't, there wasn't time. So I felt isolated.

There were formal visits from people living in more huts on the far side of the dehra. The knitting machine wallah was an insipid man who made unsuccessful jerseys and did voluntary service for Santji[4] each night and all night until Santji sacked him. On his family's first visit his wife gave me ten rupees (sixty pence), the customary gift to welcome a newcomer. I gave it back: to them sixty pence was a lot of money, and they weren't selling many jerseys. The only people who didn't come to visit were men who worked at the dehra but whose wives were elsewhere, discarded by their husbands or living somewhere more sensible. In their position they couldn't come, but

---

[3] (or Jhai Ji) name used to address or refer to an older, unrelated Hindu woman
[4] the saint: respectful form of address

they hoped I would go and talk to them instead. Jungli scowled.

Gradually our neighbours got used to me. I couldn't understand what they were saying half the time – which would have been trying for them too – for the dehra people came from all over the place, and some spoke in Hindi and some in Urdu and others in strange Panjabi dialects that I wasn't accustomed to. Running out of things to ask, and finding I wasn't terribly interesting, they came less often. Our lives settled down and I began to do my own work, researching and writing. Which started it off again. What was I up to now? They came to watch. And ask questions. And pass comments. How fast I wrote! And how small! It looked like typing. If they wrote for even ten minutes, the few literate among them said, they would be exhausted and it would pain their eyes. I stopped writing when they came and put my pen down. To the dehra people writing was work, something tiresome like sweeping the floor, only worse. In any case women didn't work unless they were very poor: I would be grateful for the interruption.

Not normally an especially gregarious person, the lack of privacy at the dehra turned me positively antisocial. To survive, I withdrew into myself. Nor did the conversations, or what I could catch of them, interest me particularly: they were usually about people I didn't know at the dehra, naughty neighbours, what things cost and watches. The men were fascinated by watches. Sometimes people didn't talk about anything but sat together in silence, finding solace in each other's mere presence. They hated being alone. Every spare minute the women gossiped in each other's huts. Jhai did nothing else. It was the only social life they knew.

The things I found fascinating – where people came from and what their lives had been previously, the machinations of the dehra, indigenous ways of doing and making things, the bullock carts crossing the plain and the plant, animal and human life it supported – were never touched on. I had to ask, and I rarely got satisfactory replies.

Most of all I was fascinated by the saint. With the exception of Karam Chand's family, the hundred-odd people living at the dehra were supported by the offerings of the crowds who came daily to be blessed and healed. They lived in below minimal or way below minimal conditions, yet man, woman and child they worshipped the dust beneath his feet.

Why? What power did he have? Why did all these people come? Were they really healed?

Life in our hut row revolved around Santji. Santji said this and

Santji did that and look there's Santji just coming out of the office door. He's got a new shirt on. People revered him like a god. They watched his every movement, held sacred some nice thing he said to them maybe eighteen months before, and believed he could cure their sorrows. And all the time he remained somehow aloof from everyone around him.

At first I watched him too, from the cover of Karam Chand's yard wall, for I was loath to give him the satisfaction of knowing I was interested. They would point him out to me, the tallest figure among many, in the whitest, most immaculately pressed clothes. He held his head high and did everything with a style all his own; he was a king among serfs; a spiritual raja.

One of the big functions at the dehra was held on Guru Nanak's birthday. That year it fell on 4 November, soon after we arrived. Tents were erected for the langar, the sangat[5] and for keeping the shoes, and linked by a processional way. The gurdwara was transformed overnight from a construction site into a usable building, and Santji gathered up his pathis to inform them that anyone late on duty tomorrow would get the sack.

Jungli went on duty at eleven in the evening and returned at five next morning. He went on again at seven and came back at midnight. I was handed over to Paramjit-next-door and, having sat in her hut for an hour while she washed and dressed her unattractive children, we moved off in a clan, barefoot, to pay our respects at the gurdwara, take langar, and join the big sangat.

It was miraculous how where only yesterday there had been a patch of dust, today was a magnificent canopy of brightly coloured patchwork fabric stretched high over poles, with mats to sit on, an ornate podium, fluorescent light and microphones. The saint sat cross-legged on the stage in his spotless white shirt and pyjamas, his arms hanging loosely over his knees. He spoke quietly and undemonstratively for about an hour and a half, as if there had been eight people listening instead of eight hundred, giving a sermon such as any preacher might give on the duties of a Sikh and the greatness of the Gurus. The women on my side of the tent sat adoringly and listened (while they knitted or shelled peanuts) as though it was the first time they had ever heard it.

When the discourse was over, everyone lined up to prostrate themselves before their saint. In the evening Santji sang kirtan[6] (he

---

[5] congregation or religious gathering
[6] Sikh hymns

sang well) and people fell asleep on the floor. He sang until midnight, and mothers curled up around their children, and men lay on their backs, turbans for pillows, and snored while Santji sang. By seven next morning the place where they had lain was once again just a patch of dust.

3

Neighbours

OUR LANDLORD KARAM CHAND and his wife Jhai were Partition refugees from Rawalpindi. Since 1947 they had lived in Chandinagar but had nowhere of their own. When Santji first came to UP they attended sangat and became his disciples, whereupon he gave them a plot of government land beside the dehra on which to build a hut: our hut. They came with their children, Moti Lal, Jagannath and Prakash, all boys, and their daughter Kamala. And we all squatted on the government's land.

The family rarely left their hut. Karam Chand had a low opinion of schools and wouldn't have allowed his children to attend even had there been one to go to. They were all of school age: Moti and Kamala in their teens, Jagannath not quite a teenager and Prakash, the bossiest, about ten. It was hard to tell exactly and the children themselves didn't have much idea.

'How old are you, Prakash?' I once asked.

Prakash looked surprised at such a pointless question. 'I don't know,' he answered. 'Ask my mother, she can probably tell you.'

I was curious as to the source of Karam Chand's income. There they were, wearing respectable clothes and eating food as nourishing as we ate, and nobody was working! Jhai was a nurse but Karam Chand forbade her to get a job: it would reflect badly on the fact that he wasn't doing anything himself.

Most of the time Jhai stayed with her eldest son in a fashionable Ramnagri suburb. He was a diamond setter (the family were goldsmiths by caste) and the theory was that he supported Karam Chand's household in addition to his own wife and child. I found it hard to believe, in spite of the bad reputation goldsmiths had for mixing other metals in with their gold to make it go further. There was a little extra income from the sale of ayurvedic medicines,[1] and after we came from our rent as well, but it couldn't have been sufficient: there was more coming from somewhere.

Because she didn't stay with her family, people at the dehra said Jhai was a prostitute, a most damning thing to say of someone, I felt,

---

[1] indigenous Indian remedies

when based only on vague suspicion. I very much doubted it: she was an intelligent and sensible woman – though a bit snobby about her son's address and inclined to talk too much – with a great deal of self respect.

Later Jungli gave me another explanation for her absence that was far more plausible. He had learnt it from the neighbours who had heard it from the children themselves. Apparently there were two girls from Santji's sangat who sometimes came to collect medicine from Karam Chand. He would tell the children to make themselves scarce, and they would slink out of the yard. But one day they peeped through the chinks in the wall to see what he was doing, and saw their father feeling those girls' breasts! Kamala told her mother and Jhai, quite rightly I thought, walked out on him and didn't come near the dehra for four months. She still came infrequently. The ones that suffered were the children, who loved their mother and knew that when she was around their father wouldn't beat them. We would sometimes hear him laying into one of the boys with a leather belt, and the terrified screams of the victim. I hated it, but Jungli said it was no use my making a fuss. 'It's his child,' he said. 'He owns it and he can do what he likes with it.'

'He doesn't own it,' I retorted, 'and there are other forms of punishment.'

But Jungli didn't know any; in his opinion if a child misbehaved the only way to reform it was to beat it. Had I ever considered having Jungli's child, all such thoughts would have been dispelled the first time I saw him hit Kaki. But Jungli had never spoken of children: presumably, to him, they were part of the marriage that was not to be.

When Jhai came home there was nothing but rows, mostly about money. She would screech at Karam Chand and he would retaliate by telling her there must be something wrong with her brain.

I later learnt that he lay awake all night and only slept just before dawn, and again at midday. 'Why?' I asked.

'Because he's a smuggler,' said Jungli, as if it were a matter of course. So that was where the money came from! 'He's afraid to sleep at night: people engaged in dirty work must stay alert.'

I knew Karam Chand used to go to Pakistan from time to time, and it was presumably to buy gold which his son could sell for him. He didn't go now: the police had blacklisted him and confiscated his passport. But men would sometimes turn up at the hut late at night and talk in low voices long into the early hours.

In many ways I had more respect for our landlord's household than the other families in our hut row. Although the boys were sometimes a nuisance to us in the first few months, always hanging around goggling at whatever we were doing, they generally kept to themselves, functioned as a self-reliant unit and refrained from sponging off the dehra. At the approach of winter I would see the three boys out scouring the scrub for dung. I asked Jungli if I could go too: it looked fun, and was the kind of land-based activity that would have related me to the landscape in which I lived. I would have liked that. But Jungli was a Jat, and collecting other people's dung was a mark of poverty. He just laughed. 'You've no need to do that,' he said. 'We'll get some paraffin from somewhere.' He thought I was trying to be helpful: there was a paraffin shortage and sometimes we couldn't cook. I watched enviously as Jhai plastered her wet dung buns on the side of their yard wall to dry.

Karam Chand was meanwhile chiselling noisily away at a lump of granite, mostly at around eleven and twelve at night in the room adjacent to ours, fashioning a mortar in which to prepare his ayurvedic remedies. Although Kamala was the hardest working of the family, responsible for all the cooking, washing and cleaning since her mother left, Karam Chand was the most versatile. He was passing his resourcefulness on to his sons, who had nothing else to do but watch and help. He had built our hut, laid its roof, fitted its doors, wired it up and constructed some basic furniture. He grew spinach and onions in a plot in the front (the boys tilled and weeded and slopped buckets of water over it). He looked after his family's health, and prescribed ayurvedic remedies for others. He knew the tricks of the smuggling world, and the trade of the caste into which he was born. When he had finished chiselling the mortar he turned to blacksmithing, and forged some new tools using a length of railway line as an anvil. He built a podium of unjoined brickwork in the yard for the boys to sleep on, and an outdoor kitchen – a brick wall, sandstone shelves and a little mud hearth – for Kamala. What he couldn't do he refused to acknowledge as being necessary: when Moti had a hole in his tooth he swabbed it with antiseptic and told him to forget about it.

Our lives were interwoven with theirs, for they could hear everything we said or did, and we them. We could hold conversations through the wall without having to raise our voices, and it was Jungli's job to keep Karam Chand informed of what was going on at the dehra. We got up, spent the day and went to bed to an accompaniment of loud Hindi film music on their ancient wireless, of Karam Chand swearing at the children, of Kamala slapping chapattis in the kitchen and the entire family scolding their mongoose. Sometimes as we sat talking we would see a plate coming through the hole in the wall followed by a hand, and on the plate there would be some delicacy, spinach pakoras[2] or a special sabzi. And sometimes there would be a cup of tea for Jungli. We would roll Kashmiri walnuts (Jungli's favourite food, a rare extravagance at seventy pence a kilo) through the hole into their kitchen, or sweetmeats that had been given as prasad. On the rare occasions that Karam Chand went out the children stuffed themselves with pakoras, shouted, sang and shrieked with laughter. Much of the day they spent with us, to be called sharply to heel on Karam Chand's return.

Soon after my arrival at the dehra I had a dose of Delhi belly, and Jungli took me to Karam Chand to get some ayurvedic medicine. Karam Chand felt my pulses. 'Very bad,' he said significantly.

Jhai took me inside and pressed her hand over my digestive organs.

'*Very* bad,' she echoed. 'Liver and stomach. No food for a week, except rice, yoghurt, whey, apples and pomegranates.' Apples and pomegranates were out of season. 'We'll give you some powders – we've got all kinds of medicine.'

I could see that. The dusty unlabelled bottles and yellowing packages dominated their one habitable room and the family fitted themselves round them. There were bottles almost toppling off shelves, wedged into holes in the brickwork, on the floor, on ledges, and ranged in rows along the sides of the charpoys. Their bedding was on the floor.

'Don't listen to the so-called doctors,' they cautioned me. '*They* don't know anything – they'll tell you there's nothing wrong with you. *We* know all about diseases. For years we've been prescribing ayurvedic medicine and everyone we treat gets cured.'

So they gave me a dose of foul brown powder every three hours and waited while I took it. Jungli was suspicious.

'Give it to me,' he said on an occasion when, having just eaten, I had persuaded them to let me hang on to it to take later. He sniffed it and tasted it on the tip of his tongue. 'Sulphaguanidine!'

Sulphaguanidine is a common allopathic[3] drug taken for diarrhoea, just the sort of medicine I was trying to avoid.

'Don't be silly!' I scoffed, but when Karam Chand came on one of his slinking see-if-I-was-fair-game visits (having made sure Jungli

[2] deep fried chickpea flour fritters
[3] Western medicine

had gone on evening duty), I asked him what the powder consisted of.

'Oh five or six different ingredients,' he said vaguely, and I could see I wasn't going to get any more out of him. When later he demanded ten rupees for the treatment I began to be suspicious too, the more so since by that time I had been acquainted with some of his other dubious activities. Thinking that perhaps Jungli did know what he was talking about (he had once lived with a doctor and knew a bit about medicine), I asked him again. He said he had seen Karam Chand grinding pills with a pestle and mortar, and that it was a common practice in India for quacks to buy cheap allopathic medicines, reduce them to powder (in which form ayurvedic remedies are usually given) and resell them at a profit to their gullible patients.

In the morning I rooted out the last of some sulphaguanidine tablets that I had once been given by an allopathic doctor and ground it up. In colour, texture, smell and taste it was identical to the ayurvedic medicine I was receiving, the only difference being that it would have cost a quarter as much had I bought it in a shop. I showed Jungli.

'Didn't I tell you so the first morning?' he snapped. 'But you wouldn't listen.' And marched off.

He had been ill himself. A few days after I arrived he was sick all night, sick on the floor (I threw earth over it), and sick into a balta that I carried over and over out into the scrub. He called through the wall to Karam Chand for medicine, which was brought wrapped in little squares of a Hindi copy book. I went to the dehra for drinking water but hadn't got a third of the way before whistles were blown and searchlights put on me and men approached with sticks. When they heard Jungli was ill they came to the hut (they were the night watchmen), and Jungli's cousin Khazan came, and Karam Chand and Jhai came and we all sat till dawn watching Jungli being sick. What cured him then, he said, was a simple glass of water someone brought from the dehra, over which Chhota Santji, the substitute saint, had recited a mantra.[4] Only Karam Chand said it was his powders that had done it, and I thought (but I kept it to myself) that whatever poison it was had naturally worked itself out.

After a week at the dehra, when I was beginning to be allowed to lead my own life for part of the time at least, I decided that after all I quite liked it there. Days began to merge, and our home had taken

---

[4] word or words to be repeated to bring peace, protection and spiritual power

shape. We had put the charpoy in the corner receiving the most daylight (I sat on it to work) and the stove on the floor at its feet. Tins of ghee and sugar, the spice box and storage jars were ranged along the wall on a plank next to the stove, and the water bucket was tucked under the charpoy beside it. A shelf for soap, coconut oil and medicines, and another for books, were fixed higher up. Our clothes, towels and blankets were draped over strings along the dark wall, and the food, bundled in turban cloths against rats, was suspended between them. There were hooks and nails in logical places. The baggage was slung on metal rods driven between the bricks high in the darkest corner.

I was happy with the utter simplicity of the room, a replica of everyone else's and created with almost nothing but our ingenuity. Our belongings were hung on nails, wedged into holes in the brickwork, looped over strings and crowded on cracked planks. It was so wonderfully fragile, spontaneous, home-made and temporary-looking; like living in a tent. Everything was small. Everything was blue, orange, muted or white. And everything belonged to the shoddy factory-produced culture of modern India. For I was a designer by training, and a purist: if half the things in the room were fragile, functional, cheap and not a bit beautiful, then the other half had to be too, if only to maintain unity and rapport. The ugliness created its own kind of harmony. A single attractive object would ostracize itself by making me dissatisfied with everything else: if I had anything nice I gave it away.

But the room never remained static for long. Jungli was always having better ideas, fixing more planks and acquiring new things. When someone died at the dehra Jungli, having been promoted to the position of head granthi,[5] often got the spoils. People liked to die in the company of a saint, and their bodies would be burnt beside our hut. We accumulated a handwoven Panjabi khes, the traditional gift to the granthi presiding over a death, more tins, cloth, beakers, a clever tin made from an oil can with a tight-fitting hinged lid for the flour (it was meant to keep out weevils but we still got them), a broken steel trunk to keep the food in, old tins, mulberry twig baskets for onions and potatoes and bits of sacking (on which to wipe our feet) for the floor.

Occasionally things disappeared. Some of the dehra people were petty thieves and it wasn't safe to go out leaving the door open for

---

[5] reader and caretaker of the Sikh holy book in a gurdwara: the Sikhs do not have priests

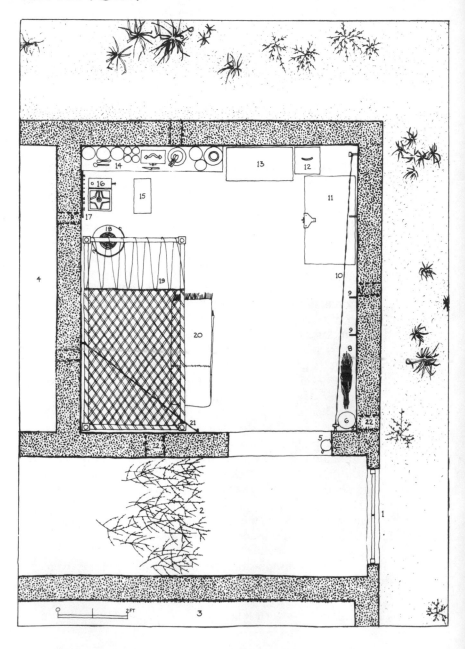

1 DOUBLE DOOR
2 HEAP OF RUBBISH AND THORN BRANCHES BLOCKING PASSAGE
3 KARAM CHAND'S LIVING AND SLEEPING ROOM
4 KARAM CHAND'S KITCHEN
5 WATER JUG FOR LATRINE
6 RUBBISH TIN
7 STICKS (FOR SELF DEFENCE)
8 DATE PALM FROND BROOM
9 RODS FOR HANGING BAGS
10 DOUBLE STRING FOR HANGING CLOTHES AND BEDDING
11 METAL FOOD TRUNK
12 FLOUR TIN
13 'PICKET FENCE' SHELVES, WITH PLANK SHELVES FIXED TO WALL ABOVE
14 LOW PLANK FOR POTS, PLATES, BOWLS AND SPICE BOX
15 1½" HIGH PLANK SEAT
16 PARAFFIN STOVE WITH PLANK SHELF ABOVE
17 RACK OF NAILS FOR COOKING IMPLEMENTS
18 WATER BUCKET
19 CHARPOY, WITH BAGGAGE SLUNG ON RODS ABOVE
20 FRAYED SACKING FOOT MAT
21 DOUBLE STRING FOR DRYING TOWELS
22 4" × 4" VENTILATION HOLES 4-5' ABOVE GROUND

longer than it took to pump up a bucket of water. So we buried the money under the floor. We removed the plank on which the plates were kept and Jungli dug out a brick with his knife. He scooped out some earth, wrapped the money in layers of polythene and buried it in the hole, replacing earth, brick, shelf and plates. Each time we needed more money the entire process had to be repeated.

At first we lit the room with candles. They were appropriate to the style of our existence, but it was difficult to cook by their light: my eyes became swollen. We were promised electricity almost daily, and I looked forward to being able to read in the evenings. It did arrive, a month later, in the form of a length of wire, a bulb and a socket, which were fixed up by a band of dehra men. Later on Jungli rigged up various side lights. He stood the charpoy vertically against the wall and shinned up it like a gorilla, digging his big toes into the gaps between the woven strings. When he had finished there was a very untidy jumble of seven different kinds of wire; it was the first thing you saw when you came into the room.

In Western terms our living conditions would undoubtedly have been classified as something well below a slum. We had under thirty square feet of living space each, very little natural (or unnatural) light, no sound insulation from our landlord's family, no foundations, no privacy, no tenant security, no window, no water supply, no proper door, no sanitation or drainage, no furniture, no dustman, no heating or cooling system, for the first month no electricity, and no outside yard. The walls weren't even waterproof. Apart from privacy, none of these things mattered to me, but they meant that everything took a long time. Nothing could be left lying about, for there wasn't room, water had to be fetched in a bucket from a communal hand pump, milk had to be boiled several times a day to prevent it going sour, the room needed sweeping and dusting at least once daily, rubbish had to be thrown in a pit fifty yards from the hut, waste water slung into the dust, candles lit and relit when the wind blew them out. . . .

It took a while to get used to such a residence. I had to discover where to put everything so I could reach it when I wanted it; I had to learn how to manipulate a very temperamental and antiquated primus stove; and I had to be taught a totally alien method of household organization. Only when I had assimilated all these new techniques could I feel the room belonged to me and be at peace with it.

At first my morning household duties would take me several hours. I would get up (most likely after everybody else), shake the bedding and remake the charpoy, keeping a look out for the arrival of Ram Pal the dudh wallah.[6] He would come cycling over the plain from a nearby village, his dirty dhoti[7] flapping behind him, four small churns of adulterated milk hanging from his handlebars and saddle-rack. 'Come and take your milk!' he would shout gloomily from the other side of the huts, but I was out of earshot and had to keep going to see if he had come.

Having collected our kilo I would boil it, cool it to blood heat and prepare yoghurt for the evening, burying the pot in the flour tin during the winter to keep it warm. I would fetch water and sprinkle a few mugfuls over the floor to settle the dust, and sweep very thoroughly because of rats and because things got caught in the open joints between the bricks. Our broom was a bundle of date palm frond tips tied with string.

Then came the washing up, the only job I resented. I would carry the dirty utensils and a bucket of water outside and perch on a brick by a patch of loose soil. Each object had to be swilled with water to loosen the dirt, scoured with handfuls of earth and rinsed clean. My hands aged and my nails chipped and broke, but the pots never shone as they should – the labour never seemed worth it. I bellyached about

6 milkman
7 long piece of white cotton ingeniously looped and tied to make a species of baggy trousers

the washing up at first, and sometimes gave up when I got to the pans, encrusted with burnt milk or slimy with ghee. They would be sitting on the doorstep when Jungli returned from the dehra. 'You're so good at cleaning pots,' I would tell him. He was, and it usually worked. To encourage me he made a scourer by unravelling a length of coarse rope, and when that disappeared I used a loofah I had picked up under a tree in Panjab.

I liked to do as much of this as possible while Jungli was out of the way so he couldn't chastise me for not doing things thoroughly or in the correct Panjabi manner. Occasionally he helped, but we had to be careful: if I shirked my duty the tongues would wag. As far as our neighbours were concerned the considerations that I had other work to do and supported myself were quite irrelevant.

Only when all these chores were done and the clean washing drying on the dub would I prepare the first meal. The stove often took five minutes to light, fiddling with knobs, pumping paraffin and unblocking the nipple (as they called it) with a thin wire pin that usually broke. First I cooked the sabzi, then the chapattis – always one thing at a time, and the cooking took more than an hour. By the time we had eaten the sun would be creeping over our doorstep and the day half gone.

In the village almost everything we ate was produced on Pitaji's land and was pure and wholesome. Here we were suddenly at the mercy of the shopkeepers, their dirty and cheating habits and food from we knew not where. There was water in the milk, grit in the dal and rice, sawdust in the flour, animal fat and motor grease in the ghee, mouse droppings in the sugar and dust in the spices. We were very much aware of the difference.

I was expected to cook Panjabi food. Jungli was doubtful at first. 'You can't make good chapattis. It's very difficult,' he said.

Left alone I made them as I had so often watched them being made: I knew how stiff the dough should be, how big the dough balls and how to make them perfectly round. Jungli when he came in looked at them suspiciously, as if wondering if I had borrowed them from next door. After that he made no further comment.

Being new to me I was very conscious of whatever task I was performing, and I found the housework drained much of my mental energy. Later it passed through a stage of being a bit monotonous, to emerge on the far side as a series of unconscious therapeutic exercises that hardly disturbed my thoughts and, demanding less of me, left me free to get on with the things I really wanted to do. Outsiders, with their comparatively rich and varied experience, have often interpreted the Indian woman's tasks as being monotonous. It wasn't so: they were more varied than many men's, and women had the advantage of being able to chat to their neighbours while performing them. Monotony was a thing I never once heard an Indian complain of.

The outside of the huts was identical to the inside: raw misshapen underfired bricks, chipped and disintegrating. Karam Chand's was about twenty feet square, the size of a large living room, and it housed eight people: we had a quarter and Karam Chand's family of six used the remainder. The next hut, across a pit where people threw broken glass and waste paper, was a third the size of ours (nine feet by twelve) and was also inhabited by eight: a Sikh family of parents, three children, a son-in-law and two grandsons. They were a gregarious family, always in and out of other people's huts or surveying the scene from their charpoys in the afternoon shade. And they were incorrigible spongers, coming to ask me for this and that when they hadn't remembered to get it or didn't want to. At four thirty every morning they were up, the men clutching pots of water and disappearing into the darkness behind the huts, returning to bathe under the pump and catch the first bus to Ramnagri, where they worked as ragis.[8] The women minded the children while they were gone, and at nine at night the men came home.

The married daughter, Paramjit, was our age, and in spite of her scrounging we got on well with her. Happily sagging from recent childbirth, she was friendly and smiling, though sometimes explosive. The pump the hut people took their water from had been installed by her family, and she tolerantly suffered us all to use it until one evening a row broke out between her and Karam Chand. Fanned by the other members of each family it blew into a feud lasting three months. Karam Chand installed his own pump in his own front yard and the two families avoided all further contact.

'They were nice before,' Kamala explained to me, 'but they aren't nice now.'

The next hut, nine feet by twenty, was split into four small rooms and occupied by twelve people. In the first, rent free, lived a tiny Muslim lady and her three grown-up children. People liked the Muslims in that there was nothing to dislike about them: they kept to their room and minded their own business. They stayed inside all day and even on the hot summer nights, speaking politely to each other

---

[8] gurdwara musicians, who accompany their singing with harmonium and tabla

THE HUT ROW

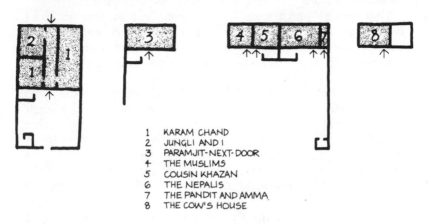

1 KARAM CHAND
2 JUNGLI AND I
3 PARAMJIT-NEXT-DOOR
4 THE MUSLIMS
5 COUSIN KHAZAN
6 THE NEPALIS
7 THE PANDIT AND AMMA
8 THE COW'S HOUSE

and sleeping on the floor. I think they thought it shameful to live in public as the others did: they were true Muslims whose womenfolk were kept hidden from the male world.

The mother only ever emerged in full purdah, and refused to go to the langar because she couldn't eat in front of others. Like everyone at the dehra (apart from us and Karam Chand's lot) she and her son and two daughters took langar food three times a day, but she was the only person allowed the privilege of eating in private.

Adjacent to the Muslims was Jungli's cousin Khazan, his wife and her younger sister. I didn't like Khazan, hadn't liked him from the start. Being younger than Jungli he couldn't address me, and I don't think we ever held a conversation. Khazan had a cold cunning look in his eye and he treated his wife roughly. But whatever he was, she was worse. Nobody liked her: the hut people said she was mean and bitchy and always picking fights with the other women. She hardly spoke to me either, except on my second day at the dehra, green dupatta pulled seductively down over her eyes (for Jungli, an elder male relative, was present) to remark, 'Your clothes are very dirty.' So they were: we had been finishing off the building of the room we lived in, but it's not the sort of remark you make to a new acquaintance.

Then a few days later she gathered up the women from her end of the row of huts and called me to the room. The men were at the dehra. She proceeded to make fun of me, parodying my strange Panjabi accent and anything else she could find to pick on in order to make the others laugh. Which they did. Karam Chand's son Jagannath was listening in the doorway and told Jungli later.

'Dog people!' Jungli spat. 'Ignore them.' So from that time on I avoided going near her end of the hut row and even walked to the front of our own hut on the wasteland side away from the main community. For months I was to have little contact with any of the people in that hut.

In the next room there was a young Nepali couple, Hindus, who several months later produced a baby boy. He was the night watchman and earned £12 a month; Jungli used to give him another pound out of his own salary for he found it hard to manage with so little. He respected Jungli and was grateful. His wife, like others at the dehra, only possessed one sari, which she would wash in the bathing cubicle, drape around the walls till it was just damp, and put back on again.

Finally, in the end room there was an elderly Brahmin couple, a funny old man with stilt-like legs (respectfully known as the Pandit,[9] though he had never been one) and his sharp-eyed wife Amma. I couldn't believe that two people could exist in such a room. It was tacked on to the end of the hut, the length of a human body and the width of the door frame. Fortunately they had no belongings, and the two of them sat on the floor by day and then lay on it at night.

Their coming to the dehra was tragic, though their story was not uncommon in India. The Pandit had owned a house, animals and land in a nearby village, and being an old man he had decided to hand over the deeds to his sons rather than wait until his death. The sons had families of their own, and the daughters had married and left the village. On being made the legal owners the sons had thrown the Pandit and Amma out of the house without a paisa, with nowhere to go and unable, at their age, to find work. They came to Santji, who took them in, gave them the tiny room free of charge (it wasn't his but no-one dared contradict him), and fed and clothed them. In return they did what they could for the dehra. Sometimes in the early morning the Pandit would come trotting into our hut on his rounds, so quietly I didn't know he was there until he warbled 'Good morning Sahib,' (they were the only two words of English anyone at the dehra ever spoke to me). Then with a few 'Satnam Waheguru, Satnam Waheguru's'[10] he sloshed half a dozen handfuls of holy water over us and our belongings and was gone. He sprinkled more holy

9 Hindu (Brahmin) priest
10 'God's name is true'

water (muttering 'Satnam Waheguru' all the while) over the outside walls of the hut too, I noticed, over the thorny scrub and over the broken glass and dusty wastepaper in the rubbish pits.

The last hut in the row, by far the nicest, with a window, a sloping roof and tiny private yard, housed Santji's cow.

Beyond was a gap and over the gap was a timber yard. It had nothing to do with the dehra and I used to ignore it. I liked to imagine myself in wild and undeveloped country. But it was really no more than a large piece of plain with the dub and thorny bushes still growing on it, fenced in with barbed wire. Here and there were small piles of timber.

In each corner of the timber yard was a hut made of bits of wood all different shapes and sizes, bits they probably couldn't sell (just as our huts on the brickworks side were built of brick rejects) and occupied by a good many people. At five in the evening, when the day's business of selling was over, the men would gather at tables fitted between the dub tussocks and begin the evening's business of drinking. They would entertain us with their earthy music-making, lewd chatter and occasional drunken brawls until we fell asleep, and then they would entertain the night watchmen. They didn't seem to sell much timber.

Beyond us on the other side, across the broad gap where Karam Chand's family strewed their rubbish and dug feeble channels for their waste water, was a long low hut with a grass roof, again twenty feet by nine. In it lived three families, one Hindu, one Sikh and one Muslim, hardly a recipe for peaceful existence. There were fifteen people in all, giving each one a living and sleeping space of a little over ten square feet. They were our hut people's shariks; nobody from our huts ever crossed the broad gap to theirs, nor they to ours. I couldn't have recognized any of those fifteen people in spite of their being our next door neighbours and living only forty yards away, for I was forbidden to go near them.

One of the women living in the thatched hut had gone mad recently after giving birth for the fourth time. She ran around meaninglessly, and I often heard her crying as her husband beat her out of the hut with a big stick. Rough on her, I thought, and rough on those who dwelt alongside her. But Jungli didn't agree. 'Where's the difficulty?' he would ask irritably whenever I expressed horror at other people's living conditions. 'Lakhs[11] of people are living like that. They don't complain.'

---

[11] hundreds of thousands

The men of that hut were our superiors at the dehra and ordered Jungli about, as did the little colony of men, mostly the saint's relations, who camped semi-permanently on his office floor. So also did the man in the last hut of all, the Big Ragi or dehra musician, who went around boasting that he was a reincarnation of Hanuman the monkey god. This man, it was said, had robbed a bank of thirty thousand rupees, killing a clerk with a knife in the process, and had come running to Santji for protection, swearing he would never do it again. And Santji had taken him in and made him his ragi and treated him like a brother, and so far he hadn't done it again. There were many such people in our community; the place seethed with smugglers, bandits and petty thieves who had supposedly come to the dehra to turn over a new leaf.

Santji had selected a wife for the Big Ragi out of the girls who attended his sangat. She was too good for him, a classic Indian wife always smilingly doing more than duty expected of her. They lived with their small daughter in a big one-roomed hut, a brick cube like ours, and it formed a full stop to the line of dwellings. Beyond was the plain.

The plain stretched as far as the eye could see. As a visual panorama it was supremely satisfying, majestic in its vastness, unlimiting to the passage of the mind. Standing in our doorway I watched the animals grazing; cows and buffaloes, mules and donkeys, horses, goats and wild rabbits. I watched bee-eaters and drongos, wagtails and three kinds of myna. Sometimes a flock of vultures flew noisily overhead like a lot of people shaking out their raincoats. I watched high-loaded, creaking bullock carts rumbling over the plain, slender dark-skinned southerners scanning the ground for dung, tattered boys perched side-saddle on the rumps of laden donkeys, and grey, tinkling Brahminy cattle filing home at dusk to the distant village in the acacia trees. Just to record such details is to romanticize them: in India they are commonplace.

The figures and the grazing animals, the thickening sepia sky before a storm and the colours of the landscape changing with the seasons; all these I could watch from my doorway. They were my greatest solace during the time I lived at the dehra.

No-one else seemed to derive any pleasure from our surroundings. To the hut people their environment was an open piece of wasteland where they relieved themselves, that harboured snakes, sometimes produced firewood, and got muddy when it rained. So they slung their rubbish from their doorsteps to shrivel in the fiery sun, be gobbled up by the first hungry animal or get blown away in the wind, and turned a blind eye to the children who made their arrangements within a foot of the hut walls, and the stinking pools of stagnant drainage water they constantly had to pass. Their interest centred on the other side of the huts, on Santji and the dehra.

4

Dehra

FROM KARAM CHAND'S FRONT YARD we observed the activity at the dehra. What we couldn't see, Jungli described for us.

A hundred yards away, across the dub and bare silt, over the pits that would one day become a sacred tank and within which two flagpoles, one white, one orange, stood as if on small islands, were the buildings which comprised the dehra. To the left was a corrugated iron shed, the langar, and beyond it the gurdwara itself. Facing us was the office and the saint's inner sanctum, with the public washing cubicles and latrines extended along one side. Set back and a little to their right a broad colonnade they called the verandah faced the langar. Here the saint held sangat.

Akhandpath, the non-stop readings of the Sikh holy book, ran most of the time, normally two days out of three. The third day was a so-called holiday. With the exception of Santji's healing sessions in the afternoons it was the main function of the dehra.

Each complete two-day reading of the *Granth* was for a particular purpose, usually the curing of an illness, and was paid for by the recipient. Really he was at Santji's mercy, for he might be told (told, not advised) that four, six or eight readings would be necessary for a complete recovery, each costing four hundred rupees (twenty-five pounds). Once to my knowledge, and maybe there were other times, the number of readings deemed necessary was seventeen. The patient was a girl with bad arthritis, Panjabi but living in California, and fortunately her father was rich. . . .

Soon after I arrived Jungli was promoted to the position of head granthi. His cousin Khazan who had held it before was demoted to the ranks, and very put out he was about it. From being Jungli's closest companion, following him around like a devoted slave and always in our hut drinking tea, cousin Khazan became his sharik, gathering up the other six pathis to make things difficult for him. The only one to remain true to Jungli was Jatedar, a tall young pathi, thin as a wire, whose clothes hung from his bony shoulders as if there were nothing but a coat hanger inside.

I was rather relieved about it. I had never cared for cousin Khazan being constantly in our hut and holding loud conversations with

Jungli over cups of tea at three in the morning when they came off duty and the rest of us were trying to sleep.

Although Jungli's position at the dehra rose, his pay certainly didn't. Most of the pathis he was in charge of earned more than he did; it was all according to Santji's whim. It was also Santji's habit not to pay the pathi's monthly salary direct to the pathi if he had a home somewhere else: he would send most of it to his wife or mother, keeping back fifty rupees (under five pounds) for the pathi's personal use. 'Three cups of tea a day and the rest on soap and hair oil,' said Jungli. That was all it would cover. But it kept them off booze and bhang, and it kept them at the dehra.

I felt sorry for the pathis. Apart from Khazan they were all unmarried or living apart from their wives, and they lived solely on chapattis and dal. Sometimes I cooked something special for one or other of them, and I offered to prepare a meal for them all once a week. Jungli was pleased. 'If I were a rich man that is what I would do with my money. There's no better service a man can give than to feed and help those less well off than himself.' Big words, and commonly enough heard in India, yet Jungli was serious. But soon after that the pathis turned against him.

Jungli was in fact on duty twenty-four hours a day, for which he was paid sixty pence, or two and a half pence an hour. Eighteen months previously when I had last been working I had been earning three hundred times as much an hour, often more, than Jungli was now getting. But I never told him. One quarter of his salary went on the ghee in which we cooked. The alternative was oil at half the price, which nobody cared for, or less ghee, but we didn't care for that either. One quarter went on milk, for yoghurt and those endless cups of tea. Sugar went up to nearly fifty pence a kilo. Had I not had money of my own (which Jungli was always loath to use) it would have been difficult to manage: without being in the least extravagant we would spend twice his salary each month.

I still couldn't quite take Jungli's poverty seriously. We had a roof over our heads. We didn't go hungry. Had I not been there Jungli would have been just as well off. But one day he went to Ramnagri to buy a turban to wear on duty. He had only one white one and it was too short. He returned with twenty-five feet of crisp white voile and three quarters of his weekly wage gone.

My living expenses at the dehra averaged out at around fifty pence a day (£180 a year), which covered my share of the rent, my clothes, medicine, soap, stationery, bus fares and half our food. It was all I could afford if my money was to last out.

I told Jungli that had I been in England without a job I could have been receiving social security benefit. He was astonished. 'You mean your government just gives it to you? You mean you could get more in one week for doing absolutely nothing than I earn in a month being on duty twenty-four hours a day?' I'm afraid you could.

As head granthi it was Jungli's job to organize Akhandpath – who came on duty when and to make sure they did – to mediate between the other pathis and the saint and be responsible for their behaviour on and off duty. If their clothes weren't clean, if they were late on duty or coming back from leave it was Jungli who got the brunt of the blame. The routine was strict: the pathis had two hours on and six hours off day and night while Akhandpath was running. So they could never get a proper run of sleep. Jungli, in addition, had to supervise sangat in the afternoons, prayer and the preparation of prasad at two thirty in the morning and evening prayer at seven. And he could be called at any moment by those senior to himself to do this job or that job, fetch this or deliver that, call someone or deal with a visitor; he was rarely allowed any rest.

'Santji wants you,' came the frequent command, and he would have to get up and go, meal or no meal, sleep or no sleep, and be kept waiting while Santji saw to something else, and then there would be a job to do or an admonishment to listen to, after which it would be time to go back on duty. Santji could and did call him at any time – 11p.m., 3a.m., 5a.m. – and sometimes I would just laugh; it was beyond my comprehension that a supposedly religious person could be so inconsiderate.

The pathis had to be clean when they went on duty, in fresh clothes, spotlessly white and ironed. Jungli would be reprimanded for wearing creased ones. But we had no iron, nor any means of ironing had we possessed one. They had to take a bath *and wash their hair* three times a day, immediately before each session. If someone didn't, the office wallahs got to know about it. They bribed the youngest pathi, a child of thirteen, to spy on the others and report back. They kept their own eyes open too, and it wasn't difficult to know what was going on. For apart from Jungli and his cousin Khazan the pathis all lived in a tiny space in a half-demolished building beside the dehra. They reached it by means of a ladder, and if they all lay on their sides there was just enough room for everyone to sleep. It didn't make for brotherliness, and they stole from each other's bags and pockets and ganged up on whoever was weakest. Which happened to be Jatedar. Their activities could be observed from outside through the gap that was the door, so that when they were sleeping the dehra people knew about it, and when they were taking opium they knew, and when one of them was fornicating with the knitting machine wallah's wife they knew about that too.

The washing facilities were equally public, and there was every chance that someone would take mental note if a pathi wasn't seen to be making use of them at the correct times, or if his hair was dry. How could that long thick hair ever get dry if he had to wash it three times a day, and coil it up wet under his turban, in the humid monsoon heat or on a winter's night when temperatures were below zero? When there was a special function Jungli's hair would stay wet for days as he would be at the dehra maybe twenty hours out of the twenty-four: at such times he would spread it out in a great wet fan on the pillow as he slept. I often grumbled about the insanity of such a dictate, until three months later Jungli persuaded the other pathis to sign a petition and they presented it to Santji and the rule was rescinded.

At the inception and completion of each reading of the *Granth* it was Jungli's job to recite the Sikh prayer in front of the assembled sangat and distribute prasad. Once begun the recitation couldn't stop, even for a few seconds, as the pathis changed shifts. At night candles and gas lamps were kept burning in case of electricity failure and a man was employed to look after them.

Between readings the room had to be cleaned – not merely swept but turned inside out – and that also fell to the pathis. They did much of the dirty work at the dehra and were at everyone's beck and call. Their superiors resented their being paid for what they considered was not work at all ('All they do is sit reading the scriptures now and then'), and would do everything to make their lives difficult. Several times the pathis were threatened with no more payment. They were given extra jobs to fill all the free hours those in charge thought they had. And in May it was announced that Akhandpath would stop for a month in June (the hottest month with temperatures of 110° and more), and the pathis were to do labouring work instead. I thought it was very naughty.

Everyone living at the dehra had to follow its rules, and that meant me too. There was to be no consumption of alcohol (those who were caught drinking were sacked), or any other intoxicant (though half of them took opium and smoked ganja). There was to be no eating of meat, fish or eggs. How stupid, I thought, and for a time bought eggs anyway. Jungli adored eggs. Feeling like criminals we bolted the door, cautiously cracked, cooked and ate them, and carefully stowed away their shells in newspaper to be buried in the rubbish pit. After

the crows discovered them I used to take the shells with me to
Ramnagri: had we been caught, Jungli would have lost his job. But in
the end we gave them up.

The entire community was supposed to get up at half past two,
attend morning prayers and repeat mantras. And we were all meant
to accompany the boundary pacing sessions to keep out the evil eye. I
would see everyone thumping past our hut row in procession, two at
the front holding spears and the rest banging drums and chanting.
From April onwards they were doing it every day at three in the
morning, and Santji told Jungli my presence was also required. It
reminded me of the territorial marking practised by certain
mammals, over which others of their species pass at their peril. All
the same I didn't go.

Another rule stated that employees were not to leave the dehra
premises more than twice a month. While Akhandpath was running,
even Number Nine was out of bounds.

'How are people supposed to get their shopping then?' I asked. For
if the men couldn't go out, their women wouldn't go without them:
they were afraid of the crowds, of pickpockets, of being cheated by
shopkeepers and of losing their way. Most of all they were frightened
of the number nine bus. Men touched you up in the fight to get in, but
if you didn't fight you didn't get a window seat, and then more men
in the aisle would press themselves against you in such a way that
you couldn't be sure they were doing it on purpose, so you couldn't
say anything. But you knew they were.

The point was we weren't meant to need any shopping. We were
supposed to eat in the langar and weren't expected to require
extravagant things like fruit and vegetables. The dehra had its own
shop selling basic commodities like soap, hair oil, paraffin, sugar,
spices and grains. That, surely, was all any of us could want.

The last thing we all had to do, and this really was compulsory,
was kneel down and place our foreheads on the ground each time we
approached the saint, or even if he crossed our path. Jungli
prostrated himself on leaving him too.

'Well I'm not going to,' I said.

Jungli looked a bit worried but he held his peace. At heart he
agreed with me.

When Santji showed no sign of interest in the first white person ever
to set foot in his dehra (and possibly the last), I ventured closer.

One day when I returned from Chandinagar he was sitting in his
office while a small group of admirers crouched on the ground

outside, watching. There happened to be a power cut and the outsiders were in darkness; I joined them unobserved. Santji was sitting at his desk cleaning out his ear with the pointed end of a paper dart. Sangat looked on in wonder. It was the first time I had had a close view of Santji, and I could see why there was always a preponderance of women at his sangats. After fifteen minutes when nothing had happened, I went home. The rest sat on.

Next time I joined one of the big Sunday gatherings, held in the open air. I sat at the edge, where the thin film of buffalo dung, specially spread, met the dust. Again I watched him, the expressive movements of his elegant hands, the relaxed way in which he sat, and the apparent power he held over his congregation. As long as Santji sat, no-one was allowed to move: I later witnessed two or three hundred members of his sangat sitting motionless through a thunderstorm.

There was sangat every afternoon. People came from nearby villages, from Ramnagri and even beyond for his blessings and, having taken their food in the langar (Santji, like the Sikh Gurus, had a rule that all who came before him must first partake of food in his kitchen), would gather on the verandah. Sangat began with kirtan sung by the Big Ragi, followed by Santji's discourse, during which sangat would be exhorted to repeat God's name, do seva and attend further sangats. The last two would be of benefit to him too, for it was through his followers' sweat and generosity that the community expanded. They dug silt from the pits around the flagpoles, and carried it in baltas on their heads; they carried bricks here and there (often the same bricks here and there, for something would be built one day, and he would want it moved the next); they cleaned the dehra and served in his langar; and they brought offerings of food and money which piled up in front of him as he sat on his podium at one end of the verandah after his discourse, surrounded by plush cushions. They came before him in ones and twos and threes, clutching their bottles of holy dehra water, and prostrated themselves before him. They deposited their gifts and handed him their bottles. Santji put his palm over the open top, inverted the bottle and returned it to them blessed, and they would go home and drink it, trusting that his power would protect them. Some devotees stayed on. They were in trouble of some sort, most often concerning an illness but sometimes a family problem, lack of money, or a business failure. Someone would say, 'I've got a headache.' Or whatever. The saint would wave his hand in front of them. 'Have you still got it?'

'A bit.'

'Now?' waving his hand again.

'No, it's all right now.' They wouldn't have dared say yes.

'Off you go then.'

But usually I couldn't hear what was the matter. People were embarrassed and spoke in whispers, and my command of Panjabi and Hindi (for he switched from one to the other) wasn't that good. They would all be told to repeat God's name, drink their water, attend sangat and do seva. To most of them he would say 'It will be all right,' and people said things did come right when he had said they would. And of some he would ask 'Do you eat meat and drink alcohol?' And those he asked always did, or he wouldn't have asked them. He would say 'Give them up, repeat God's name, drink your water, attend sangat, do seva and your problems will be over.'

Sometimes I attended sangat and observed: I wanted to see some demonstration of the power that people were so adamant Santji had. Until I saw it for myself I wasn't prepared to believe it. But nothing much seemed to happen.

On the holy day of no moon there were some new proceedings. It was dark, and I had gone to the dehra to fetch drinking water. A line of men and a line of women were seated crosslegged on the verandah: Santji stood at the back of the line of men. The last man got up and Santji lent forward and whispered something in his ear. Then he sat down again, and Santji patted him on the back. What the hell is he doing now? I wondered, and stopped to watch. He went up the line of men doing the same to each, and then started on the women. Only he didn't pat them on the back and he kept at least a foot away from their ears. Jungli, who was standing guard, noticed me watching and motioned to me to go away.

He later explained that the saint was giving each person a mantra, a group of words to be repeated by the possessor just as Waheguru is normally repeated. Daily repetition was supposed to bring peace of mind and also, through Santji, a degree of spiritual power. But the mantra must be kept secret and never uttered out loud before others: hence the whispering and privacy.

Mantras were only given on the holy day of no moon. Many requested a mantra, and having assessed each candidate Santji either accepted or discarded them; it seemed a bit cruel. It was also a departure from true Sikhism, I complained to Jungli, as were various other aspects of Santji's teaching: the emphasis on meat and alcohol when all intoxicants were equally banned and meat wasn't forbidden at all, and the very dependence of his sangat on a healing

saint who was neither Guru nor God. The Sikh Gurus had severely
reprimanded their own kin for performing miracles – just tricks, they
said, showing off – and constantly told their followers to have faith
in the one God and none other. For those who had belief, the Gurus
said, He would take care of all.

Jungli had no answer.

Santji was a Brahmin, from a poor Hindu family in Panjab. His
father was a sabzi wallah who walked from door to door selling
vegetables. They had no land of their own but rented a little to grow
fodder for their buffalo. One day about eight years previously Santji
had been out in the fields cutting clover when a vision of Guru Nanak
appeared in front of him. Guru Nanak told him that the world was
full of pain and sorrow and that he was to give up his job as a bank
clerk and go out to heal and comfort people. He gave him the power
to do so.

So the story goes. People began to come to be healed, and when
they got better they said it was Santji who had cured them. So more
people came and his reputation grew. And they called him a saint. A
small dehra was built on the site of his vision, where people could
come and receive his blessings. People came from greater and greater
distances, until there came a message from Guru Nanak telling him to
go to Uttar Pradesh and construct a gurdwara on an unused piece of
government land Guru Nanak claimed as his. Santji left his wife and
young children in Panjab, and with some close friends and disciples
came and squatted on the land in a few temporary huts and shacks.
His disciples multiplied and the rich ones donated money.

As the dehra grew larger people thought, 'This must be a very
powerful saint,' and more and more they came for his blessings.
They came from far off in UP and Panjab. Many were healed, and a
few stayed on at the dehra to do lifelong service to the saint to whom,
they believed, they owed their lives. Such a one was the dehra
secretary, who had had terminal cancer and been given two weeks to
live by the doctors. He had tried everything, and come to Santji in
desperation. In a month he was completely cured.

At first Santji had remained visibly a Hindu. Only in the last two
years had he stopped shaving, grown his hair long and tied it in a
turban. He looked a Sikh, though Jungli said that as far as he was
aware, and he remained close to him for a year so he should have
known, he didn't follow the Sikh religion that he preached. He went
to bed at five in the morning and got up at one or two. He neither
read *path* nor repeated God's name, and when no-one was looking

he smoked cigarettes. But at first he had done seva, helping to build his own gurdwara.

The government didn't like people helping themselves to its land. None of us had any right to be there. They filed a court case against the hut dwellers living outside the dehra boundary, and every month there would be another day-long sitting which Karam Chand and the rest would have to attend. But against Santji they were powerless, the hut people believed: Guru Nanak owned the land and had directed him to it. Even the government couldn't evict a saint.

It could though, we found out later. Santji was attending the court too, or at least the secretary was, and the dehra people assumed that in the end he would be required to pay for the land. But by that time he would be rich.

So we went on living there and the community went on growing. Santji made the decisions and no-one had the right to dispute them because, he said, they came straight from God. Perhaps it would be a building he would want moved. Several times in as many months he became dissatisfied with the dehra uniform and wanted it altered overnight. He would make all kinds of promises too, and forget about them. He had seen the room we lived in and asked Jungli how he expected an English girl to put up with such conditions? He, Santji, would provide us with two new rooms at the dehra, free of charge. Nothing happened, but the next we heard was that we were to live in Santji's own house that he was having built. When still nothing happened and Jungli enquired, he was told by the substitute saint that we were quite free to build our own house; there was plenty of land. I regretted then not buying the cow's house, which had originally been offered to us for £60.

Santji was strict with his employees, often threatening the sack and sometimes giving it. The meetings he called his pathis to were never to thank them for their long hours of labour at such low pay, but to chastise them for being improperly dressed, for being late, for not doing their jobs properly and for not obeying Jungli. Sometimes the pathis fell asleep on duty; sometimes they weren't fully literate (though they wouldn't admit it), and sometimes they would turn over the pages of the *Granth* without reading them. Jungli said Santji knew these things by instinct.

At one of these meetings he threatened to close down Akhandpath altogether if the other pathis refused to do what Jungli told them. A small sangat was sitting outside the door, all ears. He accused one of them of reading carelessly, missing out passages and not concentrating. Then to another he said, 'Harcharan Singh stand up!' The pathi got up; he was a Mazbi, very black. 'Tell us what you have been doing!'

Harcharan Singh was taken aback. He knew at once what Santji meant, but couldn't think how he had got to know about it. 'Come on!' said Santji impatiently. 'Hurry up and tell us.'

The pathi knew that if he didn't confess Santji would tell everyone himself, which would be worse. So he said 'I've been misbehaving with Karnel,' or words to that effect. Karnel was the thirteen-year-old pathi and Jungli had brought him from Amritsar.

'Pritam Singh, did you know about this?' the saint demanded.

'Yes,' said Jungli.

'Then why didn't you report it?'

As usual the blame fell on Jungli. For Jungli wasn't one for telling tales. Everyone at the dehra had a good laugh about it, but they were shocked too. Homosexuality is illegal in India and verbally condemned by almost everybody: 'God made woman for man,' and all the rest of it. Poor Harcharan Singh!

Santji was smart. He retained his position of absolute dictator by not allowing anyone to hold power in any office for more than about a year. He demoted the president to the rank of pathi under Jungli, and the Big Ragi (formerly important, then building labourer and now ragi) became president in his place. If a disciple or employee became too cocky he would be put down: people worked better, and were less of a threat, if they were afraid. When Santji went to California he bought two tickets for Chhota Santji and the Big Ragi to accompany him. But Chhota Santji said, 'Santji's taking me with him because I can speak English,' and the Big Ragi said, 'Santji's taking me because I'm such a good ragi.' Santji got to hear of it and tore up their tickets.

But he had spiritual power: everyone was quite adamant about it. He could exorcise spirits and he had even (so they all said, and they had seen it with their own eyes), raised a couple of men from the dead. He could prophesy the date of people's death, and on several occasions had done so.

A man came to our hut one day and sat for hours talking to Jungli. Jungli had had a sleepless night on continuous duty and needed those hours to sleep in, so in the end, assuming they were engaged in the usual idle chatter, I curtailed the conversation so Jungli could rest.

I shouldn't have, it turned out. Our visitor was not a local peasant casually attending sangat, as I had thought, but a wealthy smuggler from Jullundur in central Panjab. The poor man was in despair. His wife had been seriously ill and only able to take food through a pipe leading into her stomach. He had brought her to Santji and Santji had said she would be all right, and she had got better and was able to eat normally again. But she grew careless, began to eat meat and other things that both Santji and the doctors had forbidden her, and for a second time became very ill. Her husband brought her back to Santji. This time he said he could do nothing: they should have paid more heed before. The woman would die in twenty days' time. They should go back home where she could be properly looked after.

But this man deeply loved his wife and was terrified of losing her. He said that if she was to die she would die here, at Santji's gurdwara. Maybe he hoped that Santji could still cure her. They stayed, and on the twentieth day when her death was near Santji told Jungli to sit by her and recite *path*. She lay in a room in the gurdwara, and the other pathis, whose sleeping space was close by, got scared and ran away. Jungli rested her head on his arm and while Jatedar, who had been made to stay, recited the Sikh Psalm of Peace he repeated the mantra Santji had given him and splashed water into her open mouth to keep it moist. He didn't know at what moment she died.

5

Langar

'HAS ANYONE at the dehra ever insulted you?' Jungli asked me.
'They don't speak to me at all,' I replied.
'That's good,' he said. It meant they didn't dare. They were on
their guard against both of us, me for my affected seriousness and
him for his very real temper.

Jungli didn't want me speaking to other men, and I respected his
wishes. Luckily there weren't really any worth talking to. I noticed
over the months that each time I commented, however mildly or
offhandedly, that a man was either all right, quite pleasant or had a
nice face, Jungli would tell me something frightful about him, for
instance that he had murdered his mother, in order to put me off.
'*Very* dirty man,' he would always preface his remarks. He was
trying to scare me, the way parents did with their children when they
told them of evil Panjabi spirits with their feet on the wrong way
round that could turn you into a lizard.

Jungli was particularly irritated about Karam Chand's transparent tactics. 'If Karam Chand comes round again while I'm at the
dehra tell him I said he's not to come unless I'm here,' he shouted. I
daresay Karam Chand could hear perfectly well through the wall,
unless my stern face had already put him off, for he didn't come
prospecting again.

The hut people pitied me because I was childless. I was older than
the other young women in the hut row, all of whom had children
and/or were pregnant. They hoped to encourage me.

'Bharjaiji,[1] come and see!' said Paramjit-next-door mysteriously.
All the younger hut people called me Bharjaiji, and Jungli Bhaiji.[2] As
the older ones didn't call us anything it was only Jungli who
addressed me by name.

I followed Paramjit. In front of the huts, on a dusty piece of worn
grass sat her two fat baby sons, dolled up in dresses and bonnets,
totally unaware of the attention they were attracting and picking at
bits of rubbish. 'Don't they look sweet?' the women asked me
meaningfully.

[1] respected elder brother's wife
[2] respected elder brother

'Very pretty,' I lied. I had never seen such self-absorbed children as Paramjit's.

'When you have one they'll all be able to play together.' Paramjit grew bold.

'Won't that be nice,' I said. The babies were stuffing earth in their mouths and plastering it on their faces. Paramjit let them get on with it. Her life was one long cycle of changing and washing their clothes; she did it at least three times a day. And when her husband came home the only place they could be together was the open plain at the back of the huts – no wonder she got ratty sometimes. I'm not sure which of us pitied the other more.

I had an idea that the hut people thought me arrogant and aloof, thought that because I had had a good education and had more money than they did I considered myself superior to them. Jungli denied it, though he may have been wrong or just unaware of their feelings. People thought I was a good woman, he told me, because I got on with my work, didn't fraternize with men and didn't spend the day gossiping like the other women. The men didn't like the gossip: they knew it was often at their expense.

But some of the women grew to resent my writing. It had been acceptable as a novelty but they couldn't understand it and it made me unavailable for long cosy chats when there was no-one else around. Sometimes their exasperation showed, as on the occasion (there were many like it) when a total stranger turned up at the dehra to receive Santji's blessing and, on being informed that there was an English girl living there, had walked over to the hut row, marched straight in and announced, 'You're writing!' Jhai, who had sprinted round in case it was anyone interesting, remarked in an aggrieved tone, 'It's all she ever does!' I was sorry about it for I was fond of many of the hut people and enjoyed their company for short periods, but I had to write. If I'm not doing something creative I'm miserable.

Only just before I left India did I learn that Indians mistrust writers. Writers are like crows, they say: scavenging and indiscriminate, calculating and mercenary. And Indians are hypersensitive to adverse criticism from outsiders, particularly the British, whom many still hold in esteem.

Any resentment I felt towards visitors from the hut row was caused by their scrounging. Every other person that entered our hut wanted something, and their insistency destroyed my early benevolent intentions of bringing home fruit to share out and sweetmeats for the children. '*She*'s got plenty,' I'm sure they thought, and they felt they had the right to a share in our fortune. Cousin Khazan's wife sent her younger sister, Paramjit came herself, and Karam Chand's children shouted through the wall: I was a one-man langar.

'Bharjaiji give me ghee!'

'Give me onions!'

'Give me cumin!'

'Give me tomatoes!'

'Give me vegetables! I have nothing to cook.'

'Give me sugar! My child is crying.'

'Give me yoghurt! I'm preparing kari' (curry to a Panjabi means a dish containing yoghurt and chickpea flour).

'Give me paraffin!' Never, 'Have you a little paraffin to spare please?' and when you gave it to them, 'That's kind of you, thank you: I'll return it tomorrow.' Instead they sometimes said, 'Is that all?' looking at what was offered rather scathingly as if it had hardly been worth their while walking all the way round to my door. And I would tell them there wasn't much – there usually wasn't – and that we ate too. If it was enough they said nothing: it wasn't their way.

Please and thank you had no place in most people's vocabulary. If someone asked for something it was your duty to give it; if a guest came it was your duty to feed and look after him for as long as he cared to stay. It was your duty to share your money; your duty to give up your time; your duty to lend your most treasured possession to your neighbour. When everything in life came down to duty, where did please and thank you come in? Our hut people came for paraffin in the paraffin shortage when we had very little ourselves, and they didn't want less than a litre. When we ran out Jungli went next door to ask for it back. 'We haven't any,' they said. But he knew they had.

Begging from those better off than yourself was an accepted custom, but coming from a protestant country I found it hard to take. Neither Jungli nor I ever begged, but Jungli gave selflessly and cheerfully whenever anything was demanded. Our supplies ran out. What annoyed me was that people would ask for things available in the dehra shop fifty yards away; that there was free food for everyone in the langar; that it was always the women whose men had a salary that came; that they would ask for luxuries, such as tomatoes for a garnish; that they would ask for heavy vegetables that I had had to carry back from Chandinagar; that between them they would ask for something or other several times a day; and that, excepting Karam Chand's family, they would never give anything back.

It gradually wore me down. But Jungli rarely noticed my moods.

He did his best to make me physically comfortable, but I missed the tranquillity, the uninterrupted hours we had had in the village. Here he was claimed by his responsibilities at the dehra, by Santji, by Karam Chand, by the hut people, by the pathis. . . . I came last. It didn't help that I had no role of my own at the dehra. Jungli might have been trying to establish his position or putting on a macho act for fear of being ridiculed, or perhaps he still didn't trust me: whatever the reason, we spent little time together, and our relationship was less affectionate in those first few weeks at the dehra.

Jungli's way of compensating was to give me rough, provoking, opium-induced slaps and prods and thumps in the odd moments when he wasn't on duty: concentrated attention that conceivably a Panjabi girl might not have minded. He laughed when my patience ran out, thinking I wasn't really cross. But I was. It was more satisfactory when our bad moods coincided, for then we would bolt the door and wrench and tussle until we had worked the aggression out of ourselves and were back to laughing.

It affected me though. When I caught myself getting lethargic for the first time, giving in to the invaders and lounging about like the rest instead of getting on with my work, I decided to go to Kulu. Jungli instantly became gentle and loving as he always did when I went away, saying he couldn't bear to be without me, that even if we weren't together much at the dehra his heart was always with me and it made him happy to know I was there.

On the morning of my departure he accompanied me across the scrub to Number Nine.

'Don't forget to feed the mongoose,' I reminded him. Karam Chand's family had gone to a wedding, and Raju the mongoose was tethered in our passage. 'And eat properly yourself.'

He was worrying about me. 'Trust no-one,' he warned. 'Those hills are full of bad people. Don't go to anybody's house; stay in gurdwaras. Don't ride in trucks. And come back soon.'

I disobeyed all these injunctions, as no doubt he ignored mine. But I found autumn in the Kulu Valley, in grey-brown fallow fields, in yellowing willows and robinias in wispy groves, in golden rice and maize-straw shoved into the forks of trees, and in copper-leaved apple orchards with stiff angular branches and leaden trunks. I went on to Amritsar and south Panjab and came home through Haryana on a twelve-hour bus journey two weeks later, arriving at night.

The room was full of people. Jatedar was stirring a pot of dal in the doorway and a friend of Jungli's from Amritsar was stretched out on a new charpoy that had appeared in my absence (only a Sikh could dress in ice-cream pink from head to toe and still look like a man). People I had never seen before kept appearing and being invited in for cups of tea. Karam Chand's boys stood watching. I retreated into the corner, and as my eyes grew accustomed to the dim light I noticed that everything had been moved around.

I had been looking forward to coming home, but the noise and squalor in our hut depressed me. I tried to shut my ears to the loud smackings of lips as the men tucked into their chapattis and dal and slurped down glasses of salty water, and the swearwords forming a preface to every other sentence. Was this how I lived? I felt like a stranger in someone else's hut.

Next day I put the room back as it was before. Long thin Jatedar had made himself a permanent fixture in my absence, eating and sleeping in the hut though he had space of his own at the dehra, and keeping his unwashed clothes slung untidily over our string. The previous night he had slept in Karam Chand's kitchen to make way for our guest, but he had it in mind to continue sharing our facilities. You could just fit another charpoy into the room he argued, and he would pay for the food I cooked him.

The thought of having Jatedar, goofy spineless Jatedar, as a twenty-four hour chaperone in an eight-foot-square room, appalled me. Since he and Jungli worked the same shift at the dehra they were scarcely apart as it was. I put my foot down.

Jungli was clearly embarrassed by my attitude. He seemed to find it puzzling, self-indulgent and even shocking that I should insist on having some time alone with him, if only at night. To him, so long as I was there too, our private relationship didn't seem important. Attempting to come to terms with his apparent indifference to something which to me was fundamental, I realized that it wasn't just Jungli, and that in the whole of the dehra we were the only couple with the privilege of sleeping on our own; the only couple with the possibility of anything approaching a normal married life.

Quite a lot had happened in the fortnight I had been away. Soon after I left almost everybody at the dehra had been evacuated to a city three hours journey away to set up camp and perform Akhandpath on a piece of vacant ground where Santji intended to build a new dehra. When a group of sweepers to whom the land belonged attempted to oust the dehra people a fight broke out: the police came, arrested everyone involved and locked them up in jail. There they remained for ten days, until Santji got them out.

Meanwhile only Jungli and Jatedar remained to do all the work at the dehra. Sangat continued and people came to do seva and take food in the langar. Jungli was responsible for all the normal administration, organization of seva and sangats, the reading of *path* and the preparation of three meals a day for twenty or thirty people. He and Jatedar would cook at night and fall asleep in the langar, too exhausted even to walk back to the hut. But by the time I returned the prisoners had been released and Jungli had resumed his normal duties.

Partly because of his hard work and loyalty during this period Santji came to have more and more trust in Jungli, and as a special privilege would ask him to prepare his meals and make his tea. Santji was fussy about his food and, as befitting a saint, would only allow those in whom he had sufficient faith to prepare it. He wouldn't eat alone. He wouldn't drink tea out of a glass but only from a metal beaker: he believed that if people who were envious could see what he was swallowing, their impurity could be transmitted to the food and to him.

But Jungli was fussy too. Sometimes someone from the hut row would present us with a small bowl of dal or sabzi, and when they'd gone Jungli would fling it out into the dust. 'Unless I see it coming out of the pot from which they too are eating, how can I touch it?' he would say when I complained of the waste. 'Who knows what they've put in it?'

Jungli now spent much of his free time running backwards and forwards with beakers of Santji's tea and our room became public property. Sometimes in the evenings he would be told to cook for fifteen or twenty people, for the hangers-on in Santji's office would want to eat too. The dehra store supplied the constituents when it had them, but anything lacking we had to provide ourselves. And of course there was no question of overtime. For several hours there would be constant comings and goings between us and the dehra, with everyone bossing everyone else and losing his temper. Karam Chand's boys would be peeling and chopping vegetables on the charpoy and doing more than their share of shouting, and strewn over the floor would be primus stoves, huge brass pans, piles of vegetables, a mountain of dough and droppers-in drinking tea. Not until ten or eleven o'clock would it be ready, by which time the recipients must have been starving. We certainly were, and when all the food had been carried off and we had cleared up we had to begin again, for it didn't occur to those dehra people that we might have stomachs too.

One evening Jungli was making tea for Santji, special tea that he always made with great care and our ingredients: all milk with three cloves and two green cardamoms. I said, 'I'll take it to him.' But he wouldn't let me.

'What business have you got there?' he asked. 'He can't take tea from *anybody*'s hands.' Jungli could be very blunt sometimes.

I thought I would go and see for myself, and next day at dusk I went.

Santji was sitting behind a desk in his big black plastic chair with an imitation chandelier floating like a crown above his head. Beyond was a lot of dusty space. I hovered doubtfully outside, positioning myself behind a pillar so Jungli couldn't see me from the hut row. He disliked the idea of my speaking to Santji more than to any other man at the dehra, for he knew he was the only one in whom I had the slightest interest.

The saint and I stared at each other through the door. I entered, prostrating myself before him (at the last moment my courage failed me), and sat down among some adorers on a carpet beside and below him. It was the first time I had ever spoken to him.

'Yes?' he said. I felt like a customer in the greengrocer's.

I asked if he could take food and tea from my hands, for I wanted to be able to help Jungli when he had a lot of extra work to do.

'I can take tea,' he replied.

'What about food?'

'No.'

Other people were getting interested in the conversation, and the crowd around us was gathering. They were starting to ask *me* questions, and I heard Santji telling someone that Jungli and I had had a row. It was time to leave. I had some pride swallowing to do: no-one other than my mother had ever refused to eat my food before. I consoled myself with the thought that Santji was after all still a Brahmin, and that putting everyone down occasionally probably helped to maintain his own feelings of superiority. That night Jungli again cooked for a special sangat of twenty, and I sulked on the charpoy pretending to be absorbed in a book. My mind was dominated by the disconcerting thought that I couldn't help because I was unclean. Or impure.

In the morning Jungli and I went for a walk across the plain, our custom whenever we wanted to have a serious conversation. Inside Kamala was usually listening through the wall in Karam Chand's kitchen. Jatedar came loping after us like a faithful red setter, not wanting to be left out.

Jungli explained that Santji didn't allow just any old person to prepare his food. You had to be 'tested' and you had to have a mantra. And then you had to repeat it daily. That was why I couldn't do it. But if I liked he would ask Santji if I could do seva in the main langar. He might say no though, Jungli warned me, for he was even choosy about the women who cooked for his sangat.

Permission was granted – as if it were he who was doing me the favour – and I was told that from now on langar seva was compulsory and that I was to do it every day from noon until three. No days off. It wasn't what I had had in mind, and the next day I had planned to go to Ramnagri to get the shopping.

'Why wasn't your wife in the langar today?' they all demanded of Jungli, and in the evening when I returned, weighed down with bundles and exhausted, my shoulder bag ripped in the battle to get on the number nine bus, the housework still to do and Santji's bloody dinner to prepare, yet again, they came to search me out. 'Why didn't you come to do seva?'

Next day I was on duty at noon. At that time the langar was a makeshift shed which made that noise that corrugated iron does when it hasn't been properly nailed on to its supports and the wind blows hard against it. With two other women I mixed and kneaded three enormous dishes of dough, and we hauled them to the side of the big log fire that a fourth woman was stoking. Squatting on planks with twisted torsos, the wind clattering the corrugated iron, my back aching and the smoke stinging our eyes, we rolled chapattis for three continuous hours. One of the women had a deranged adult son whom she had brought with her: he played about like a naughty boy, sang popular songs, munched carrots, fidgeted, leered and did various other things that aren't allowed in langars. The women shouted at him when they thought of it, and as they rolled chapatti after chapatti they gossiped, sniffed and wiped their streaming noses on their dupattas.

For two more days I rolled chapattis in the langar, squatting on my plank at an unnatural angle. The third day was Christmas Day, and it was by then cold enough even when the sun was out for people to keep their hut doors closed. The electricity failed so I had to sit in darkness. Our paraffin ran out and there was no more in the shops. So I couldn't cook.

When the current returned mid-afternoon I caught the faint strains of Kings College Choir singing my favourite carol *In Dulci Jubilo* mixed up with several other channels on Karam Chand's plug-in wireless. I yelled through the wall, '*Don't touch the tuning knob!*' which of course they instantly did, and my carol was lost for ever. I ranted and fumed and Jungli said this was supposed to be a happy day and what on earth was the matter with me? I just wanted to listen to that carol, that's all.

He came back from his evening duty with boxes of candles and arranged them round the walls, shoving knives and slivers of wood into the joints to support them. He said he was making Christmas for me; he remembered my telling him about candles and Christmas trees. We cooked dinner on a coal fire in a mud-lined bucket that Paramjit-next-door's family had made, with a hole at the bottom for fanning and emptying the ash, three mud peaks at the top for the pan to rest on and a grate half way up. With the candles, the coloured paper chains I had made and the warmth and smell of the coal fire it really did feel like home.

Four men from the dehra, all our superiors and according to Jungli all awful, had invited themselves for dinner since it was my Christmas.

'What are you going to cook for us on Christmas Day?' they had asked. They turned up at ten at night, just when I was falling asleep, consumed twenty-four chapattis with sabzi followed by khir[3] and held forth with a long boring story about how Santji had raised a man from the dead. I thought it could just as well have been cut to nine words: '"Get up," said Santji. And the man got up'.

By next morning my back was so painful I could hardly move. Jungli had to do all the housework. He sent me to afternoon sangat supported on a big stick, hoping that if Santji's power could cure others it could cure me too. Santji wasn't there because he'd gone to America – they were building a dehra for him somewhere in California – and meanwhile Chhota Santji had taken over.

Chhota Santji looked pleased (Jungli said he fancied me), and I was called to the front of the queue.

'What's the matter?'

'My back hurts. It's from having to sit at an angle in the langar.'

'Rub your hand over your back – the part where the pain is.'

I rubbed my hand over my back.

'Has the pain gone? Less?'

'No.'

He gave me two palmfuls of holy water to drink, and when that didn't work either, half a marigold to eat. He made me turn round and threw several more handfuls of water over my back. Then he gave me his antique Kashmiri shawl to wind round my waist.

It was at this moment that Jungli arrived and saw me sitting there

[3] sweet rice pudding with cloves and cardamom

wrapped in Chhota Santji's shawl. He gave it a menacing look. Having then to reassert his position Chhota Santji sent him off to the tea stall for a glass of hot water. 'Run!' he shouted at Jungli's back. 'Fatta fat!' ('Quickly'). And Jungli ran.

It was no use, and I returned to the hut. The langar women came to see how I was, each with a huge bundle of greens balanced on her head: Kamala said they had stolen them. Our hut people came with various contradictory advice. I was worse and in a lot of pain: couldn't stand up, walk or lie down. Jungli looked at Santji's photo in its illuminated glass-fronted box and spoke to it as if the saint was in the room: 'Come on, *do* something about it!' But Santji was in California and Jungli had to do something about it himself. He prepared a dish of hot ghee, sugar and ground root ginger for me to eat: delicious, but it didn't kill the pain. Then he heated the heavy iron chapatti pan, wrapped it in the dirty sack we used to wipe our feet on and put it, like a hot water bottle, behind my back.

In the morning we went to see the fat Sikh doctor in the village on the hill; it was the first time we had been beyond Number Nine together in the ten weeks we had lived there. I was given pills and cream, but they were no more effective than Chhota Santji's half marigold. Chhota Santji came himself in the evening with the one I called Kala Sap (black snake) for he was dark and sly, and they made themselves comfortable on the charpoy. Was I cured?

'No.'

'No faith,' said Kala Sap.

Chhota Santji squatted in front of the stove, heated some water, stirred it with a knife while mumbling a mantra and gave it to me to drink. Then he asked about the traffic in England. . . .

It went on for days. I sat on the charpoy with the hot chapatti pan wedged behind my back, and Jungli did the housework. Since I could no longer do seva in the langar I did a drawing of Santji instead, copied from a photograph. Jungli took it to show the dehra people and the secretary, the one who'd had cancer, said, 'What a beautiful drawing! Give it to me!' and Jungli gave it to him.

That sort of incident, which had already occurred several times in Jungli's company, would throw me into an impotent rage. I cursed the secretary for having the nerve to ask for it and I cursed Jungli for giving it to him without my permission. Poor Jungli! He couldn't understand my anger. It was only a piece of paper, he said; I couldn't be that mean. Anyway the secretary was his senior, and if he asked for something it had to be given him. I could do another drawing; where was the difficulty?

Softening, he heated up a pan of sand and, wrapping it in a cloth, shoved it between me and the wall. It was more comfortable than the chapatti pan. He rubbed some ointment into my back, repeating in a whisper the mantra Santji had given him. I could only catch two words: Santji's name. Instantly the pain was less.

'You should be baptized as a Sikh,' Jungli said. 'Then you would be in the Guru's care and these things wouldn't happen.' Over the months Jungli had frequently pressed me to be baptized. He said he was afraid of going somewhere horrid in his next life since he was forbidden to have an unbaptized partner. He felt he had left God's side: he wanted to get back, but couldn't. Many other people had encouraged me wherever I went, but I had always refused. I didn't think I could keep those vows and wasn't sure I wanted to: I wasn't particularly pure and my motives for doing anything were usually the wrong ones. Most of all, as Kala Sap had uncharitably or astutely pointed out, I had no faith.

I did do another drawing, believing it would turn out wooden, but strangely it was better. Jungli said he'd given me the power to do it: he'd prayed to Guru Nanak and Guru Gobind Singh to give me a hand. Chhota Santji and Kala Sap came later to inspect it. They pored over it, pronouncing the nose too small and the moustache untidy, but grudgingly allowed that the beard was all right (and Santji's only comment when presented with it, apparently, was that there was something wrong with the neck).

'Have you seen the drawing *I* did of Santji which is hanging in the verandah?' asked Chhota Santji. It was a huge toothy charcoal drawing that made Santji look like a Saturday night television comic. But Chhota Santji clearly thought it fit for the National Gallery. Karam Chand's family were lighting their mud bucket and a cloud of smoke seeped through the wall and chased them out.

In the morning I began to do a little housework again. There was a beautiful sunset that day, luminous and peaceful, with horses grazing against the light. Those were the last few hours of the 1970s.

At midnight we both got up. Jungli recited the Sikh prayer, touched the floor and went on duty. I stood alone under the glaze-cracked clouds half hiding a near full moon and sang Auld Lang Syne to myself, quietly, so the other hut people wouldn't wake up and think I'd gone off my head (Indians celebrate New Year, more sensibly, in spring). At that moment I felt no optimism.

1980, and a soft rain was falling, washing away the sins of the seventies.

6

Pilgrimage

WINTER CAME. The cold winds howled through the missing bricks in our walls and the gaps around the door. There was thick wet fog at nights which clung long into the mornings, followed by cloud and drizzle. It continued for ten days. No-one could wash their clothes for there was nowhere for them to dry. The bedding got damp. My hands were too numb to write, the floor was permanently wet, and we had run out of coal.

People went about as usual in their thin cotton clothes and sandals, a shawl thrown casually over their shoulders. Each time they came to our hut they left the door open behind them. During the paraffin shortage I had been cooking on a contraption Karam Chand used for blacksmithing, lighting some coal in a small iron bowl on a stand and turning a handle to fan the fire as I cooked. The rest of the time I sat huddled on the charpoy in my blanket, trying to preserve what little heat there was by keeping the door closed, light or no light. In a moment it could all be lost.

'Shut the door!' I said to people who came in, some of whom, notably cousin Khazan, completely ignored it, and, 'Shut the door!' I yelled after their disappearing backs.

In the end the sun came out and brought with it a brilliant English summer's day. All morning and afternoon the women were at the pump and soon there was more drying washing to be seen than huts, all hung over strings and wires and walls and spread over the hummocky dub.

Santji returned from America after a three-week absence and Jungli spent the whole of the night before at the dehra, sewing gold sequins onto a navy cloth. They hung it on poles with marigolds at the sides as a triumphal gateway to welcome him home. At eight in the morning when the cold sun was rising through a white mist and I was scrubbing the pots on the doorstep, Santji came. Everybody ran, barelegged, blankets over their heads and flying behind them, and within seconds there was a huge crowd round his car. The big drum was beaten, the conch shell blown, and there were great shouts of 'Bolé so nihal, "Sat Sri Akal!"' ('Ye who seek salvation shout, "God is Truth!"')

A few days later came the festival known as Lori, when people ate meat and drank themselves drunk on rough liquor. I was going out shopping but they all said it was too dangerous: instead there was a bus going to Dholpur (Santji's home town) that night on a two-day pilgrimage, and since Jungli didn't want to go, I could go in his place for nothing.

Dholpur was three hundred miles away in Panjab. We set off to much crunching of peanuts, shouts of 'Satnam, Waheguru!' and 'Bolé so nihal, "Sat Sri Akal!"', each person trying to outdo his predecessors as to how long he could prolong the 'é' syllable. I was tired of it: I'd had a continuous week of it on the Hemkund pilgrimage.

There was a lot of laughing and shouting, and the men took it in turns to drive the bus. I had been looking forward to making the journey by road for the first time, but all I could see was what seemed to be endless eucalyptus forest (though I knew it was only a roadside belt), and lorries snoozing along the verges.

Every couple of hours the bus stopped for those ceaseless cups of tea the Panjabis don't seem able to do without. Each time I got out to uncramp my legs. Each time it was colder. Finally, in the pre-dawn light, we stopped for a long time in the middle of nowhere, but this time no-one was anxious to get out. It appeared that we had arrived.

We were indeed in the middle of nowhere, surrounded by youthful fields of wheat and clover. It was a funny sort of gurdwara, not what I had expected of a religious place marking the spot where a saint had had a vision, but a small walled farmyard with a log pile, a heap of sand and three buffaloes. Part of the yard was covered by a corrugated iron lean-to, and there were a couple of small rooms on one side. I couldn't imagine where we were going to sleep.

Our sangat made a dash for the two little rooms and sat close together under their blankets while I took a bath out of a bucket under the cover of darkness. Since nothing had been organized until afternoon I went for a walk across the fields, so much prettier than the barren landscape outside our huts at home. Everything was fresh and green; sharp and reborn.

I walked into Dholpur. It began suddenly at the base of a ridge and rose in a pile of flat roofs. A tangle of aerials provided a roost for stranded paper kites. Through the arched gateway a maze of alleys led up the hill, lined with tiny shops selling home-made rat traps and tinsel wreaths, herbal remedies and hand-beaten iron pans. I felt as if I had taken a leap back into the Middle Ages until a motor bike came vrooming up from behind, scattering pedestrians rudely with its horn. It was our Santji in his advertisement white, with a strange apparition clinging on behind in a red and yellow woolly knitted hat with a brim. Within the next half hour Santji and I came face to face in the narrow lanes four times, and neither of us said a word.

After langar in the farmyard and scrubbing our utensils clean in the heap of sand we joined the local sangat for Santji's discourse. For the first time I noticed he was nervous. Having spoken for an hour he sent those of us from the main dehra outside to await him in the car park: we lay on daris and dozed in the low winter sun. Eventually he joined us and seated himself delicately in his royal chair. I continued to gaze out at the landscape, but the others sat in devoted attention, nobody moving, all eyes fixed on Santji – yet no words came. Then, muttering something about arrangements, he jumped up, leapt on his motor bike, and was gone. We waited and waited but he didn't return. Nor did he come after evening langar when again we sat waiting: he had promised to sing kirtan. Without him his sangat was like a body without a pulse, a dog without its master. It took no initiative; it was lost.

In the early evening when Santji had returned briefly on some pretext and I happened to be walking across the farmyard, he called me. It was the second time we had spoken.

'Woman!' he addressed my back.

I stopped and turned round.

'Me?' meaning I wasn't exactly overjoyed at the title.

'Is there anything you need?'

'Nothing.'

'If there is you ask my father . . .' (Santji's father ran the langar) '. . . bedding, tea . . .'

'I don't drink tea.'

'She doesn't drink tea,' echoed the hangers-on who were collecting around us to see what we were saying.

'Then drink milk.'

'There isn't enough for everyone so it's hardly fair if I drink it.'

But he'd had enough of the conversation. 'Off you go,' he said.

I went to sit by the fire in the langar and talk to Santji's father, a grand old man with bushy whiskers and twinkling eyes. The family's former poverty, which Santji had left far behind him, was explicit in the face of his father. He spoiled me like a child, gave me sweet-meats and the best milk I'd ever tasted. Afterwards a group of young women sang kirtan, improvising tabla on old tins while sangat napped and gossiped and the Pandit from our hut row sat eating bananas like a monkey. We slept in a pile of straw under the lean-to in the yard, warm and cosy.

In the morning Kala Sap kicked the dregs of the snoring sangat to life. 'Pack up, we're going,' he said.

We were supposed to be staying two days, and sangat had paid four pounds each for the six-hundred-mile-journey. Yesterday our saint had paid us no attention whatever, and today he was sending us back: it was most irresponsible of him.

So after much leave-taking and boot scraping we departed for UP. It suited me, for we would be travelling the GT Road in daylight. At least I thought we would be, but a few miles down the road the bus pulled up and we all piled out with orders to leave our shoes behind. We limped along a gritty road to a large gurdwara like other gurdwaras, smelling of mustiness and rancid ghee and full of flitting squawking sparrows drowning the voice of the pathi reciting a passage from the *Granth*.

The next stop was Kharanpur, Jungli's real father's village. Having paid our respects to the gurdwara we started off, only to stop a hundred yards down the road when the man driving the bus was hailed by a friend. 'Come and take tea,' he said charitably to the fifty people in the bus, so we trooped down a side lane and squashed into his yard. Within five minutes a microphone had been rigged up and the men were singing kirtan: having accepted the absence of Santji they had at last come to life. One man pedalled off on a cycle to fetch a tabla, several neighbours brought their day's supply of milk in brass pitchers – for you can't make fifty cups of tea on one family's milk – and the buffaloes looked on in absolute amazement. The postman came to the yard door with a letter and, despairing of whom among the sixty-odd people to hand it to, hurled it into the air instead. It fluttered to the ground like a feather a foot from where he had been standing. A postman ought to know you can't throw letters.

The elderly patriarch stood with hands clasped and an expression of childish joy on his face. He would be able to hold the attention of his friends for weeks with tales of how he had entertained a holy sangat in his house who had sung the Guru's hymns and recited prayers for him.

While three women wiped and polished our fifty pairs of shoes, two others brewed tea in a bucket. We drank it out of shallow brass dishes and departed. The patriarch stroked the new bus driver (he giggled about it afterwards), there was more yelling of 'Satnam, Waheguru!' and a couple of miles further along we turned on to the main road. It was almost dark, and our homeward journey had just begun.

Jungli had missed me. Akhandpath wasn't running and for once he was free from strain. We talked for hours like we used to, and he told me not to go away again.

A few days later he ran out of opium. Major disaster. His usual source had dried up and it was difficult to find trustworthy dealers. A day-long pilgrimage in crumbling buses and through the narrow crowded streets of Ramnagri brought us eventually to an opium shop with a selection of dried pods in varying degrees of disintegration. Jungli bought two kilos of the cheapest and in the evening we made opium tea to cure my cold.

Its effect was appalling. I laughed and cried uncontrollably; could neither speak nor hear. I lay on the charpoy, the ceiling rocking, and Jungli fed me pieces of salted orange.

My efforts as reformer had failed. I had hoped to be able to persuade Jungli to break the habit. Quite apart from my other reservations about our relationship, the prospect of spending my life with a man enslaved to opium, or any other intoxicant for that matter, was more than discouraging. I don't believe I ever knew the real Jungli, for his personality was transformed by opium. Boyish, teasing, high-spirited and energetic soon after taking his daily allowance, he became flat, tired, aching and morose when the next one was due. To keep me quiet he pretended he was cutting down and would show me the little black ball he had rolled between his palms, but it always looked the same to me. Mostly he swallowed it when I wasn't around, hoping I would forget. I was his conscience, he said, and it troubled him.

It was around this time that the Nepali night watchman's wife in the next-door-but-one hut gave birth: her first. She delivered the child in her hut under the supervision of some of the older women, our Jhai included. We gave the new mother some money, as was customary, and I was going to add a bag of almonds and sultanas but Jungli wouldn't let me. She would either throw them away suspecting a curse, he explained, or eat them and then blame us if the baby got ill. People's minds worked like that he said, particularly towards a childless woman. Many believed that if such a woman put a curse on a new-born baby (for instance by paying a pandit to recite evil mantras at a burning ground) and it died, she would stand a better chance of bearing one herself.

Well this baby did get ill, but it certainly wasn't our fault. For a start she had nowhere to put it. Then she refused to cover it up for eleven days. This was in January. It had to lie naked: it was their custom in Nepal and it made the baby strong. Everyone thought she was crazy: they had little respect for customs other than their own.

When the eleven days were up and the baby, fortunately, better, the Nepalis held a langar outside their hut. All the dehra people came to take their morning chapattis and dal for the well-being of the young child. That was the custom too.

Later on there were some less welcome guests: kusras. I knew there was a group of them living nearby for we sometimes saw them on the number nine bus, singing and dancing in the aisle for odd coppers, and squatting on the floor at the back in red lipstick and saris, smoking. They came one windy morning and made themselves comfortable on some pieces of gunny outside the Nepalis' door. They tied bands of bells on their ankles and danced to the singing and drumbeats, and we all came out of our huts and gathered round to watch. The mad woman from the thatched hut joined in the dancing. The old Muslim lady stood in her half-open doorway, two patches of gauze in her bourka where her eyes should have been, and the young Nepali mother, baby in arms, peeped sheepishly round hers. She knew she was going to have to part with money.

I still couldn't make up my mind about these kusras. There seemed to be more male about them than female, which could be the point of wearing saris, to redress the balance. The rattling bangles, the long plaited hair, the red lipstick, the feminine gestures, the forehead marriage mark, the padded breasts and the constant flicking of the sari fringe over the head would all be employed to undermine the man in them. And yet there was something non-male too, their delicate hands and feet, narrow shoulders and rounded women's bellies.

There was an argument about payment. The kusras demanded twenty-five rupees, half the night watchman's weekly wage, which he couldn't afford to give them. One kusra stood menacingly in their doorway and the others, sitting on their bits of sacking, gave the impression that they were quite happy to go on sitting there until they had received their dues. The hut people joined in on the Nepali's side and everyone shouted until Paramjit-next-door, who also had a young baby, gave some money too. And since neither of the babies was hermaphrodite they were allowed to remain where they were.

I had one more exchange with Santji: it was to be my last. There was a black and white film in my camera that needed finishing off so

Jungli and I went to the dehra with the intention of finishing it off on Santji.

'He may refuse,' Jungli warned. 'In all the time I've been here he's never obliged anyone by coming out to have his photo taken.'

Kala Sap came to the door of the inner sanctum and snarled when we told him what we had come for. But Santji came out smiling and pleased, took my camera and examined it, and told me where to take the picture. I said I wasn't taking it there (I noticed Jungli looking at me aghast), and led him up to the outside steps of the gurdwara. For the first time we were alone and could hold a conversation free from the hindrance of twenty or thirty eavesdroppers. I positioned him against the shade and told him to take his glasses off: since returning from America he had been wearing a pair of dreadful sunglasses through which you couldn't see his eyes.

'No,' he said. It was a battle of wills.

'What's the use of people coming for your darshan if they can't see your eyes?' I asked. Jungli would have been horrified. 'Your eyes are your soul,' I told him.

He removed them and I took the photo, but it didn't come out well. He looked lusty and not a bit like a saint. We continued talking at the foot of the steps, and people around stopped what work they were doing the better to concentrate on listening. Kala Sap was now carpenting (he was a carpenter by birth), and several women were sitting in the dust with sewing machines making salvar-kamiz. Devotees came and shrivelled up at Santji's feet, but he did little more than glance at them. We discussed the English, how they sat on trains behind newspapers and never spoke to each other.

'But you aren't English,' Santji said.

'What am I then?' I asked.

'Indian, absolutely.' Jungli had told me some time ago that Santji had said God had made a mistake in giving me birth in England: I ought to have been a born a Sikh. God sometimes made mistakes like that, apparently.

7

Wilderness

FACING AWAY from the dehra, and being the sole occupants of the hut row to do so, I only caught sight of the other hut people when I went for water or milk, or they came to visit, or when they came round the back to make their arrangements. People had their own favourite spots and would return to them day after day, just as our rats favoured the bookshelf. There was usually someone trudging off to his patch with a plastic water jar in hand.

I rarely went beyond my own territory by the dwarf tamarisks. The landscape itself prevented me, and it was some time before I began to understand why. I am normally a compulsive walker; this was a new thing.

The line of latrine territories hugged the edge of a large shallow pit from which silt had been dug. The plain was covered with such pits, their pale silty floors cracked like crazed earthenware. In places there were dry brown thickets of reedmace and an occasional lonely sentinel of windswept thatch grass. But most of the plain was covered (intermittently, like spots on a leopard's back) with parched dub, dwarf tamarisk and three kinds of small xerophytic perennial. Panjab must have looked like that once, except that there would have been trees. Around the dehra the pressure was too great for anything large to survive; if a bush or tree managed to escape being chewed to death there were plenty of people in the vicinity too poor to afford paraffin. Prakash would be sent out with orders to dismantle every poor struggling specimen of vegetation trying to be a tree and haul it back on the end of a piece of rope. Everything nice went the same way. In the hot weather when the dub threw up pale green feathery flowers the women went out with knives and cut it, every last spike, to make new brooms.

Beyond the silt pits and maybe half a mile from the hut row were two defunct brickworks, low piles of pink rubble fluttering with delicate mesquite bushes. Weeks passed by, but in the end I went to investigate. Beside the mounds and under the bushes was a small cluster of thatched mud huts. Turning back to our own hut, which to us was everything because we lived in it, I had an unanticipated feeling of estrangement. It looked so insignificant: a faceless box of a hut among huts, dwarfed by the huge sky and wide-stretched plain. I couldn't relate to it at all.

That was one thing that stopped me going out again. Another was climate and a third lack of time: the awareness of being busy all day but achieving little made me loath to part with the few hours I did have to myself. But the main barrier was the plain itself; an awesome wilderness, used but not cared for, unloved and unbelonging, endless and flat with no real incident or, more important, no point of refuge. You didn't feel safe in it. Paths didn't lead you anywhere. It was like the ocean, big and powerful, lapping the walls of our hut.

After that I had to make a conscious mental effort to go out for a walk. There was the timber yard for instance, just beyond our row of huts at the cow's house end and only about ninety yards away. I had a childlike and almost subconscious notion that beyond the timber yard there was nothing, that it went on to the end of the world. It was seven months before I went as far as its barbed wire boundary, walked along it and discovered it had an 'other side'.

One day Jungli and I walked over to the brickworks, whose smoking chimneys told us which way the wind was blowing. Most of the labourers were Rajasthanis, men, women and children, who lived in a pathetic clutch of tiny huts within the brickworks, with unmortared walls of broken brick, makeshift doors and low pitched roofs of thatch grass. We had to stoop even to see through the open doors. Inside each was a family lying on thatch grass mats, or cooking chapattis on tiny mud hearths to eat with chillies and salt. There were no belongings in the huts, no spare clothes, the children were dirty and there was no hope of anything better. A male worker earned thirty-six or forty-two pence a day (depending on how many bricks he shifted), which could have to support five or six people if his wife had to look after several young children and couldn't work herself. Everyone looked so tired and underfed – they were probably too exhausted and too downtrodden even to walk across to the dehra to get the free meal to which they were entitled. Santji always said feed the brickworks labourers first.

By comparison we lived like kings, and we certainly wanted for nothing. But somehow I felt it was only through the simplicity of our own lives that I could begin to comprehend the deprivation of theirs.

The following day we walked out past the low rubble mounds of the disused brickworks sites and past marshy hollows fringed with reedmace to the distant village in the acacia trees. Southern women were digging a drain on its outskirts, beautiful dark-skinned women with heavy silver jewellery and bottle green and indigo saris. Beyond there were trees, not just acacia trees but scented neem[1] and *Albizzia*, pipal and pomegranate, and they were full of bird song. Village women in baggy salvar and waist-length blouses were making dung buns, stacking the dried ones in cones and thatching them with a covering of reedmace. Others were building them into a drum, plastering it with more dung and scoring the outside in primitive, almost African geometric patterns. It was a different sort of village from those I was used to in Panjab, more spread out and leafy, and all the houses were pakka. The men sat on charpoys smoking hookahs and the women stoked their cooking fires or wandered lazily down the street to the pump. There were all the ingredients of my imaginary north Indian village: a green scummy tank with a banyan tree, a little spired Hindu temple, tiny shops and ramshackle tea stalls, mud-walled vegetable gardens, buffaloes ruminating at troughs, smoke rising from hearths. I felt nostalgic for village life and wished for a moment that we too could sit under a pipal tree with a bulbul singing in its branches. . . .

From the very first day at the dehra we had been kept company by rats. They lived in burrows, mostly at a respectable distance out in the scrub, but our floor became curiously undulating and strange holes appeared in the corners that seemed to go down and down. As soon as we had settled down for the night and blown out all but one of the candles, little faces with pink noses and cupped ears would appear at the top of the wall above the charpoy and twitch their whiskers. Intent on mischief they scrambled down the corner, paused to relieve themselves on the bookshelf, and spent the rest of the night rummaging through the utensils, scuttling round the walls, knocking things on the floor, sharpening their teeth on anything they took a fancy to and growing fat on our provisions. Which woke us up. It also woke me up when one chose to stand on my cheek.

I never achieved the oriental complacency towards living at close quarters with a hoard of rats (or visitors of any sort) to the extent that you felt you were presuming on their territory rather than they on yours. When I complained of the disturbance, the mess, the smell and the sharing of our food supply people would smile tolerantly and answer, 'Yes, there are lots of rats!' No-one trapped or poisoned them for, they said, if you got rid of one lot you would only be invaded by a new tribe coming in from outside. Besides which, killing rats was against the dehra regulations. Rats, to a Hindu, are sacred.

[1] *Azadirachta indica*

But the room wasn't big enough to accommodate all these extra inhabitants, and we weren't getting any sleep. So one day when I came home from Ramnagri I brought a packet of rat poison. Jungli looked at it nervously. He said nothing, but a few days later when we had been arguing about something he slung it up on the roof.

'What's the use of it up there?' I grumbled.

He explained that having poison in the room frightened him, and in case either of us should feel inclined to sample it in a rash moment he had put it out of reach.

Next time I went to Ramnagri I bought a box trap with a strongly sprung door, and we fed it with pieces of chapatti. For the first two days they approached it gingerly, but on the third night they were coming out of the heap of thorn branches and into the trap one after another: twelve in all between six o'clock and midnight. There would be a crash as the trap door banged shut and I would yell 'Jagannath!' and Jagannath would come tearing round the side of the hut with Prakash at his heels. He dug the trap out from the rubbish under the thorn branches and thrust it under my nose for approval. 'What a fat one!' he would say, looking at it proudly, and Prakash would stand on his toes so he could admire it too. One of the rats was so greedy that even caught in a trap with his tail pinned down by the door, the box waving about and a torch shining in his face, he was still scoffing chapatti.

It was an exhausting evening. Each time one of us had to get up to let Jagannath in, hand him the torch and wait until the mongoose disposed of the rat and Jagannath returned with the empty trap.

'Not in here!' I could hear Karam Chand shouting at the mongoose. 'Take your dinner outside!'

Several months passed before we were disturbed on such a scale again. This time it was mice. They made their home in a handy place near the vegetable basket and spent the day chewing little round holes in the aubergines and making constant little noises. I found it rather distracting. Little noses would be peeping round jars, tiny feet clinking glasses and teaspoons, small furry bodies skittering between my feet and diminutive teeth scraping solidified ghee off the chapatti pan. They climbed over saucepans, whisked round the flour tin and bit at the legs of the primus. There were a few big rats too but they'd gone off our trap. In the evenings when I was reading I would sometimes see an enormous fat rat coolly marching through the doorway and sauntering along the clothes line a yard in front of me, putting his dirty feet on Jungli's nice white clothes.

Outside there were snakes, some of them poisonous. A man at the teashop nearly trod on one, and Jungli made an awful fuss about putting on shoes and taking the torch whenever I left the hut at night. He never bothered himself, even after having to flick a scorpion off his foot while taking a pre-dawn bath at the pump. 'It doesn't matter about me,' he said, 'but if you were to die your father would come after me.' Jungli was always worrying about what might happen.

One evening he came back from the dehra and told me there was a snake.

'Where?' I asked. 'Let's go and have a look.'

So Jungli, rather less enthusiastic, led me to where he lay, coiled comfortably and minding his own business, in front of Sitaram's shop. He was fawn, with brown markings on his back and a white belly.

'What a beautiful snake!' I exclaimed, and the tea drinkers and loungers at the teashop came to have a look too. We stood round him in a circle.

'He's an extremely poisonous snake,' Jungli said sinisterly. 'If he bites anyone they'll be dead in five minutes.' But Santji had forbidden the killing of snakes. Snakes were sacred to Hindus.

What were we all doing standing within three feet of him then, I wondered.

Nobody moved. 'Very poisonous,' they all agreed.

Apparently the plain held other dangers. One night a thick cold fog fell and you couldn't see more than ten yards ahead of you. My stomach was upset and I had to keep going out.

'Don't go far,' Jungli said. 'Stay by the hut.'

'Why?' I asked. 'There's nothing out there.' I couldn't see why the night watchmen made so much noise all night either, blowing their whistles, flashing torches and calling 'Jagde ro-o-o-o!' ('Keep awake!'): there were two of them at the dehra and four more in the timber yard. It was difficult enough to sleep as it was.

'You don't know,' he said mysteriously. He had tried to explain once before but I hadn't understood. This time I did. 'A man was murdered,' he continued, 'and his soul instead of migrating to another body remained tied to the earth. His spirit isn't seen but it has a voice, an eerie laugh, that is sometimes heard at night. The people here are afraid, especially the women: that's why they crouch virtually on their doorsteps if they have to pee at night. And that's why they trace the dehra boundary from time to time reciting *path*. If you recite *path*, or mantras of any religion, spirits cannot harm you.'

So there was a ghost! I had previously watched Jungli mumbling mantras and sprinkling water over our room – like the old Pandit –

but he hadn't explained why. I then realized it was to protect me in his absence. As far as Akhandpath carried, no spirit could approach, but our hut was outside the sound boundary and beyond the invisible dehra one, so his own precautions were necessary too. The spirit didn't come near me because he kept me safe, he said, by reciting the mantra Santji had given him each night before going on duty.

To my mind a moonless foggy night when someone has to keep going out is the last time to tell them the place is haunted. Especially as I too had heard the sound of hollow laughter coming across the plains, always at night. I had vaguely assumed it to be a hyena, but the fault with my hypothesis, when I thought about it, was that there were no longer any hyenas: they had gone the same way as the forest a century ago.

But that still wasn't all. Besides the snakes, scorpions and ghosts that I was led to expect to bump into two steps beyond the hut door, I discovered the wilderness held a yet more real and terrible threat. Once again Jungli warned me not to go outside after dark, and if I had to pee to stay near the door. And once again he told me that people had been killed.

'What's killed them then?' I asked next evening (our conversations were always being broken up by Jungli's suddenly being called to the dehra). The great starry plain always looked so peaceful.

It turned out to be dacoits.[2] Armed gangs had raided the dehra several times recently, but our Sikhs had swords and pistols and had held them off. It put the wind up me though. My insides once again chose that night to play tricks, but thinking, in the way one does when one is alone in the dark, that there might be a tribe of swarthy men with waxed moustaches crouching in the scrub waiting to pounce, I was too alarmed to go out. I waited with considerable self-control for Jungli to return and stand guard against the wall of darkness.

After that I forgot about the dacoits. There was no point worrying about them for if they *had* chosen us as prey we would have been quite helpless. Apart from our door, thin and fragile as a wafer biscuit, which could be unlocked from outside by putting a hand through the crack and lifting the bolt, it would have been no difficult matter to remove part of the wall and get in that way. Dacoits had a special tool for hoiking bricks noiselessly out of walls, Jungli said. I was especially vulnerable, sleeping alone for hours each night and

[2] armed robbers or bandits

continuously going out to pee. Our door faced the unseeing plains and there was no secondary means of escape, the thorn branches being in the way. Anyone troubling to watch the huts for a day or two would find all this out; I was there for the taking.

Adjacent to the dehra and along the Chandinagar road was a small scattered colony of about two dozen new cement houses. One night early in the new year a gang of dacoits broke into one of them by their hole in the wall method. Inside there was nothing worth having except a young woman whose husband was away. They gang-raped her, slit her body open with a knife and dumped it on the roadside, where it was discovered in the morning.

I took the sword from its sheath and got Jungli to teach me how to hold it securely and how to swing it. Not that it would have done much good, for I found it heavy and unbalanced. Jungli said I wasn't to draw it again for it wasn't a toy: when drawn it needed blood – like the thirsty Kali. He went off to discuss weapons with Karam Chand for at that time we had no pistol, only the sword. And I, always trusting the men around me to protect me, was reassured.

Karam Chand, it seemed, had everything necessary. He boasted that he wouldn't be afraid if a hundred men came, because he'd throw vitriol at them.

'Vitriol?' I repeated, taken aback. 'What a terrible thing to have! Where would he get vitriol from?'

'Goldsmiths use it,' Jungli replied. 'You know his son's a goldsmith.'

A few evenings later on a moonless night as Jungli and I were sitting talking, he suddenly pricked up his ears. He ran outside and stared in the direction of the colony: he had eyes and ears as sharp as a fox. 'Dacoits!' he yelled and grabbed the sword. 'Bandits! Khazan, bring your stick!' And calling back to me, 'Lock yourself in!' he was off into the darkness. I could dimly see a lot of men running, and the cries of 'Chaur! Chaur!' ('Thief!') echoed across the plain. For a moment I was frightened – it was that eerie shouting and the running with sticks and swords like a cavalry charge that did it – but unable to contain my curiosity I took a pole and went round to Karam Chand's front yard to see what was going on. Karam Chand, I noticed to my satisfaction, hadn't set foot out of his yard. His family was standing in a row peeping over the wall, but the voices had died down and there was nothing to be seen. So we went inside and crowded round the mud bucket eating peanuts in silence until news came back.

There had been about fifteen or twenty dacoits, the men told us, and they had raided three houses simultaneously, seizing money and gold but fortunately this time not harming anyone. They had fled before our dehra people could get there.

That was the second time in the first three weeks of the 1980s that our small colony had been raided. And with the fighting in Afghanistan and unrest in Pakistan, north India, people said, could be in for another war. It no longer seemed a safe place to live.

8

Enterprise

SOON AFTER THE RAIDS I left for Sri Lanka, and was away for three months. Jungli was cross with me for going to Sri Lanka, quite reasonably so, and didn't speak to me the whole of the night before. But Sri Lanka had been one of my principal excuses for justifying my return to India, and I also wanted to see the south. On the morning of my departure for Bombay he told me about 16 February: there would be no sun that day, and it would be as black as night. Many people would die; the earth would open and swallow them up. Guru Gobind Singh and the Hindu scriptures had prophesied it. But I wasn't to worry. I was to go and sit quietly on my own, not speak to anyone, and no harm would come to me.

In matters of which he had direct experience, such as village life and the workings of the dehra, I had usually found Jungli's comments fairly reliable. But regarding things they didn't understand, even far better educated Indians than he were apt to believe the most wild and fanciful stories. On 16 February a large sangat consisting of all the people who had been given a mantra gathered fearfully around their saint. During the eclipse they stayed indoors and no-one ate until it was over. But nobody was swallowed up for the earth never opened, and I returned intact to the north Indian summer.

I reached Ramnagri at midnight and slept in the waiting room. Getting off a bus next morning and walking through the crowds I caught sight of Jungli in his white granthi's clothes, holding the hand of a young boy and going the other way. I tugged him from behind and he turned round angrily, eyes flashing with that who-dares-to-insult-me look I knew so well.

He was still angry when he saw who it was and had got over his momentary relief at having me back.

'Where have you been you said six weeks and you've been away three months you've only written me five letters in three months do you think five letters is enough in three months? For the last four weeks I've done nothing but wait for you each day I watch the bus stop until ten o'clock every night you ask the others if it isn't true.'

Oh Lord, I had been afraid of this. 'But I've written sixteen letters,'

I protested lamely. 'I even numbered them in case any got lost in the post. Didn't you see the numbers?'

Jungli never mentioned my absence again. No 'What have you seen?' or 'Did you enjoy it?' or 'Where did you go?': he wouldn't have been interested had I tried to explain.

What I had been doing over the last three months, besides travelling, was worrying about Jungli. My dilemma over what to do about our relationship had kept me awake at nights and moving restlessly throughout the day. Should I leave him or stay? I didn't care for either alternative, the first in the short, the second in the long term, and I was afraid of the effect either would have on him. To see how it felt I described myself to people I met as 'married to an Indian'. It was also partly out of loyalty to Jungli, to distance myself from those who might have become friends. But I didn't like the sound of being a wife: I no longer felt whole.

I had been putting off returning to the dehra, staying extra days here and there ostensibly because they were nice places but underneath, I think, because I dreaded Jungli's wrath at my remaining so long in Sri Lanka and his grief when I left for good. As usual while I was away he had been ill, with a nameless disease for which there was no cure but my return. Almost as if he became ill to escape the reality of my absence.

But I laughed at his ravings as we walked through Ramnagri, slipping back into my former role as effortlessly as a bird alights on its nest. At one stroke my responsibilities for decision-making were dissolved and I followed him about like a lamb. He chose where to cross the road, he watched the traffic, he found the bus, he told me where to sit, and he went to fetch cold water for me to drink. It was really quite pleasant: I forgot about my guilt. I forgot how I had fretted, and I thought no more of going.

Jungli had taken four days' leave, having told Santji there was a fight in his village. But the real reason was to open a hotel (which doesn't mean a lodging house but a place that serves meals) on the Haryana border near Rajinder and Gurmit's house, in partnership with the pathi who had been sacked (at last) for having it off with the knitting machine wallah's wife, and employing the Bull Pathi, who had also got the sack, as cook.

'But why?' I asked. 'Neither of those two is to be trusted.' The Bull Pathi (he looked like a bull) was a former dacoit whose old habits had not entirely deserted him: Jungli had seen him take some money out of his pocket when he thought he wasn't being watched. The other, besides being a philanderer, was a confirmed liar. I was amazed that Jungli couldn't see it: Jungli, who was always telling me not to trust anyone.

'We need more money,' he replied. 'My salary's not enough for both of us. I won't have to do anything, just supply the capital.'

'But you'll lose it!' I repeated, exasperated. 'Without a shadow of doubt those two will double-cross you!' Although we didn't need more money I could see no advantage in losing what we already had.

'It doesn't matter,' he replied calmly. 'It's only money, and not that much.'

The Bull Pathi had a wife and five children to feed and no job, that was really the point. It was Jungli's usual way of going about things, blindly and through the heart. He had what the Panjabis call a daria dil, a river heart. He felt sorry for the Bull Pathi and would do what he could, even though it would probably mean that it would be he who was worse off in the end. For Jungli was a true Indian in the sense that he lived through feeling, never through reason, as I partly did. He trusted without reason, loved without reason, exploded without reason and had total faith, also, as far as I could see, without reason. It wasn't that he was unable to reason, but that he was unaccustomed to using it. He was right in a sense, but it made him very vulnerable, and he suffered.

I had never been to Rajinder and Gurmit's Haryana lodgings. They lived on the outskirts of a village on the state border in a small rented room off a shared yard. The living quarters were on the far side of the yard from the busy main road, a long one-storey block of six brick rooms like Rajinder's, each occupied by a family of three, four or five. The other inhabitants were Haryanis, with a richer (because they were poorer) and more primitive culture than the Panjabi one I was used to. The women wore long full skirts and filmy headscarves tucked into their waistbands and falling to the ground, often (if there were men around) worn like a sack completely covering their faces. Thus they went about their daily tasks, like butterflies in their combinations of turquoise and lemon, cherry and lime, aubergine and strawberry, tangerine and tomato, washing down their buffaloes, drawing water from the pump, carrying dung up to the roof to dry and hanging their washing on the lines stretched between the pollarded mulberry trees. Their men, when not at work, lay on charpoys on the road verge watching the trucks rumble past. At midday when the sun came over the tree tops they dragged them across to the central reservation, kicked the cows and the big Brahminy bull out of their slumbers and occupied the deepest patch of shade under the big neem tree, fanned by the movement of passing traffic.

I didn't like the look of that road. There was the usual madness of everything going as fast as it could, which meant basically the two conflicting speeds of the slow lumbering bullock and camel carts of the age-old India and the fast and unreliable motor vehicles of the new one, with the added danger of traffic going both ways on both sides of the dual carriageway. For people, and especially camels, whose cart masters often snoozed and left the camels to find their own way, didn't understand the system.

My doubts were soon confirmed. Jungli and I slept on the roof with the dung buns and dried rape stalks, under the fragrant branches of a flowering neem tree. The others slept in the yard with the overflow by the side of the road. On our third night at Rajinder's, when we had just retired to the roof, we were startled by a loud wail from below, the sound of a woman crying not as we cry, but with a drawn-out roar that seemed to emanate from deep in the subconscious. I was prepared to assume that the cause was some fairly minor thing that women cry about, or at least that it was none of our business, but Jungli knew better and went down.

'The landlord's dead,' he said.

He had left the compound a few moments ago on a motorbike, and a drunken lorry had mown him down. Its driver had fled into the cover of night, knowing that if he stayed he'd be lynched by the witnesses: he could face the more lenient courts later. So the men went out to deal with the police and the women stayed to comfort the bereaved one, a girl in her mid-twenties. She roared and lamented and the others joined in, and the men when they came back cried too, but quietly, to themselves. All night she wailed and no-one in the compound slept. Next day the neighbours came to commiserate, each group of sympathizers setting her off again as if rewinding a wailing clockwork doll. 'He's dead, he's dead, he'll never come back!' Her grief, poor thing, sounded theatrical, unreal. The men, brothers of the dead man, sat on their charpoys with their heads in their hands, silent.

Rajinder's living conditions were typical of so many Panjabi homes I had seen: classifiable as slums on the basis of the amenities they lacked, but anything but slum-like in the way they were kept. Rajinder was a far more diligent housewife than I, I noticed to my shame: whereas I did the minimum to keep our bit of hut clean and tidy, she did the utmost. She swept the floor three times a day, and each time she washed it with water and a rag. Three times a day she laid out a piece of sacking and got out the stove, took the utensils down from their shelves, cooked, washed them under the pump and replaced them. She scrubbed her utensils till they shone. This endless cycle of housework occupied most of her time.

'Well what else has she to do?' retaliated Jungli. Kaki had gone back to the village, leaving Rajinder alone to cook and clean among people not her own for a man she did not love. It was quite beyond me how she could still be so cheerful.

On our last day with Rajinder she and I walked down to the state border to see the hotel Jungli had bought. Just outside the compound we found a corpse lying by the roadside shrouded in a primrose yellow cloth. Rajinder marched up to it and eyed it critically. A group of men were standing and squatting nearby as if it didn't belong to them.

'Who's this?' she asked the men. Then, 'Why is the corpse here? When did she die? What did she die of? Where was her home?' It astonished me that even death didn't put an end to the Indian habit of relentless questioning and was a public affair for anyone to join in. The girl had only been dead a few hours; one of the men was her husband and he had brought her here on a bicycle to be burned. It was nothing whatever to do with Rajinder or me.

The border was not a nice place. Clouds of dust blew about in the hot wind and trucks parked along the sides of the dual carriageway belched black unfiltered exhaust while their drivers, oily and lusty, checked their tyres, gave us the eye, and shouted abuse at other oily drivers. In the semi-desert behind was a jumble of shacks and petrol stations, and among them was Jungli's hotel. It was a tiny wooden hut on stilts, with cups and bowls and glasses ranged along shelves and a stand-up clay hearth under a small tarpaulin. In front five charpoys were stretched out in the dust.

The cuckolder was standing at the hearth, rather sulkily I thought, frying onions and ginger. His beard looked a lot thinner than it used to be – in fact he looked like a half-plucked chicken.

'He pulled parts of it out with tweezers,' Jungli told me later. 'He thinks he's more delectable that way.'

Jungli was meanwhile chopping up aubergines. The Bull Pathi wasn't there at all: he had pocketed the £15 change from the purchase of the crockery and disappeared, never to be seen again.

We went back home that day and Vitu, the Hindu boy whose hand Jungli had been holding when I discovered him in Ramnagri, came with us. For our room was now his home too. He had come to look after Jungli while I was away and Jungli was ill in exchange for Panjabi lessons which Jungli was now giving at the dehra every day to Hindi and Urdu speakers in addition to his other duties. I would have objected to almost anyone else sharing our lives so intimately but Vitu was a wonderful boy, intelligent and unimposing, and he had such a lovely face. He stayed with us for several weeks, helping me a bit, learning Panjabi a bit, and playing with the other children as a boy of twelve should. Only Jungli didn't think so: he liked him too, but he scolded him for his laziness and for running about in the midday sun.

The hotel didn't last long. The cuckolder disliked having to do the work himself, for he felt it beneath his dignity. Every other day he would turn up at the dehra whining and wheedling: he wanted more money, he wanted the sword to protect himself with and he wanted Jungli to provide a servant. In desperation (there being no money), Jungli went to Ramnagri to find Jatedar.

Jatedar had left the dehra some months previously, unable to cope with the pressure put on him by the other pathis. He was working in the Ramnagri gurdwara, and as a prop to his frail sense of identity had spread it around that he had been having an affair with Santji's head granthi's English wife, i.e. me. Jungli, having had to be physically restrained from knocking Jatedar down (he looked as if he would snap in two like a dry stick), hadn't spoken to him since. Overjoyed by this sign of forgiveness, Jatedar quit his gurdwara job that minute and went off to work at the hotel.

A few days later he appeared at the dehra, mumbling something about a disagreement. His clothes were filthy, but he never noticed his appearance, did Jatedar. His brain scarcely seemed to function at all: at the dehra he had always relied on Jungli's decisiveness to carry him through. 'Should I take my bath under this pump or that one?' he would ask him. Or, 'Should I have a cup of tea or not?' It was only when Rajinder and Gurmit turned up with the tale that everything from the hotel had gone and the cuckolder with it that Jatedar, in terror – for Jungli held the holy knife with which he had been stirring prasad at his throat – admitted his part in it. Having paid Jatedar to keep his mouth shut the cuckolder had gone, nobody knew where, taking everything of value with him. And that was the last we heard of him too.

It was two months before the hotel and remaining charpoys were sold, but the money raised was just enough to cover Gurmit's losses (£20) and Jungli's (£30). Only Gurmit decided to keep it all for himself: to Jungli, his brother-in-law, he refused to return a single paisa.

8

Heat

'WHAT'S HAPPENED since I've been away?' I asked Jungli on the way back to the dehra with Vitu. During my three month absence the temperature had risen fifty degrees.

'Nothing,' he answered. 'I've got a pistol now though.'

'A pistol! What do you want a pistol for? Are there any bullets?'

'Bullets are expensive. Ten rupees each.' It seemed we didn't have any bullets.

'Well what else has happened?'

'We don't pay any rent now.'

'Why not?'

'Santji said so.'

'What's it got to do with Santji?'

'Everything at the dehra is to do with Santji. The rest of us have no choice in anything.'

One day Santji had called Karam Chand to his office. 'We aren't paying you any more rent,' he had told him. *We* aren't paying you any more rent, not, 'I think you're charging too much rent,' or even, 'Pritam Singh won't be giving you any more rent.' Karam Chand's nose was put distinctly out of joint.

According to Jungli everything else was just the same as it had been three months ago, so when we arrived and I found it wasn't I got rather a shock.

The first thing I noticed was the plain. How green it was! I was expecting it to have curled up and gone bracken-dry in the heat. Even nicer was the new herd of camels swinging-limbering across it, right outside our door. But of all the changes, they were the only nice ones.

With Vitu there were now three of us living in our quarter of the hut. An extra charpoy had been acquired which took up most of the rest of the space. There was a fan on a floor stand, borrowed from Santji, a raised cooking surface Jungli had made from loose bricks, a couple of stone slabs to save my back and a large circular chair.

It was all very well, but there was nowhere to put your feet and it was impossible to get at things because something else was always in the way. Whereas before it had been like living in a fairly pleasant potting shed it was now more akin to camping out in someone's garage, stacked with the junk no longer required in the house and with the car in the middle. Jungli had painted a big notice on the door in mis-spelled Panjabi which said, 'ENTRY WITHOUT PRIOR ANNOUNCEMENT IS PROHIBITED'. I rather liked it.

And I liked the ingenuity of the Indian landscape chair. The materials of its construction – criss-crossed thatch grass stalks, twisted and woven thatch grass fibre and cast-off bicycle tyres – were there for the collecting. It required no specialized tools. It was comfortable to sit in. The combination of thatch grass and bicycles were so very evocative a symbol of the north Indian plains.

Everyone was inside in the heat and a new silence hung over the hut row. The next door hut people were away, cousin Khazan had left – he'd also been given the sack – the Nepalis had returned to Nepal and we had two new families as neighbours. One of them had even had the cheek to oust Santji's cow. And Karam Chand's children, who normally came rushing round to see us even if we'd only been gone for a few hours, were nowhere to be seen. I learnt that they weren't speaking to us any more because of the business over the rent.

The thatched hut next to ours across the gap had disappeared altogether. It had housed three families, one of which had moved to the cow's house, but the other two, and I felt very sorry for them, had gone into a big hall adjoining the gurdwara in which half a dozen other families were also permanently lodged. They had partitioned themselves off from each other by blankets hung on strings, giving them each an area half the size of our room. Every word could be heard and every movement monitored from above by anyone going up the dehra stairs. It was far worse than living in the huts, and reminded me of the semi-permanent camps one often sees on Indian station platforms.

Where the thatched hut had been there was now a wall, the new dehra boundary, ten feet high. Men were still building it, squatting unprotected on the top, laying bricks between their feet. It ran along in front of the huts like a prison wall, effectively cutting us off from the activity within. Karam Chand's family used to spend half their lives standing in their yard gazing at the comings and goings at the dehra, and I at least liked to know I could see it if I felt like it. On our side of the huts the only innovation was a most inelegant pissoir made of sundry bits of sacking and the Muslim women's old bourkas. Each time the wind blew it fell apart, and the Muslim women would emerge from their hut and squat beside it, sewing up the sacking and redraping their bourkas.

I went to say hello to Karam Chand's family in spite of Santji and the rent, and found them moping in their yard. How lonely it was here now, they gloomed, and what a dreadful wall! Santji must have taken leave of his senses. And what a long time I'd been away! They talked as to one to whom they weren't speaking, coolly and distantly. It saddened me, for on the whole we'd got on well.

To sort out these new events in my mind I went to take a bath at the dehra. It had worked before – been a stilling process I mean – on my first day there. But it wasn't so now. It had been raining and water was lying on the surface, turning it to sticky slithery mud. The verandah had been painted a frightful lurid pink. And where there used to be three bathing cubicles there were now only two (it had been bad enough with three when they all got in there with their piles of washing, and I had often had to stand and wait for an hour). One of the cubicles had had a door: now neither had, and I like a door when I'm taking a bath in a public place. By this time I had worked myself up into a thoroughly bad mood.

'You're lucky no men walked in,' Jungli smiled. He liked it when I was cross, for he found the things I came out with terribly funny. It was nothing compared to his anger, and therefore nothing that needed taking seriously.

'Why?' I asked indignantly. 'Why should men go inside the ladies' bathroom?'

'Because it's the men's bathroom now.'

I had yet to discover the ladies' one, a single cubicle with a perforated piece of metal without a bolt for a door at the end of the row of usually unswept latrines. Santji retained several out of work sweepers on very low pay, but they couldn't be sweeping all the time.

A thick layer of dust clung to the walls of our hut and blanketed our belongings. 'What a lot of dust has collected in four days!' Jungli kept saying unconvincingly. And there were copious signs of rats having made themselves at home. In the morning we carried everything outside, beat it, shook it, brushed it, wiped it and, having swept the floor and the walls and thrown bucketfuls of water over every surface to cool and moisten the air, carried it back in again. I couldn't bring myself to use anything until I knew I'd cleaned it. We washed everything made of fabric and we didn't sit down all day. It struck me that the only decent things we had were our clothes and a borrowed sheet. All our other cloths were rags, variously torn, frayed and stained. There were little rags for lifting pans off the stove, wedging in the tops of lidless tins, blocking holes in the walls, pressing chapattis, cleaning shoes and dusting, and long thin rags for use as strings and fiftis – the coloured band that goes under the turban and shows in a triangle at the front. There were middle-sized rags for keeping chapattis warm, wiping utensils and winding round Jungli's head as a house turban. There were old clothes used as cleaning rags, and lastly big rags for keeping food in, carrying shopping in, tying round Jungli's mouth when he read *path* (so that no spit should fall on the *Granth*), drying on, wrapping the holy books in, lining the shelves, keeping the dust off our clothes, hanging on the walls when we needed privacy for washing, and wearing over our heads. They were all blue, white or orange, and there must have been two or three dozen of them.

We slept outside because of the heat, with the sword under the pillow in case of dacoits: they had been again in my absence. In the morning, 'Miaow miaow' came the distant wail of wild peacocks from the villages over the plain. Five o'clock and dawn had come and the air was full of the song of larks.

Sometimes we still slept inside, for it was the season of summer storms. But that wasn't successful either.

'Whirr whirr,' went the fan (if we were lucky).

'Chirp chirp,' went the cicadas.

'Tinkle tinkle,' went the bell round the neck of the mongoose, rummaging for rats in the next room.

'Clatter crash,' jangled our utensils as the rats knocked them on the floor.

And 'Squeak squeak,' (or 'Shung shung,' as they say in Panjabi) went the myriads of little mice. It was like living down on Macdonald's farm.

Life now followed a different rhythm. People went to bed late and got up early and slept during the middle of the day. I cut physical work down to the minimum, bathed in the hut by day and washed the clothes at night: they would dry, inside, within an hour. We sat indoors with our feet up, for we were plagued by giant ants who bit them sharply almost as soon as they touched the floor. We had a big ceramic pitcher to cool the drinking water and between us we drank a bucket and a half a day. We made jal-jira, a mixture of salt, a dozen spices, lime and mint, ground and mixed in water, and another potion of jaggery and satu (barley roasted in hot sand and then milled): they cooled the body and tasted delicious.

Usually there was a wind, a fierce burning wind, but it was better than no wind for it at least kept us dry. When we cooked we had to draw the curtain across the doorway or the stove wouldn't work, and if there was no electricity it would then be almost dark: on stepping outside the light nearly blinded us. We took to soaking the curtain in a bucket of water and fixing it, dripping wet, to nails on each side of the doorway: then for ten minutes until it dried the air in the room would be a blissful ten degrees cooler. There was often no current, sometimes for days, and when it did return it would be at quarter ebb; the hundred watt bulb was too dim to read by and the fan feebly fluffed up the air for a foot in front of its nose.

Some days there were storms. The wind blew up and the sky went brown, thick brown in the direction of its source. Then the dust was upon us, stinging our faces and sneaking through the walls to settle in a moss over everything I had just cleaned. I peeped out through the holes in the door and saw the plain transformed into a wild beast, its hair dust-tufted, crouching low and torn against the wind. Brown sky, brown earth, brown grass.

Then came the rain, slashing the door, seeping through the open joints. The sky turned green, washed clean of its dust. The rain poured down and lay in a film over the crusted earth, pulling the sky down into itself; green sky, green earth and once again green grass.

Then all was peace; the watery landscape and the green-washed sky.

'Kashmir has come to us,' said Jungli.

Or it might be that the most dramatic part of the storm was the lightning, sheet lightning that flickered like a dying light bulb in an attempt to return daytime to the plains. Or it might be the dust clouds, dark swirling chocolate clouds in layer upon layer that appeared on the horizon and swallowed up the forget-me-not sky; once upon us the light was metallic, the colour of burnished bronze. Or it might be the wind itself, ferociously tearing at the door while Jungli and I, feeling fragile, crouched in the darkness inside.

'Will the hut fall down?' I asked him. The mud mortar couldn't have been very strong.

'No,' he smiled, 'but the door could go.' Lumps of broken brick came flying through the gaps in the walls and landed beside us, and on us. It was the fiercest dust storm I had ever seen.

That summer it was Jungli who felt the heat more. The sweat soaked his clothes and ran in rivulets from beneath his beard. I remembered it as being much hotter in Panjab the year before, but they all said no, no, last year was a cool summer and this is an especially hot one. Besides which UP was hotter than Panjab and our huts were built of fired bricks. The difference was that I had accepted the heat and forgotten about it; I was concentrating on whatever I was doing. If you fought against it, it was bound to win; if you let it become part of you there could no longer be any battle.

But the heat did queer things to people's stomachs. There was a steady stream of hut people using the arrangements area: we often had to wait for someone else to finish and come back. One day I produced a nine inch worm.

'*I've got worms!*' I shouted when Jungli came back three hours later. I had meanwhile been sitting in the hut, feeling unclean.

'Has one appeared?' he asked mildly, not nearly as shocked as I felt the situation warranted.

'Yes,' I said meaningfully. 'Nine inches long.'

'That's nothing. When you were in Sri Lanka I had two, and they were eighteen inches long. It's the water. Children often get them, for they're always eating earth. Was yours alive?'

'No.'

'Mine were. One of them only half came out and hung there wriggling. I had to pull it.'

'How dis*gus*ting!' I shuddered, in English. I reverted to it when I couldn't think of a forceful enough Panjabi word.

'Ser*cus*ting!' he echoed in a high squeak, for he liked the strange English (his English vocabulary consisted of the terms I used under stress).

In case there were more worms inside (which there were), we went to the fat Sikh doctor in the village on the hill. There were monkeys in the trees in the village on the hill.

'*I* didn't take any medicine for *my* worms,' said Jungli.

While I was in Sri Lanka Jungli had also had a bad tooth. A doctor had told him to collect sap from the poisonous desert apple (*Calotropis procera*) as a remedy. Some of it had spurted into his eyes, and for two days he had been unable to open them. They were still red and sore when I returned and there was a big hole in a back tooth.

When the infection entered his bloodstream he agreed to go to a dentist. According to Jungli India was full of unqualified practitioners who got round the law by paying a hefty sum to a qualified dentist in order to be able to operate under his name. They would work with him for a month or so to learn the very basics of the trade and then set up in business. Such a man, it seemed to me, was the dentist we went to.

For the first half hour he never stopped talking, mostly (as he examined Jungli's mouth) to a woman who had come after us and was complaining of a filling falling out. Jungli held a small hand mirror to watch what the dentist was doing and the woman was called over to watch too. To demonstrate a point to her (he wasn't much interested in Jungli's mouth), he picked up a grubby tooth from a row of extractions he had ranged along a rusty pipe in the wall: then he carried on working without washing his hands. I had only just time to take in the little cubicle opening directly on to the street, the old-fashioned dentist's chair, the total lack of dental equipment as I knew it, the hammers and pliers hanging on nails, the piles of dusty Urdu newspapers on the floor, the rat trap, the dentures in a chipped enamel bowl, the bucket of dirty water, the list of prices, and spoons, tins, jars, boxes, screwed up rags and more dentures, before the filling was done and we were out in the street. Jungli had been charged the equivalent of three days' wages.

When he opened his mouth I could see a very crude filling that looked like cement. It was even called cement. All the man had done was wipe round inside the hole with a wodge of cotton soaked in disinfectant, mix up the filling cement in the palm of his hand and shove it in the hole. He hadn't drilled the tooth to remove the rotten part, there was no suction pipe or mouthwash and no polishing afterwards. The tooth began hurting again two minutes after it was filled but the dentist was unruffled. No problem, he said, the filling would last for fifteen years. Jungli's last filling hadn't survived fifteen days.

Jungli had switched our morning milk supply to a government milkman who came from Chandinagar and supplied the dehra. The machine milk, as he called it, delighted him, because it had not been diluted with water. He could go on making cups of tea from half a kilo all day and it never seemed to run out and, having used the remainder for the night yoghurt, he could scrape out the pan with the handle of a teaspoon. Meanwhile Ram Pal's milk got thinner and thinner until it must have been three quarters water: the drought may have had something to do with it. We still took it in the evenings because Santji gave it to us. Finally Jungli gave the dudh wallah a talking to.

'Ram Pal, you're putting far too much water in your milk. It doesn't even boil over any more.' It was dirty too, full of unidentifiable floating objects. 'Yes,' he went on, 'and it's full of dirt.'

Ram Pal was silent. Low caste Hindus don't answer back.

'Are you going to do something about it?' Jungli asked.

'It will be all right from now on Sahib.'

But it wasn't, and the wonderful government milk was soon to come to an end. For many Indians are unable to believe that something they buy can be unadulterated. This milk was so thick and creamy that the teashop wallah, who took our half kilo each morning with the dehra supply, decided it must have flour in it. You could even smell the flour if you put your mind to it. And he closed the account.

10

Invaders

FOR THE FIRST SIX MONTHS of our time at the dehra we saw nothing of Jungli's relatives. Fortunately they lived a long way off. Probably they had been warned not to associate with us. Our only visitors were people from the dehra and Santji's sangat. But after our stay at Rajinder and Gurmit's on my return from Sri Lanka, things changed.

The first to appear was Mama,[1] Mataji's younger brother. Mama was a truck driver, a man of Jungli's age, square-framed with soft flesh and thick short hair; a larger version of Balwant. Like Balwant he was vagrant and unreliable, he drank and took drugs, and he formed liaisons with a succession of loose women. As with Balwant his relatives made feeble attempts to reform him.

It was the first time Mama and I had met. Our relationship was to be a silent one, much like the tacit arrangements I had with Jungli's other male relatives in which I pretended not to exist somewhere in the background and never caught them casting so much as a glance in my direction. When Mama presented Jungli with a lump of opium he had bought for himself and found wasn't very good, I began to have my doubts about him. When Jungli warned me that on no account was I to leave him alone in the hut while he was on duty since Mama was prone to theft, they were confirmed.

Soon after this Rajinder and Gurmit turned up, late at night, tired and hungry, just as Jungli and I were finishing our evening meal. They repeated the performance two or three times, Gurmit sitting cross-legged on the charpoy swigging from a bottle of rum while I cooked him a sustaining meal. Gurmit, when drunk, could put away a dozen chapattis. But one morning Rajinder arrived alone, her luggage knotted in a handkerchief. She sat down and burst into tears. Gurmit had stayed out all night and had come in early in the morning and beaten her in front of the neighbours. He said she hadn't cooked or washed his clothes. She hadn't: she was ill.

'Dog!' spat Jungli, and a lot more besides. Again, instead of showing sympathy and comforting Rajinder he ranted on about Gurmit. This wasn't the first time it had happened.

[1] literally mother's brother

There was a lot of discussion about what should be done next. Jungli said Rajinder was to go home to the village and fetch Pitaji. Pitaji could then go to Kanpur, more than a hundred miles away, and speak to Gurmit's father. That was the normal way of dealing with marital problems: the elders arranged the union, let them sort it out! I couldn't see that it would do any good. Gurmit was a bad lot and could only change through his own volition. He spent all his salary on liquor, leaving Rajinder to beg the money for food and clothes from Pitaji. She had left him for two years out of the three they had been married and returned to the village, only to be fetched back by Gurmit's relations.

Rajinder was sitting in Karam Chand's yard having treatment for her sprained foot when Gurmit turned up with Mama. I was forewarned by one of the children, who could see them coming across the plain, and I dived round the other side of the hut to tell Rajinder to run for it. But she had her foot in a bucket of water and didn't seem inclined to. I raced to the dehra to inform Jungli, knowing that if he returned to the hut and saw Gurmit he might go for him. Then there'd be trouble: Gurmit's five military brothers would come after us and there would be no end to it. When Jungli did arrive, the seventh to squash into the tiny room, I could almost hear him seething. He kept his mouth grimly shut in case the wrong words should come out. The two men left and came back, left and came back, and Gurmit was jumpy as a grasshopper but hadn't the courage to tell Rajinder to come home with him in case she said no and made him look silly. Instead he said – his first words addressed to her – 'Where's the money?' and when she told him where she had hidden it he left. Rajinder went with Mama, and Jungli was too distressed to work again that day.

What at first seemed obvious to me wasn't at all obvious to any of them. If Rajinder left Gurmit what was she to do? Go back to her village in shame because she hadn't been able to make her marriage work? Live alone and be labelled a whore? Sponge on some other relative? There was nothing she could do: she went back to her husband.

He really was a most disagreeable character. There was the saga of Jungli's watch. Jungli had an English watch he was very fond of – not, fortunately, for the status it represented but because it told good time. Gurmit had his eye on it; his own watch was a cheap and scratched Indian one which didn't work very well, and didn't match up to the opinion he had of himself.

'Swap watches for a bit,' he said to Jungli, and Jungli, being Jungli,

wasn't able to refuse. He said it was out of respect to Rajinder. But he
was very upset.

'You idiot!' I accused him. 'He won't give it back!' I had brought
that watch from England, and I hadn't brought it to boost Gurmit's
already over-inflated ego.

'Never mind,' he sighed. 'It's only a watch.'

About a month later Gurmit did give it back: I expect Rajinder had
told him to. But while I was out he took it again, and this time was
less eager to part with it. In the end, and going against social mores, I
intervened. 'He needs a watch that keeps proper time,' I told Gurmit.
'Yours doesn't go at all.'

It washed over Gurmit's head and the subject was dropped. So
when he was about to leave I stood in the doorway.

'Give me the watch!' I said.

'I'll return it later,' he muttered evasively, clearly irritated that I'd
had the cheek to interfere.

'We'll have it now.' I stood my ground. And he took it off and gave
it to me.

'Don't let him have it again,' I warned Jungli when Gurmit had
gone.

Once eight visitors turned up on the same day, from three different
sources. It was a religious festival that only occurs once in thirty
months, when the holy day of no moon coincides with the slightly
less holy day of a new Indian month. There was a special programme
at the dehra, and the coloured tents went up and people came from
near and far.

Our first guests, three people I had never seen before, arrived at a
quarter past five. Luckily I was up. I made tea and khir for breakfast,
and they came and went all day between us and the dehra. They used
our hut as their base and talked and snoozed (visitors always slept
when they came) and drank tea and changed their clothes while
Jungli went to the village on the hill to buy something to feed them
with, for we had run out of vegetables and the flour tin was full of
maggots. The first three visitors produced another two, women with
shrill voices who watched my every movement with a disturbing
insistency until, to avoid them, I removed myself to the doorstep. But
Jungli said, 'Don't sit on the doorstep.' When I asked why, he didn't
answer, so I went on sitting there, chopping up the vegetables. Next
time I did it though he told me that people only sit on doorsteps when
someone has died.

'But you're always sitting on the doorstep,' I accused him, 'and
no-one's died!'

'Someone's bound to have died,' he answered. 'People are dying all the time.'

Meanwhile Jatedar had turned up, and after him Rajinder and Gurmit. I crouched over the primus stirring curried aubergines with ants biting my feet and sweat pouring into my eyes, for it was noon in the hot weather and we were ten in our airless brick hut. I slunk round to Kamala's kitchen with the flour tin where, in whispers, we sieved out the maggots. I kneaded the dough and cooked thirty or forty chapattis. By then things had begun to happen at the dehra and our guests had gone to watch. The food got cold. Over the next three hours, in twos and threes, they came in to eat, and they gobbled it down for their minds were elsewhere. . . .

They came again in the evening, by which time I had a headache and was trying to get some sleep. The shrill women's voices grated on my nerves. They came again at five in the morning when I was still half asleep, my hair unknotted and the floor unswept. Once they were in there was no room to clean it, no place to wash (for there would be long queues at the dehra), and no chance of having anything unorthodox for breakfast. I still had a headache so I hid behind Karam Chand's urinating enclosure watching Moti being sick by the yard wall until they'd gone. I couldn't stand any more of it. We'd had unexpected visitors for three whole days on end.

Jungli was cross. He said it looked bad and what must they have thought? Several times he admonished me for my antisocial behaviour. He was absolutely right. Other Westerners might have adapted to it better than I, though they in turn might have thought twice about the physical conditions that to me were no obstacle to contentment. I could alter my ways of doing things but not my way of being.

Privacy is an alien concept to unemancipated people of the third world, whose conditions of existence deny its possibility. Traditional patterns of living and working are physical and gregarious: the desire for privacy arises from a need for mental concentration or for protection from the threat of a less well-off majority. My love of being alone and my preoccupation with writing remained riddles to Jungli to the last.

It was the one huge way in which I couldn't adapt to Panjabi culture. Imprisoned day after day in that tiny room crowded with people all asking what everything cost, having to run backwards and forwards to the dehra fetching buckets of drinking water, spending half my waking hours cooking and clearing up and the rest in idle conversation and not even being allowed to sleep or work was just not the sort of life I wanted to lead. For there was no escape: the scrub held no shade, and in the whole of the dehra there was no unused corner where I could work undisturbed.

But in other ways it was a very positive existence. Life was full and demanding and I rarely thought of anything, anywhere or anybody outside the dehra. I didn't pause to reflect on whether being there would change me, or what my family and friends would think, or what would happen afterwards, or even why I was there. Had I questioned such things, been anxious about them or found my situation incomprehensible – as others might find it – I doubt whether I would have stayed, or even arrived. The events that led to my coming had followed what to me seemed a natural sequence: the dehra was my logical home.

Apart from occasional letters to and from England, my writing and my attitudes, I had no contact with the West and missed nothing it could offer; even the books I read were by Indians and about India. Only once had I tried to make contact with my roots, and Karam Chand's plug-in wireless had outwitted me. The weird goings-on at the dehra, the mysteries it guarded and the dramatic ups and downs of my relationship with Jungli, on whom I could never rely to react as I expected and who was alternately loving and gentle, boisterous and provoking, angry and petulant or in quiet depths of despair, were as much as my imagination could cope with. No, I was never bored – except when there were visitors – for I was busy and there was always something interesting happening. I enjoyed sitting in the doorway writing, the wilderness stretching from my toenails to the horizon, the sunsets that faced us, the sound of the larks, the grazing animals and the wonderful summer storms. I loved being allowed to lead such an uncluttered life (if anything its simplicity didn't go far enough), to live among unsophisticated people in a culture so different from my own. I loved India, its wealth of philosophical experience, its huge landscapes and compelling detail, its teeming cities and simple villages. I loved all this. But in the end I learnt that the traditional Indian way of life, rigidly defined on a basis of religious ethics and duty, was not for me.

It wasn't often that Jungli and I left the dehra together. Leave was hard to come by and it took so long to get anywhere. Occasionally we paid return visits to the relatives who came to see us, but neither of us enjoyed it. We only went because people would go on and on and on. 'Come and stay with us,' they would plead. 'Come back with us now.' 'Why not?' 'Oh, he can look after himself for a day or two.'

'What?' 'Then come tomorrow. We'll be expecting you.' Jungli would say yes yes, we would come – out of politeness – and then I would feel we had to. When we didn't go the very next day, someone was sent to fetch us, wanting to know why. So we gave up and went.

Mataji's sister, the one responsible for Rajinder's disastrous marriage, was staying in a village five miles away organizing a second wife for Mama. They were staying at a doctor's house and had been there a month, making nine of them in the doctor's one room. But it was larger than ours and stood in a garden. Chickens pecked between neat rows of okra, marigolds bordered plots of pumpkin, and there were young papaya and guava trees. It was nice to be in a garden, lying on charpoys in the afternoon shade.

When the sun was almost touching the horizon I got up to go for a walk: it had been too hot before.

'Where are you going?' they called.

'For a walk,' I answered.

'Are you going to the latrine?'

'No. Just a walk.'

'Sit down!' they said. 'Go later.'

Jungli came to my rescue. 'Let her go,' he persuaded them. He knew I'd go anyway.

'The light will soon be gone,' I added over my shoulder as I went.

Jungli's aunt came running after me: they weren't going to let me get away with it. She kept me in order as one would a wayward child. 'Don't look in there, that's someone's house.' There was a man hammering something and I wanted to see what he was doing. 'We don't go in other people's houses,' she said.

I turned into a little alley. 'Not that way!' she called, continuing straight on. And if I paused to look at a plant or bird it would be 'What are you stopping there for?' I felt like Opu in *Pather Panchali*, going with his father in search of the blue-throated jay. There was so much of interest all around but the grown-ups seemed to have lost the eyes to see it.

Further on we came to a grove of beautiful *Ficus benjamina* trees, within which was a space full of dried leaves. And of course faeces; lots of them.

'If you want to sit then sit,' said Jungli's aunt, meaning that if I wanted to make use of the amenities now was the time. I didn't.

'Well I'm going to sit,' she said, squatting down without ceremony beside me. 'You go on and come back in a little while.'

Overjoyed, I escaped, and crunching through the leaves to the far side of the grove of trees came out into the plain. You could just see our dehra and the hut row beside the smoking brickworks chimneys. But there just in front of me, all alone in a patch of young reedmace, was an elephant, munching. And smiling. I couldn't take my eyes off him. I walked carefully round the reedmace to get a better view. It was the fact that he looked as if he belonged there that delighted me, that nobody was with him, and that there he was helping himself to the natural vegetation, tearing up clumps of leaves and stuffing them untidily into his mouth.

By this time Jungli's aunt had finished her business in the trees and come after me. 'What are you doing over there?' she shouted. 'It's time to go back.'

Still watching the elephant I walked, as slowly as possible without seeming to be disobedient, over to her side.

'Whose is he?' I asked.

'How should I know?' she replied. She couldn't see what I found so interesting.

'Does he belong to those people over there?' There were four rather strange-looking people sitting in the grass with double gourd-shaped brass pots and coarse homespun blankets. She followed my eyes and screwed up her face in disgust. Low caste. Not worth commenting.

At five o'clock the men had started drinking, visitors being an excellent excuse for procuring a bottle of rough liquor. What vexed me about it, then and every time it happened, was not so much the excessive drinking – though that was bad enough – but its exclusiveness. I would be sent to sit on my own on the furthest charpoy or into the house to join the women. Being a woman, of course, I wasn't allowed any.

When you're visiting it's your host who decides how you will fill your time. An acquaintance of the doctor's had a television, and the doctor was intent on seeing a Panjabi film that was on that evening. I daresay what he really wanted was to show me off to his friends. 'We'll go and watch the film,' he announced. Neither Jungli nor I liked Panjabi films and Jungli was tired and needed to sleep. We both said so. 'No no, come and watch the film. It's a good film.' Our wishes were irrelevant. We tried to back out but he insisted, so we gave up and went to the television house.

There were two rooms in the television house: the family lived in one and the television in the other. A lot of villagers were sitting on the floor in front of it, but they got up when we arrived and trooped outside to have a look at me instead.

At first I thought it was a colour television and was surprised to find such a thing in an Indian village. But there was something wrong somewhere. The colours didn't fit their subjects, nor did they seem to change position. Proudly the owner lifted a sheet of plastic from the front of the screen – it was broadly patterned with transparent colours – to expose the black and white image beneath.

Only once before had I ever watched Indian television. They were showing *David Copperfield* in Panjabi, dressed in salvar-kamiz with middle-class modern town houses as a setting. In the background was the kind of piped music I would expect to hear in a reps' hotel.

Next morning I slunk off early while they were all too busy douching their noses, shaking their bedding and rolling their beards to notice my absence. Having disturbed half the men in the village in their early morning squat on the stream bank – it was also where I wanted to be, for there were hoopoes and black-tailed drongos there too – I came back and lay down on a charpoy.

'Why are you lying out there?' they called to me. 'Come and take your tea.'

'I don't drink tea, thank you.'

'Why not?'

'I don't like it.'

'Well come in and take it; it's all ready. You can't stay there in that sun.'

I was quite happy where I was, and very tired of being ordered about. I had drunk numerous cups of nasty Panjabi tea just to humour people. When I didn't move someone else took over.

'Drink your tea. Here it is.'

Then the first, recharged, would start up again. 'Take some tea, just one cup.' You'd think it was a matter of life and death. And the more they went on the less was I going to drink that cup of tea. I didn't see why I should. I don't drink tea, and what's more I consider that what I put in my stomach is for me to decide.

My determination to discriminate puzzled people at the dehra too for, as every good Indian knows, one's life is not one's own to do what one likes with, but God's to manipulate as the fancy moves Him, and society's to fashion into the mould it has cast. A Panjabi is carried along by the tide, eating when he doesn't want to because people force it on him, going to places he has no interest in, doing work he doesn't enjoy and spending a fair number of his waking hours hanging around waiting for other people. For no-one can bear to do anything on his own. If there's no-one to cook for a woman won't eat; if there's no-one to accompany him to the cinema a man won't go.

Visitors *must* drink tea. Jungli was as bad: if anyone came to the hut for the slightest thing it was, 'Sit down and take tea.' When they replied, 'No, don't bother, I've just had a cup,' he would say 'Drink, drink! It'll only take a minute to make,' and when he'd said it a few more times they would be forced to sit down and wait while I made it. Whether they wanted to or not.

Serving others brings merit.

11

Mama

BEING SO SPONTANEOUS, Jungli was undisciplined. He could not have known that a relationship such as ours required mental effort and adaptation. He was as he felt. From time to time he suffered from depressions, when he would lie on the charpoy facing the wall and refusing to talk.

During one gloomy interlude he hardly spoke to me for a week, and if I went too close he got up and moved away. I couldn't bear it. I didn't know why he was behaving like that – I was being no more than usually foul – and possibly he didn't either: anyway he gave no explanation. Having put up with it for a week I packed my bags, expecting him either to beat me, cry, or coldly tell me to go where I pleased: anything would have been better than the stalemate situation we were in.

I had underestimated Jungli's passion. He did all three. Having hit me a couple of times he thought better of it and smashed his hand against the wall to punish himself. 'Go then, go, if that's what you want!' he said, but his face screwed up as if he had bitten into something sour and he wept like a child, at which I joined in. He took my things out of the bags, put each one back in its place, and wept so much I hadn't the heart to leave. My sorrow was manageable, but I couldn't bear his.

But it would not have been that simple to walk out on my home, my closest friend and the life I had led for the past eighteen months. Many people whose relationships have deteriorated far beyond the level of incompatibility that Jungli and I had found existed between us still remain together for the rest of their lives. And Jungli could not yet have coped with our parting. For in spite of these inexplicable periods of torpor and delusion and his frequent stance of taking me for granted, incidents like this illustrated that his inner feelings towards me were as steadfast and unprecedented as the day we met. I had discovered, to my embarrassment, that to people at the dehra he built me up into some kind of superbeing, to the extent of telling them I was the most wonderful woman in the world.

The only other outward change in our relationship was that Jungli now responded to me as an individual. He transgressed the unspoken rules of his community by asking my opinion in matters concerning his responsibility at the dehra. No other man did that. But Jungli had decided I was clever, and having reached that decision, being what he was, he acted on my advice unquestioningly, which was as bad as not taking it at all. He had also found that I was careful with money and would hand me his wage packet the moment he received it. To which I objected, believing he had a right to do with his money as he wished, even to give it all away.

It was me that had changed. I had become more affected by Jungli's teasing, his sulks, his temper, his addiction to opium, his indifference to my work, his inability to discuss and his growing dependence on me; and more sure that ultimately our attachment could not be intellectually sustaining. It is one thing to be with a man you love when the potential for creative exploration lies ahead, another to spend the rest of your life in his company when that love is perforated by doubt, and you have uncovered nearly all there is to know. What I still loved about Jungli, and dreaded losing, were those qualities that initially attracted me, the generosity and loyalty, instinctiveness and adaptability, directness and spontaneity, his truth unto himself. Not caring what the rest of the world thought or did was a rare enough quality in the West, but exceptional in a man with a background like his. I cared for Jungli as a friend, respected him as a human being, liked him, even loved him. But I didn't love him enough.

That afternoon the doctor from the nearby village in whose house Mama had been staying turned up. He was crying. 'Mama's gone!' he said. He had left the house two days ago on a short errand and hadn't been seen since. His lorry was standing at the state border. The doctor's family feared him dead.

The next week was spent searching for Mama. Jungli took leave and we went to stay at the doctor's house. Jungli and the doctor went round the local police stations and hospitals and Mama's acquaintances. No-one knew anything. The doctor and his wife wept: they had taken Mama in as a friend and loved him as a brother.

Being too upset to work, the doctor had no money to feed his young family. He borrowed ten rupees here, five rupees there, and we lived on chapattis and dal. I learned that there was a further cause for alarm: Mama had had 2700 rupees (£160) in his pocket, the proceeds of a load of cargo, for which the doctor, having given a security to the transport company on Mama's behalf, was responsible.

Having tried all normal methods and failed, and being Indian, the doctor then turned to the occult. He and Jungli visited four saints, all religious masters with supposed spiritual or supernatural powers, to see if they could throw any light on Mama's whereabouts. Each one thought for a moment before giving his answer, and was quite adamant about his reply.

Number one saint said, 'He got into a fight and was beaten up. But he's all right. He'll reappear.'

Number two saint said, 'He left the village in a scooter rickshaw, and was waylaid by a dacoit. He managed to escape but is now in hiding. He still has the money, apart from two hundred rupees which he's used for expenses. If you go to the temple at Shantipur between half past four and six tonight and wait there you'll find him. Otherwise, he'll turn up next Wednesday.'

Number three saint said, 'He's with a woman, a whore, somewhere near Agra. There's only seven hundred and fifty rupees left of the money. He'll come back in time.'

Number four saint, our own Santji, was brief and to the point. 'He's dead,' he said.

The second saint was rather like Santji, a young Hindu dressed simply in white who had built a temple to Ganesh, the elephant-headed god. He had a wide reputation as a healer and solver of mysteries, and every day scores of people went to consult him. Jungli and the doctor got there at three in the morning so as to be first in the queue but they weren't seen until noon.

This saint knew of our Santji and wasn't very complimentary about him. 'He is a very dangerous man,' he cautioned Jungli. 'Be careful of him.' Perhaps he was just jealous, I thought, for by now our saint had a big gurdwara lit up at night by blue and white neon tubes, red fairy lights and green strobes in praise of God and himself (whom he recognized as being one and the same) and a hundred men working and doing seva for him full-time. The Hindu had no fairy lights and only three or four men.

But Jungli didn't think it was jealousy. The Hindu saint had known that we lived in a newly-formed community without being told. He warned Jungli that everyone at the dehra was 'dirty' and that it would be ill-advised for us to stay there much longer. In two or three months Jungli was to consult him again and he would tell him where to go.

Jungli asked if his life would be happy. The saint seemed to think present contentment was difficult because there was something wrong with our room. 'It contains an evil spirit that's causing you

trouble,' he told him. I wouldn't have put it past Karam Chand to
know a few spells. 'You should change it if possible, or have
Akhandpath performed inside.' I could just see myself taking my
bath, sweeping the floor and cooking lunch round a two-day relay of
men reciting the *Granth*. 'Take this ash,' he continued, 'mix it with
water and sprinkle it over the floor. That will help too.'

Each supplicant was given ash, some to sprinkle and others, like
myself, to eat. It was the equivalent of Santji's holy water; the
powdered ash of burnt cow dung. He gave me peppercorns to eat
with it, and it didn't taste bad.

The doctor told the saint his wife was perpetually ill. 'Get rid of
her and find another one,' was the counsel. We had a good laugh
about it.

While Jungli and the doctor were out foraging for saints, I stayed
with the doctor's wife Jasbir – she was, it was true, perpetually ill –
and their three small children. Theirs was a love marriage, Jungli
thought. Jasbir was fair and beautiful and Jat; the doctor was small
and dark and probably Mazbi. Thirteen years ago they had eloped
and come to Chandinagar.

I was fond of Jasbir but less enamoured of the idea of living on
stage in direct view of the surrounding houses and passers-by down
the lanes and across the grass patch. The continuous clamour of
violent domestic squabbles depressed me: neighbours screeched,
servants cowered, mothers beat their children and children whacked
other people's buffaloes. The food was awful, and at night there was
no wind; heat and mosquitoes ruled out sleep. I longed for the
relative calm of the dehra and the freedom to live as I chose.

So when Jungli announced he was going to Panjab for two days to
look for Mama and that I was to stay on at the doctor's, I said I was
going home. I resented their deciding for me. They argued and
cajoled but I stood firm. The doctor was puzzled. Jasbir looked
aggrieved. Jungli, for some reason, didn't want me being at the dehra
without him. He thought I was making a fuss about nothing.

When he set off for Amritsar I returned to the dehra. No more
chapattis and dal! I feasted on *Xanthosoma saggittifolia* fritters with
lime, and they tasted like scampi. I worked in the peace of our room,
spent longer than usual with the neighbours and slept in the open air
dormitory in front of the huts.

I saw in those few days that the women lived in anticipation of
their men coming home. Only Jungli and the old Pandit were there
all the time: Paramjit-next-door's little black Buta Singh and Jai
Singh in the next-door-but-one hut worked as ragis in distant

gurdwaras and stayed away for several nights in a row. The Muslim boy only appeared at weekends, and Karam Chand had bribed his way into a new passport and gone to Pakistan on a smuggling spree.

Jai Singh's wife was a loud-mouthed young woman with a malevolent gleam in her piggy eyes. She padded her breasts and wore tight-fitting clothes. Nobody called her anything but Jai Singh's, even when calling to her along the hut row.

I had had to get used to women being considered as appendages of their men.

'Whose is she?' I had heard newcomers to the dehra ask, looking blatantly in my direction.

'Pritam Singh's.'

Whose is she; never *who* is she. I didn't exist in my own right, though because of my wish for anonymity I didn't really mind.

Paramjit-next-door was a warmer person than Jai Singh's. She was too good for Buta Singh, who a year before had left her with a small baby and pregnant with another, without money, to go off to Singapore and Bangkok. To pay the fare he had had to sell what little land they had (Jungli thought they were low caste people, probably water carriers), but he got round Paramjit by telling her how rich he would get in the Far East and how much he would bring back for her. He did make money working as a ragi, but he squandered it on drink, high living and child prostitutes. After six months he'd had enough and came home with a cheap watch for Paramjit, telling her how difficult it had been and that he'd been unable to find work.

Neither in the village nor at the dehra did I ever notice a husband and wife touch each other or display any verbal intimacy in public. I wondered if the other men were as affectionate as Jungli normally was, always kissing and hugging me and telling me I was the light of his life and the only star in the sky, etc. Somehow I doubted it.

Although tenderness was a fundamental aspect of our private relationship I had long ago developed a distaste for its public expression. Once, when Jungli, Kamala and I were sitting on our charpoy in the morning sun outside our hut, Jungli had put his arm round me and kissed me on the cheek.

'Hey hey, this is India,' I reminded him, genuinely shocked by this show of irreverence.

'Is it wrong to be fond of your wife?' Jungli asked Kamala. 'Is it bad to express your love for her?'

Kamala giggled in embarrassment and looked away.

There was no question of my not being accepted as part of this community. In the village it might have been different, but here, where everyone was transient, where I lived as they did and belonged to one of their men, they treated me as one of themselves. I felt privileged to belong to an Indian community, however unattractive many aspects of life at the dehra may have been, because it allowed me to live not just *in* India but *within* it. As a dutiful Indian wife I was quite passable and Jungli was proud of me: I neither laughed loudly, nor ran anywhere, nor acted extravagantly in any way. I tried to behave with dignity and restraint. I was – for me – moderately docile. And I worked hard. Unlike many high caste Indians Jungli didn't regard manual labour as degrading, but as humble service through which one raised oneself in the eyes of God.

Women at the dehra were not inferior, just different. They took pride in their role of serving their men, as their men took pride in serving their families by providing for them. Neither had any scope for changing their positions, and their lives were equally harsh.

The one Indian practice I didn't always follow was to eat after Jungli had finished. While I would not have considered doing anything so heretical as having my meal before he came in, I preferred to eat in his company. It was foolish of me in a way, since the woman who eats only after serving her husband has the triple pleasure of watching him enjoying the food she had prepared for him, the self-righteous glow of martyrdom – which somehow deepens her attachment for him and is probably designed to do so – and the relish of her own meal at the end. That is, if he hasn't eaten it all.

In time I started judging people and events by Indian standards and ceased to measure their ways of doing things against my own. I stopped noticing our differences as differences of race and only saw differences as the dehra people saw them in each other, in terms of temperament and relative virtuosity. I saw no Indians; I saw only people. Sometimes I had to remind myself that I was living in a foreign country with people not my own, and the knowledge would surprise me.

Few of the people living at the dehra had any conception of what life was like in the West, that houses or food or landscape were any different from what they knew in India. It made it easier for them to accept me. They were simple enough not to be prejudiced by the normal Indian expectations of a foreigner's behaviour, so I escaped being treated with condescension as someone from a superior race who had demeaned herself by choosing an inferior Asiatic lifestyle. And sometimes I thought, 'Thank God the Raj isn't still here!': what with bad-tempered sahibs, prim snooty memsahibs and obsequious Indians, I would have courted ostracism on all sides.

I would like to believe an experience of this kind could alter one radically, but in my case I doubt if it did. I would have liked India to change my outlook, my self, instead of subtly influencing my attitudes. It is the writing about it that has changed me, by forcing me to explore my feelings to a depth I would not have done otherwise, and further, by having to express them. Naturally secretive, I have spent my life avoiding exposure to the world.

India taught me to be a woman. I discovered how much more simple, pleasurable and dignified life became when men and women had separate, and clearly defined roles. If Jungli and I sometimes trespassed over the boundaries of our traditional roles, it was through our own volition, not the other's nagging. We each did all we could for the other, expected less than the help we received, and never argued over who should do what.

Because the other women didn't like to be without their men they felt sorry for me in the three days I was alone, and as soon as someone spotted Jungli walking across from Number Nine they all ran round, happy for my sake, to tell me he was coming. Jungli was tired and had discovered nothing in Panjab. He emptied a shoeful of bullets on to the floor and produced a small revolver to go with them which he said was for me. They had been Mama's. He taught me how to shoot – he seemed to think I ought to learn – and fired dramatically into the scrub to demonstrate the revolver's effectiveness before burying it in the wall.

Nothing was heard of Mama. The doctor talked of trying some more saints. He had heard of one in Agra, a Muslim who charged £10 per consultation but offered to refund the money if what he prophesied proved incorrect. There was another in Kashauli, a village outside Ramnagri. But Jungli had tired of saints: they hadn't been his idea in the first place.

About a month later Mama reappeared. His story went that the day he disappeared he had been arrested by the Hyderabad police, who had come all the way to Ramnagri to apprehend him. It was an old charge – something to do with a fight and a fraud. He was jailed for it but his transport company had bailed him out.

Jungli shook his head: he knew Mama's wiles. It was far more likely that Mama had been off with a floosie.

Since I first came to the dehra a lot more huts had appeared, not on our side of the plain but between the hut row and the main road, and more on the far side. They were poor people's huts like ours, kept at a discreet distance from the up-market cement houses of the middle

classes. They each comprised a small plot of land demarcated by a
low wall, with an eight foot square unplastered brick hut in one
corner. As money became available the occupants would raise the
boundary wall and extend the building: the yards would grow leafy.
This was the bald stage, of unearthly pink cubes scattered at random
over the green plain.

Sometimes I would wonder how it was that I could be happy in
such surroundings. For I *was* happy up to a point; I had grown fond
of the place that at first I had thought I wouldn't be able to stand for a
day. I had got used to living in semi-darkness or by artificial light and
no longer hankered after windows. It was only when I went away
that the thought of returning to our dingy hut alarmed me, and then
only because I was staying in the comparative splendour of station
waiting rooms and gurdwaras. And when I came back I wouldn't
stay despondent for more than an evening.

Previously I had lived in a succession of houses in different parts of
England: old, attractive, spacious houses with no noise coming from
the neighbours. Everything inside had to be visually pleasing, at least
to me, and I wouldn't suffer one nasty chair or saucer. There had to
be trees outside the windows, and flowers and flowers and more
flowers in the rooms. And there *had* to be a garden.

The hut didn't have a garden. It didn't have a window either and
there were no proper trees for miles. The plants in the plain had
flowers not much larger than a pinhead. For a time we were three in
the hut with only twenty square feet of available floor space between
us. And nothing we had was attractive.

So what was it about that hut? In the first place it may have been
that we had no choice. The hut was our home. But it had real
advantages too.

One of the things I liked was that in that tiny space we could do
anything and everything we had to do. We cooked, ate, lived,
entertained, worked and slept in it. In the hot weather I took my
baths in it (with the bucket and the green plastic beaker), for the
water ran straight through the open joints. Occasionally when Jungli
was on night duty and I was feeling paranoid about dacoits I must
admit I peed in it too, aiming down the mouseholes. I poured water
down them afterwards and the floor never smelt of anything but
damp bricks. By that time we had taken to washing up each
non-greasy crock as we used it and throwing the water over the floor.
Ants and mice did the rest. The floor never got dirty, for it had never
been clean. It was the sort of floor you could spit on: Jungli often did,
so I spat a few times as a token gesture, rather than get cross with

him. But when he blew his nose on it (as people did), I turned the other way.

Because the room was so small everything was always within reach; nothing ever got lost. I could almost sit in the middle and do all my work without moving. And because things were arranged logically the room was always tidy; it never felt claustrophobic.

We had nothing inessential, except for the Guru Nanak calendar and the framed pictures of the first and last Gurus, which to Jungli were most essential – and a funny rag lotus which people placed as an offering at the feet of Buddha in Sri Lanka.

'What's that?' asked every man, woman and child that came into the room. 'Where did it come from? How much did it cost?' It had cost three pence.

'Take it down,' Jungli ordered: it was too cheap. But I liked it and it stayed there, the single non-functional object. And when I tried to think of anything else we or I needed, I couldn't. I enjoyed the discipline of that austerity, the more so as it wasn't going to be permanent.

There was an endearing ugliness about the room and everything in it, engendered by the total lack of pretentiousness. The unendearing ugliness comes when people try and fail, or when sense and function get lost in a book of rules. Because it was *all* ugly, the oozing walls didn't matter, nor the screws of paper in the joints, nor the tangle of wires, nor the ghastly shape of the plastic ghee jars.

I liked the relationship between dwelling and landscape. Or rather the lack of relationship. Having been taught that there should be a link between inside and out, between home and garden, and always having lived where there was one, I found it exciting to dwell for a time where the two were totally separate and opposite. The hut perched in the plain with no sense of belonging whatever: where the building stopped the landscape began. Crossing the threshold one passed in a single step from the absolute refuge of small, dark, crowded and enveloping room to the unbroken prospect of boundless light-flooded space, potentially hostile and lacking the ordering influence of man.

People used the plain all right, in fact they over-used it: it was treated as common land, a free-for-all landscape. Grazing animals munched the tops of the tender growing shoots and replaced the goodness they had taken from the land, only for it to be quickly scooped up by some marauding villager or one of Karam Chand's children. Young trees all went for firewood. Even the silt was appropriated by the shifting brickworks and on a minor scale by hut builders for their mortar. What was already a semi-desert became even more barren and infertile.

To me the interaction of land, people and animals was endlessly intriguing. I could compare the vegetation of the open plain with that of the recently fenced-in timber yard where rabbits hung out, away from the heavy competition from the big herbivores, and where young trees were gaining a foothold. I could watch different plants being eaten by different animals at different times of year, and the plants themselves coming into season at different times, briefly dominating, and quietly receding. There were burrows and nests; Jungli found a lapwing's nest, a shallow scrape in the silt containing four brown speckled eggs. There were spotty beetles and imperial dragonflies. And there was the constant summer sound of the high-singing larks.

12

Removal

PARAMJIT AND HER HUSBAND had acquired a dog, a pleasant-looking affectionate black and white mongrel. To hear them talk, Jungli said, you would think no-one in the world had ever owned a dog before.

The dehra had become home to a pack of pariah dogs, feeding them its leftovers and sheltering them in the rain. The dehra people stoned the pariah dogs and beat them with sticks, and the dogs learnt to slink round the mean ones in wide cautious circles. But Santji was fond of them: he gave them all names and they would obey him without question.

Every few days I would go and look at the lapwings' nest to see if their babies had hatched out. One day there were three fluffy black and white chicks crouching in an unprotected huddle. To my alarm, the hut people were being led there in relays by Prakash, who poked them with his finger. He had discovered them too and wanted to assert his importance by showing them off.

By next morning they had gone, for Paramjit-next-door's black and white dog had eaten them. Everyone felt sorry for the sad lapwings and cross with Paramjit for not keeping an eye on her dog. But she was like that – careless about the things she cared for most. She would put her baby on a charpoy and go off to do something and it would fall off, usually head first and two or three times a day. The Muslim women would come storming out of their hut and admonish her for not looking after it properly, but she said she had nowhere else to put it. Or she would lay it down to play on the sandstone slabs round the pump, beneath which a family of scorpions had their nest. And she said nothing to her brother Karamjit who had been having it off with Jai Singh's piggy-eyed woman over the last year or two, astoundingly – for everyone lived so close – without the knowledge of either Jai Singh or the neighbours.

It was 1 July. The rains were approaching and the sunset was gorgeous, with a great rift in the slate grey clouds through which, like a vision of a sugary heaven, strawberry cumulus clouds garnished a pink blancmange sky.

As night fell Jungli and I were sitting in the hut talking, I with bare feet on the ground, when Jungli suddenly shouted 'Lift your feet up!' and simultaneously stamped on the floor. There, fortunately dead, was a small scorpion, black poison spurting out of its side, the same sandy colour as the sack across which it had been scampering in the direction of my feet.

'I keep telling you to be careful of snakes and scorpions,' Jungli said severely, 'but you think it's all a joke. You've no respect for them at all. In the rains hundreds appear, especially at night. Before you came I was lying one evening on a charpoy in Khazan's room and a scorpion ran right over me.' Leaving me to ponder his warnings he disappeared round the side of the hut.

'That's nice,' I thought, and for the first ten minutes was careful where I put my feet. But you can't be forever watching your feet, and we couldn't afford unlimited torch batteries.

The scorpion was a bad omen. Jungli came back an hour later saying, 'Come on, we're moving!' He picked up a charpoy and carted it off.

'What?' I asked, when he reappeared.

'Yes,' he said. 'Bring the bedding and hurry up. We're moving to Khazan's hut.'

'I don't want to go!' I protested. This hut was my home. I sulked and snivelled and Jungli shouted and Paramjit-next-door came and consoled me.

It was the shortest notice of having to move house I had ever had. Jhai had been giving us trouble for some weeks, complaining daily to the neighbours that we gave them no rent – as if it was our fault – and saying (untruthfully) that she needed the room. I had preferred to put up with it rather than lose the relative privacy of living at the back of the huts and the view across the plain, but Jungli had had enough. He had confronted her. 'If we're causing you trouble why don't you talk to me about it rather than grumbling to everybody else?'

Which had set her off. She accused him of drinking and eating meat and said she was going to tell Santji to give him a beating. I expect Jungli was disrespectful too, for the outcome was that we had to get out. While we carried what we needed for the night across to Khazan's room, the second of four in the next-door-but-one hut, we saw her running from neighbour to neighbour to claim her total innocence in the affair.

'I never told them to go,' I could hear her saying. 'They left of their own accord.' She had been working herself up into a rage about the room, mostly, I suspected, because she had nothing else to think about. Having handed the housework over to Kamala she had all day to sit about and grumble. And the more she grumbled the crosser she became.

I didn't like the idea of living in Khazan's room. He might appear at any time and want it back. The entrance faced the main road (along which there was a steady drone of lorries) and a degraded area of plain between the dehra and the industrial estate, crossed by electricity lines and dotted with new huts. And it meant living one brick-thickness away from Jai Singh's and her constant hysterical shrieks of 'I'll beat you!' the louder the further away her children happened to be. Her staccato threats were interspersed with the characteristic Panjabi sarcasm, designed to make or break any weak heart, and which I also received, and thoroughly resented, from Jungli. He'd had his share from Mataji: now it was his turn. If I asked if he would like his food now he might say, 'What else is there to do?' Or if I forgot to place a glass of water beside him it would be, 'Are you a cripple that you can't bring me any water?' Sometimes I thought Jungli was a dreadful man.

But it was worse to hear a mother using such words on her young children. Jai Singh's' little daughter Sona, of two or three, was being sick.

'Well what have you eaten that you're sick?' she screamed. 'If you've been eating earth it serves you right! Why do you make such a face – are you dying?' And Jai Singh, fat and back from Ramnagri, roared with laughter. The child, unforgivably humiliated, made no murmur, being used to it. She knew if she cried she would get no comfort, though cry they all did, all three, much of the day. The eldest, a boy of four called Mani, ran away when his mother told him to stay. She caught him and beat him, and when he cried she beat him again for crying. He wept uncontrollably but the more he yelled the more she beat him. Then she dragged him out of the hut, covered with dust, and proceeded to tie him to the wall by a rope. Hearing his unrelenting screams the Muslim women put on their bourkas and came out of their den. 'Let him free,' said the old woman quietly. Under pressure Jai Singh's untied the ropes.

It was this aspect of Khazan's hut that disturbed me most. I hated to see such cruelty: it had been bad enough listening to Karam Chand strap-beating his big sons while they cried for mercy – 'Papaji, Papaji, don't do it! Please Papaji!' And when we got Khazan's door open I liked the thought of moving there even less. No-one had lived in the room for three months and it contained a lot of dusty junk belonging to Khazan that would take up precious space: it was slightly smaller than our old room. The floor was littered with pieces of torn sacking, snake shit and recently discarded contraceptives, the result of the illicit affair between Jai Singh's and Paramjit's brother Karamjit.

We set up our charpoys on the patch of trodden silt in front of the hut. The Muslims in the end room slept inside and the old woman, suffering from bad lungs, coughed and coughed. Everyone else slept outside; Jai Singh's family were next to us and the old Pandit and his wife on the mud floor, bricks for pillows and sacks for a mattress, beyond them. People took it in turns to get up for a pee, the Pandit looking scrawny without his Congress cap, the Muslims putting on their bourkas and the Pandit's wife Amma, bangles jangling, flicking her sari over her head as she clambered to her feet.

I lay awake for a long time staring at the cloudy sky, feeling numb and confused about this new state of affairs. By the time I woke next morning Jungli had got rid of the snake shit and contraceptives and was shovelling up basketfuls of dust and loose dung from the floor. I wondered when the snakes would decide to make their appearance: there were some suspicious-looking holes by the wall. By seven we had moved in, cleaned the room, put up planks and covered them with remnants of old turban and set out our belongings. There wasn't enough room, what with Khazan's rubbish, and our things were wedged under the charpoys and piled on top of each other. But it looked nice when we had finished, nicer than the old room. The walls were half-covered in giant and colourful Guru Nanak calendars which blocked the peepholes through into the Muslims' room on one side of us and Jai Singh's' on the other and hid the oozing mortar. Our remaining possessions were stacked on shelves above and below them, and the crowning glory was a length of plastic lace I had acquired as a present for someone in a cut-price store in Kentish Town Road, now adorning the longest plank. Everyone admired it.

Encouraged, I gathered grasses from the plain (there being no flowers), but Jungli clamped down. 'Panjabi people don't put flowers in their houses,' he informed me. 'Flowers are messy. If you want some get plastic ones. I've seen people selling them outside the Hindu temple in Chandni Chowk.' So had I.

We found there were other advantages to cousin Khazan's room. It had a strong rustic looking door that couldn't easily be broken into. It had a dung floor that was simpler to sweep. It faced the prevailing summer wind so there was sometimes a breeze (our electricity supply was switched off for four or five hours each afternoon). And, best of all, it had a window! Even Jungli was happy about it, Jungli who had been surprised when long ago I had asked whether we could have a window if we moved. Its wooden frame was fitted with a swirly piece of wrought iron that looked as if it would have been better off as a front gate in Surbiton, and over it hung a thatch grass chick that could be rolled up to let in the light. We hung a piece of white homespun over the door and that looked nice too, but it blew in the wind and people could see in. The Muslims next door had an infallible visual fortress to protect the virtue of their women: a cloth covered the window and a curtain the door; another curtain hung at an angle inside it, and the women sat on the floor behind yet another giant curtain that spanned the centre of the room.

I went out in the sunset to collect dung for the floor. Following the homegoing line of pale grey Brahminy cattle I scooped up their fresh deposits in my hands and returned, happy at last to have gathered something useful from the land, with a large pitcherful of fresh sweet-smelling dung on my hip. I dung-smeared the floor as I remembered Mataji's sweeper doing it in the village, while Jungli lay on his charpoy looking amused. He couldn't do it, he said – I was delighted there was something Indian that I could do and he couldn't – but next morning he effortlessly surpassed my attempts by smearing on a second coat twice as smoothly and in half the time. Jai Singh's stood in the doorway with her arms folded, looking as if she thought him a bit of a pansy.

Jungli defended himself. 'Is a woman a servant?' he asked her. 'A woman should be given respect.'

That day I went to Ramnagri, and when I came home in the evening Paramjit had gone. She had moved house as unceremoniously as we had two days before. Buta Singh had returned from his new job on the far side of Ramnagri and said to her, as Jungli had said to me, 'Come on, pack up, we're moving,' and she had packed their belongings in a big metal trunk and, leaving their black and white dog Nasty at the dehra to fend for himself, they had picked up a child each and balanced them on their outside hips and borne the trunk between them across the scrub to Number Nine.

We now had to temper our conversations to the probability that people from three different faiths would be listening through the walls. Often I would glance out and see someone hovering by the door, obviously all ears but pretending to be doing something else. Jai Singh's would join in from her room if what we were talking about was of any interest to her, and Jungli gave a few sermons for the benefit of the occupants on the other side about how Muslims were all right really and just because there had been a few despotic emperors one shouldn't blame them all. I thought it quite unnecessary, but I strongly objected to our lives being thus monitored: we might as well have been living in the street.

It was awkward at night too. We would be tired and wanting to sleep but Jai Singh's would need the outside light on until half past eleven while she scrubbed her pots and pans with noisy gritty ash. I had unconsciously become sufficiently Indian in habit, and sufficiently mistrusting, to object to sleeping in front of men in case my clothes should ride up and expose my calves or I should move into an undignified position to keep cool. I wouldn't lie down until the light was off, and still felt uncomfortable if there were strangers sleeping close by. In the end we decided to sleep inside and suffer the heat.

Living in Khazan's room was an opportunity to get to know the other people sharing the hut. The three families – one Hindu, one Sikh and one Muslim – were a closely-knit group and almost lived one life, thought it was more an obligatory communal existence than one founded on mutual love.

Everyone was addressed in his or her own language: I was Bharjaiji, the two Muslim sisters Didi (Hindi and Urdu for sister), their mother the Urdu Ammi, for mother, and the Pandit's wife Hindi Amma, also mother. The only people to be called by their names were the children. They ran about in dusty knickerless tribes, those of four and more tending the younger ones, and their toys were the huts themselves. They dismantled walls, dug holes in the paths and pulled canes out of our window chick. If they could scrounge a lump of firewood they would drag it along the ground on a piece of rope, and an old tin lid nailed to a stick made a wheel. But nobody had a spare tin lid, and Jungli rebuked me for giving one to Jai Singh's' son Mani: what we were going to do with our rape oil now, did I think? But to those children, anything was something.

The conversation in our hut followed established patterns and rules. It was employed to occupy space and time; the need for communication with nothing new to say. To break out of the convention of acceptable topics or, worse, to question them, was to disturb the known order, to alienate oneself from the group. Conversation was relaxation: it heightened reality and reinforced the status quo. It neither provoked thought, nor required it.

'What are you cooking for tonight?' Jai Singh's would enquire. Earning a living outside the dehra, her family was not supposed to eat in the langar, though they usually did.

'We're having chapattis and dal tonight.'

'I'm preparing chapattis and dal too.' People very rarely ate anything else. But the familiarity of such an exchange was reassuring, therapeutic.

The Pandit's wife Amma was like a nosy old aunt. Thin and fidgety, wrinkled and bird-eyed, she flitted anxiously between her bed-wide house and the dehra in fear of missing something, her faded mauve sari billowing like a spinnaker behind her. When there was nothing better to do she sat on the ground in her doorway picking her feet and watching other people scrubbing clothes at the pump.

I liked Amma. She was generous of spirit and a steadying influence on Jai Singh's. She and the Pandit never quarrelled. I wish I had thought of buying her a new sari: when someone else did, out of duty, she was thrilled.

Because of Amma I had to revise my standards of dish washing. Amma's two pots were spotless and shone like mirrors. She would scrutinize my lacklustre ones as I returned from the pump having rinsed off the earth, trying in vain to conceal them from her view. In the end I was shamed into giving up a morning to scouring and polishing, but the effort was worthwhile for I could now display my pots proudly like the other women, rather than tucking them behind something else in embarrassment.

But I never reached the level of scrupulousness of Sultana and Didi, the Muslim sisters, who cleaned their tea glasses with a toothbrush and seemed to wash every piece of rag, cloth and sacking they possessed every single day. One or other of them was always squatting in front of our door removing the last speck of dust from the soles of her feet with a trickle of water from a spouted nickel pot. It was fortunate for me that Jai Singh's wasn't so fussy: her room looked like a rat's den, with onions and dusty knickers strewn over the floor and bedding in damp crumpled heaps.

Jai Singh's enlivened her household chores every now and then by belting her children. The sound of them crying seemed to drive her up the wall. 'Who are they to cry?' maybe she thought. 'Haven't I enough trouble without them crying all the time? What responsibilities and difficulties have they got in this world?' So Sultana and Didi befriended them, and played with them in their own room until Jai Singh's came and hoiked them out, fearful lest they should be having a good time.

She had her good points though. She was genuinely fond of Amma and Sultana, the younger Muslim sister: the three of them would sit chatting for hours each day. She would feed Jungli if I wasn't there and be nice to visitors and anyone who was ill. That people's worst sides came to the fore in such conditions was not remarkable; overcrowding and no privacy, very inadequate hygiene, insubstantial diet, no money, and possibly people in the next room you couldn't stand: I wasn't at my best myself and I hadn't three children to bring up as she had.

But I didn't forgive her easily for her churlish behaviour towards Jungli. She had never liked him: he was outspoken and unsubduable and she liked to have her neighbours under control. Her children frequently made a nuisance of themselves, getting up to such pranks as putting earth in the lime pickle we had prepared and put out in the sun to accelerate the diffusion process, and hacking at our lump of Pakistani salt with a brick when I had washed it and put it out to dry (it was beautiful, like a piece of rose quartz). In the end Jungli chided Mani, the culprit, but Jai Singh's was down on him in an instant. *She* could beat her children all day if she pleased, but no-one else was to utter a single harsh word to them. She and Jungli were the most volatile of the thirteen people in our hut, she the more so, and the incident developed into a violent slanging match in which he had the upper hand. So, dragging Sultana and Didi behind her she went off in a huff to report Jungli to the dehra president.

I believe a lot of the friction at the dehra had to do with sexual frustration. Half its inhabitants were single, and the rest had scarcely more opportunity than the first half. During the hot weather when people slept outside, if you suddenly disappeared into your hut with your spouse and shut the door everyone knew what you were up to. So you didn't. During the day most of the men weren't there, and in any case someone might walk in at any time. And anyway it was too hot. And anyway one or other of you was too tired, or too inhibited by the proximity of the neighbours, or felt ill.

What people's tension did not have to do with was boredom. An Indian lives as part not of a family or even an extended family, but of a community, and among the hundred or two hundred or five hundred of his daily acquaintances there will always be someone being born, someone marrying, someone dying: people falling ill and getting better, going away and coming back, falling out and making up. Most Indians' lives are synonymous with struggle, and anyone who has ever struggled will know how it fills the mind and leaves no room for boredom. Hunger, illness, family feuds; these things are all-absorbing. Boredom creeps into the emptiness of having, and no longer needing.

Ammi, the elderly Muslim lady, never came out of her fortress except to relieve herself. She lay on the floor at the back of their room behind the three curtains, her grey wispy hair disarranged by her bourka, her tiny legs clothed in old-fashioned skin-tight Muslim pyjamas that Jungli said were called bangle pyjamas because of the way they clung to the calves in bangle-like ruckles. Her tiny square face, which Jungli never saw, was inquisitive yet serene; there was a light and vitality in her eyes, in spite of long illness, that no-one else in the hut row possessed. Maybe she was the only truly religious person among them. Every day she read the *Qu'ran*, a huge tome that completely dwarfed her, and sometimes she talked – very quietly, almost in a murmur – to her daughters. Why weren't they married, those two? At first I had assumed they were in their teens, but when I looked more closely I saw lines on their faces and grey in their hair. They were very poor and proud. They were orthodox Muslims who prayed five times a day at the specified hours. They avoided charity. They didn't shout at each other and they said sensible things. I felt more pro-Muslim than I had felt in years.

All the hut people, in fact all the dehra people, affected religiosity and took from the dehra what they could, but I doubt if many of them felt it in their hearts. In India it was almost a duty to pretend and quite unacceptable to admit non-belief. People found it difficult enough to care for each other: where then was there room in their hearts for God?

For they were always telling tales on each other; it was like being in a boarding school. Being divested of responsibility they couldn't cope with their quarrels and took them to a higher authority. Those who had a grudge against Jungli reported him for things he wasn't guilty of; they reported the pathis for this and that, and Sitaram the shop wallah reported Kali, queen of the cow's house.

Kali and her family of six, untouchables turned Christians, shared the cow's house with four or five single dehra men. Mercifully there was a four foot wall between our hut and the cow's house, for Kali was a real harridan beside whom Jai Singh's appeared almost docile. She was black-skinned and cross-eyed but as conceited as they come, slyly admiring herself in the eye-catching new salvar-kamiz she always seemed to be wearing (to the annoyance of the other women) and flashing her good eye at the seduceable males. She barked at anyone who complained about her leaving her squalling children lying around in front of our hut when she couldn't be bothered to look after them herself, but she changed her tune when she came to beg. 'Just three potatoes!' she gushed with an artificial simper, and when I said we hadn't enough she took them anyway. Kali was the name Jungli and I gave her; Kali the goddess, the black destructress.

Sitaram reported her for being forward and facetious. He loathed frivolous behaviour in a woman (once I had smiled, not at him but alone in his presence, and he had been most upset), and Kali was known to be very free with her favours. She should have known better in a place like that, for the men she seduced made disparaging remarks behind her back and everyone got to hear. In traditional Indian communities such as this – traditional in practice if not in age – if such were a woman's inclinations it didn't pay to succumb.

13

Rains

THE RAINS CAME EARLY. The sudden explosion of cool refreshing storms into which people ran and soaked themselves in relief never happened. It just rained more than it had been, and there were always clouds somewhere in the sky. But every day there were spectacular sunsets which I would stand and watch – I was the only one to do so – while the clouds glowed richer and brighter against the darkening blue in fruit salad colours: pale green grape and the even paler green of cut apple, peach and apricot, strawberry and mango, and the creamy white of peeled banana.

The plains didn't exactly go green overnight as the parks and gardens of the cities did – ours weren't those sort of plants – but things grew faster. Inside the timber yard the dub frothed out in luscious tussocks, while on our unprotected side of the fence hungry animals chopped it at various untidy lengths like badly cut hair. Snakes came into the huts out of the wet; one into the cow's house and another, four feet long, into Jai Singh's', which she discovered coiled neatly round the sugar tin.

Some days it rained hard for hours on end, slashing the plain into misty white streaks as it filled up the hollows and bounced back from the surface of newly created pools. After the first long rain we all emerged from our huts when it stopped and looked at it silently, for it surrounded us in a shallow flood, cutting off the dehra and leaving nowhere for us to make our arrangements. I tiptoed around feebly looking for a place to pee, but there wasn't a spot even for that: the huts stood like islands on the low earth banks that served as their foundations. The women started sweeping water away from the walls with their little bundles of dub stalks, for if it got underneath and washed out the soil they could collapse. The men, meanwhile, dug an impressive system of shallow ditches, and the water fell in a cascade into the big peeing pit behind the next door hut and streamed away across the plain. Where there wasn't a fall they loosened the earth and dug up the dub to encourage it to seep downwards instead.

A pair of pheasant-tailed jaçanas, birds of Parisian elegance, swam peacefully across a large pool that had formed in the arrangements pit among feathery strands of submerged tamarisk bushes. At nightfall a multitude of frogs set up a resounding stereophonic chorus from muddy puddlesides. Jungli caught fireflies and we watched them walking about inside his cupped hands, quite ordinary little beetles silhouetted against the bright greenish flashing light emanating from their undersides.

The rain formed a lake on the roof and poured into the hut. It seeped through the walls and spattered over the pillows. Streams of liquid mud trickled down our clean clothes and the back of the books and dribbled onto the charpoys. We rolled up the bedding, stood the charpoy frames on end, and crouched in a dry patch until the rain stopped. Then Jungli fetched the bamboo ladder from the dehra, undammed the lake and carried up baltas of new mud to spread a four-inch thick sealing layer.

But the rain still came in, making delicate tendrilly patterns on the walls like stranded seaweed clinging to rocks. It stole under the door and lay in a pool. It flooded the plain and created a swamp. Everything was permanently damp, for even when it wasn't raining water lay all round and saturated the air; Ramnagri for once seemed preferable, with its wet green scented gardens and drains for clearing the floods. The door expanded and refused to close, matches wouldn't light and clothes didn't dry. Our drinking water was suspect because it was no longer properly filtered; people got ill.

The environs of our new hut had never been very savoury. We were able to keep the apron of land in front of our old one fairly clean, but we now had to make allowances for others. Jai Singh's' children seemed to have permanent diarrhoea, and they had it immediately adjacent to our room or, failing that, on Ram Pal's parking pitch where it greeted us when we went to collect our milk. I was used to and could put up with a fair amount of squalor, but once or twice when it exceeded even my level of tolerance I came storming into the hut slinging abuse at Jungli, the least to blame of all: '*Filthy* people! There's shit everywhere! *Everywhere*! With all this open space why do people have to go two inches from their doors? It's like living in a latrine!'

It wasn't very fair of me, for the floods had cut off the arrangements area and we had been forced to find new spots much nearer the huts. And the children didn't know any better.

All the fun had been taken out of making one's arrangements, that was the other thing that annoyed me. I would squat for ages in my old territory by the dwarf tamarisks contentedly watching them come into flower, or following the progress of dung beetles as they rolled tasty morsels nowhere in particular, or observing the hut people trotting back and forth to the pump, or gazing into the distance wondering about the meaning of life. I knew for sure that no-one would ever, ever disturb me. But now all I had to look forward to was calf deep water and mud.

But the mud nurtured a garden. Young pumpkins nestled under the dub. Tindur, a round green vegetable smelling of mown grass, burgeoned in the ditches. Tiny neem and mesquite trees rooted in walls and bare patches of silt. Behind our hut a sleek carmine-leaved mango seedling came up from a stone someone had pushed through the wall.

'Ooh!' said the children, and pulled it up. And, 'Ooh look, here's another one! This one's different!' they cried, and pulled that too. And, 'What's this one?' snapping it off. My garden wasn't to be. They uprooted every one.

At night the hut swarmed with biting insects. They dropped into my hair, crawled under our clothes and littered the floor. I scratched and cursed and couldn't get on with anything. A rat bit Jungli's foot, hoping he might be dead, and Raju the mongoose skittered about under the charpoys trying to run it down. Nasty the dog lay outside our door, leeches dangling elegantly from his eyelashes. A family of lizards set up camp above the beam directly over my head and sent down well-aimed missiles.

The monsoon brought all kinds of rain. Besides regular Amazonian downpours there were long steady English rains, short sharp squalls with steamy breaks in between, and hours and days of low cloud and drizzle. Once it rained all night and half the next day, and to fetch water, collect our milk or make our arrangements we had to get wet. None of the women owned an umbrella; they went sloshing about in the mud like baby buffaloes, towels over their heads, their cotton clothes plastered to their skins, soaking wet and actually laughing. I couldn't get over it. They had no means of getting dry again for everything inside was wet too, so what did they have to be so merry about? I'd never seen them so gleeful. They got out a rope and started skipping, clapping their hands and trying to outdo each other in prowess.

This incident was unique. In the taut repressive atmosphere of the dehra it was difficult to let go. There were few real bonds of friendship, for the place didn't nurture confidences. One could never be quite sure of anyone else, of what they really believed, of whose side they were really on. People laughed, but their hearts weren't in it.

Next day things went back to normal. The women scowled as they put out their sacks, daris and khes to dry in the thin watery sun. Jai Singh's' children howled lustily and Jai Singh's howled too. 'You dogs, what's the matter with you now? Oh I'll give you such a beating!'

It had been a disturbed night. Our electricity had been cut off and the air was muggy and windless. Mosquitoes were feasting off my feet and hands. At half past twelve there were sounds of shouting from Number Nine and we all got up. People were running from the dehra, and Jai Singh signalled to Jungli, and Jungli extracted the pistol from the underside of the Indian landscape chair and they ran too. But the dacoits, who had this time practised their art on a member of Santji's sangat, had already been apprehended at gunpoint and Jungli soon returned. At three we were woken again by enthusiastic sounds of eating coming from the next room.

'What on earth are they doing?' I whispered to Jungli: the Muslims never cooked for themselves.

'It's the first day of Ramadan,' he replied, and I understood. I had been in Muslim countries before during Ramadan, when people got up at unearthly hours to bolt down as much food as possible before the sun rose.

Over the next month they cooked every evening and delicious smells came through the wall; they were totally absorbed in their preparations. Even an earthquake couldn't shift them, as I discovered one day when I felt my charpoy shaking. I assumed it was Nasty rubbing off his lice on the fibre beneath, yet when I looked he wasn't there. Finally when my charpoy started bumping up and down I began to wonder if I was being set upon by an evil spirit. But Jungli was already out of the door, crouching in a huddle with the other hut people and shouting at me to follow – huts like ours with no foundations were liable to collapse like a pack of cards.

Everyone was there. Except the Muslims.

'Come out!' we called. 'It's an earthquake!' But they were engrossed in their cooking and didn't answer: it was almost half past seven and time to break their fast.

I had never seen so many mosquitoes as, by that time, we were harbouring in our room. They bred in the swampy plain, slunk in the brickwork joints and in the folds of our clothes during the day, and emerged in clouds at dusk. It was hardly surprising that people caught malaria; at one time there was a sick female in each of the four rooms of our hut. Amma at the end was still suffering from her bronchial something, and Jai Singh's, Amma and I all had malaria.

Lacking their built-in resistance to it, I was knocked out for ten days.

Up until that time my health at the dehra had been reasonably good. Though undoubtedly thinner, run down by the heat and sallow-skinned through lack of fresh air and exercise, I hadn't suffered anything more serious than mild stomach disorders and bouts of ill humour. And yet, while often a bit grumpy, I was never depressed.

When the fever first appeared (Jungli had leapt up saying my skin was on fire) we went to the fat Sikh doctor in the village on the hill. At the surgery there was the usual crowd of sixty or seventy local villagers in the waiting room, watching the fat Sikh and whoever it was he was examining. His one room surgery was open to the street where new patients were arriving laid flat out in bullock carts. When my turn came I was dismissed in thirty seconds with pills for fever and the standard Indian diagnosis, 'It's the weather.'

Two days later and having got worse we went again, this time to a Hindu doctor who was actually qualified (Jungli said the fat Sikh had picked up his knowledge here and there). By this time I had high fever, abdominal pains, a cold, a racking cough and nausea. I hadn't eaten for three days. Jungli supported me through the swamp the three quarters of a mile to Number Nine. In the rickshaw that carried us from there to the village on the hill everything suddenly went dark – though my eyes were still open – and for a few seconds I was unable to breathe. I collapsed onto Jungli, who held me up and delivered a no-nonsense lecture. 'Don't be so feeble!' I was dimly aware of him shouting. 'There's nothing wrong with you: you're imagining it. You need a strong heart.' There was a lot more besides but I wasn't listening: for a minute, and for the first time in my life, I thought my end had come. The rickshaw wallah was staring straight ahead, pedalling on as if nothing had happened.

Back at home with an assortment of pills, I collapsed on my charpoy under a blanket. Even immediately afterwards my memory of the next two or three days was hazy, but I remember a lot of women coming and going, massaging my legs and arms, feeling my wrists to see how high the fever was, sticking Vicky fingers up my nose, feeding me lumps of wood to chew for my cough and tucking my feet under the blanket. The outside temperature was way up in the hundreds but I was frozen.

'Put a sweater on,' I recollect saying to Jungli. 'It makes me feel cold just to look at you going about in that vest.' Each time I lifted a corner of the blanket an icy draught blew in.

I lay there covered in sweat, with no means of drying. It poured with rain hour after hour and water trickled down the walls and dripped from the roof. Whatever Jungli did it still came in. My clothes were filthy: sweaty, grimy and stained with menstrual blood. Jungli surreptitiously began washing them with a stick and a bucket of water, but a troupe of women swept in unannounced and caught him at it. With a horrified shriek they bore them away to the pump: it was unheard of for a man to be washing a woman's clothes. To me it was unthinkable that strangers should be doing it, but I hadn't the strength to protest.

Meanwhile our electricity supply had been taken down and hidden, for the government electricity wallah was coming on an inspection and our huts were wired up illegally. By the time the electricity was reconnected, two days later, my fever was down. The dehra electrician, Baldev Singh, ex-dacoit, house breaker and highway robber, appeared with the end of a roll of tape, a bundle of sundry lengths of wire and a couple of wonky poles. The men came out of their huts and dug holes for the wonky poles, and Baldev Singh shinned up the bamboo ladder and fixed the wires (which he had joined with bits of sellotape) to their tops. Like all electrical jobs at the dehra it was finished in about five minutes.

Shortly after that we lost our fan. They needed it at the dehra, they said, only they didn't really, they'd just given up trying to ingratiate me. There followed a succession of sweltering windless days and nights when I didn't attempt to sleep until after midnight and spent half my time mopping up sweat and extricating insects from my hair and clothes. Jungli cared for the rains no more than I did, though some of the others seemed immune to being permanently soggy: I would watch Jai Singh's and Amma bathing under the dehra tap and putting their clothes back on while the water was still running off their skins.

For some months Jungli had had a distended and painful stomach for which he had refused to take any medicine. He said no-one could cure it. Then Baldev Singh, the electricity wallah, told him of a certain hakim[1] who would know what to prescribe and, suffering from some obscure ailment himself, they went off together to consult him.

What Baldev Singh didn't divulge was the hakim's whereabouts, and to Jungli's horror he found it took them nine hours and five buses to get there. They alighted from the last bus on a minor road in

[1] ayurvedic doctor

Rajasthan, from which there was an eight-mile walk across the fields to the hakim's village. The paths were ankle deep in mud and the air was hot and breathless pending a storm. Elephant-high sorghum cut off what little breeze there might have been, and for the last five hours they had had no water to drink (Jungli said I wouldn't have survived it, when I complained of being left behind). When at last they arrived they found a queue of people waiting for consultations, but the hakim put them up for the night in his hut, fed them on chapattis with a chutney of ground chillies and salt (which was what he lived on), and in the morning made his diagnosis and gave Jungli some pellets to cure it.

That evening when I was washing his shirt I discovered – rather too late – the semi-dissolved package, containing what now looked like a nest of slimy reptile's eggs. Jungli cursed me and cursed the hakim, but mostly the hakim.

'I'm not taking that sort of medicine! Who knows what's in it? It could contain beef fat for all I know!' Jungli's stomach would remain distended. He seized the package from me and thrust it through the wall.

Jungli was a man who either got on well with people or didn't care for them at all. When we first came to the dehra his generosity, charm and lack of caste consciousness earned him the respect of everyone, everyone that is except cousin Khazan's wife, who wanted her man to herself. Gradually he lost his popularity, mostly, I believe, through forthrightness and hot-headedness. For Jungli had no guile. And disliking him they ostracized me too; not openly, but I felt the change.

There had already been a certain chilliness in their attitudes towards me. My writing was incomprehensible to them. My long disappearances to far away places leaving Jungli to fend for himself, would without doubt have been misinterpreted by almost everyone at the dehra: if an Indian woman goes off on her own, there can only be one explanation for it.

In the end, out of all those in the hut row, only Paramjit-next-door's family remained loyal. So by this time our visitors had become more manageable. There was Sitaram the shop wallah and Baldev Singh the electricity wallah. There was also – and this gave Jai Singh's something to get her teeth into – an exceedingly pretty girl, a friend of Sultana's, who lived on the far side of the dehra. At Jungli's invitation she came to the hut and drank cups of tea. He teased her and she laughed.

This wasn't done. No decent married man (as Jungli was supposed to be) solicited the friendship of pretty young girls like that. Jungli sank lower in the hut people's esteem and earned the further derogatory title of philanderer. The girl was told in no uncertain terms to keep away and have nothing more to do with him. No-one could understand why I didn't mind.

But I didn't mind: on the contrary I was delighted. Knowing Jungli's history I was pleased whenever he trusted a girl enough to consider her a friend. He was close to Inderjit's sister. He had been close to Kamala until Kamala overdid it: she was a little in love with Jungli and I think had tried to seduce him while I was away. When we left their hut she cried and cried, for Karam Chand had forbidden her ever to come near us again. She had been one of my greatest allies and I missed her.

Not once in two years did Jungli or I ever question each other's fidelity. Twice we were apart for three months, but it never crossed our minds. There was much to be said for that.

On Independence Day Hindu-Muslim riots broke out in Ramnagri. When I got there next morning to do some shopping I found it in curfew. Those from our hut row who worked in Ramnagri were concerned about what might ensue, and our Muslims (in their precarious minority) got a bit jittery, but the rest were wrapped up in the capsule of dehra life. No-one thought of buying a newspaper, and the news that reached us was all hearsay.

It was a few days later. Jai Singh had just returned from work in the evening, and Paramjit's brother Karamjit from tramping the streets in search of it:

Jai Singh: 'I've heard there's trouble in Kashmir now too.'

Jai Singh's: 'I haven't slept a wink all day!'

Karamjit: 'The curfew's still on in Ramnagri. There's no-one about, and the police are patrolling the cordons.'

Jai Singh's (to Jai Singh): 'All you do is sit and read *path* for half an hour and snore yourself silly the rest of the day. You call that work?'

Jai Singh: 'The situation could be dangerous; the Indo-Pakistan wars started with small incidents of this sort.'

Jai Singh's: 'I'm stuck here with these children and can't get a minute's peace. Listen to them, do you like the sound of their screaming? Then you come back demanding dinner! Where's the paraffin to cook it on I ask you? And have you looked at the flour you brought? The dirty dogs put millet in it! Take it back and demand some decent stuff.'

Karamjit: 'It's this country: too many religions. Religious wars are the worst. People can't live together in harmony.'

Jai Singh's (to Jai Singh): 'You lover of your sister! What's the use of trying to tell you anything? You don't listen to a word! I said the flour's full of millet: take it back!'

Jai Singh took the flour, borrowed Sitaram's bicycle, and pedalled off across the plain.

14

Saint

THERE HAD ALWAYS been fighting at the dehra. When there was
no threat from outside to ward off, the dehra inhabitants fought each
other. Even the women had fight in them, but they found release in
nagging their husbands, quarrelling with each other and haranguing
their children. Jungli believed the cause was illiteracy: like so many
inhabitants of the third world he saw education as the answer to all
their problems. But it wasn't that at all. Our community was
unstable, only just over two years old, perpetually expanding and
changing in composition. It comprised former criminals, people
separated from their wives, their husbands, their children or their
parents, Partition refugees, villagers whose families had outgrown
their land or quarrelled, single people with physical deformities (like
the man with no legs who minded the shoes), and the simply
homeless jobless poor. Being predominantly Sikh, physical aggression came naturally to them, and in addition to the usual oppressions
living conditions at the dehra were far from ideal. People were in
constant competition with each other to rise in Santji's favour: but
he held them down, every single one.

Occasionally it was Jungli who started a fight, but his adversaries
knew better than to hit back. One day a member of sangat came
before Santji waving his head from side to side and complaining of
being possessed by a Pathan spirit: he wanted it exorcized. When he
insulted Santji calling him a fraud and a trickster, Jungli (at that time
very loyal) grabbed the man by the hair and gave him a mighty swipe
across the face with his palm. Everybody laughed; even Santji
seemed to approve, and the man's head stopped waving about.

'Are you still possessed by a Pathan spirit?' Jungli asked. But the
man had picked himself up and was making off, at a rather
undignified pace, towards Number Nine.

Jungli clouted the gatekeeper. He belted the waker-upper (who,
being embarrassed by the sight of us sleeping on the same charpoy,
had failed to get Jungli up on time). Sometimes he took a swipe at me.
But his conscience always plagued him afterwards.

Other dehra men were worse. There was the time when the
teashop wallah announced he was going to kill Kala Sap. He took a

dagger and went after him, but Kala Sap managed to slip out of his way. Then one morning when I had gone to the tailor (Jungli loathed my going, for he knew the tailor would have to touch me), and Jungli was stocktaking in the dehra store with Sitaram and that same teashop wallah, an argument blew up, an exceedingly trivial matter concerning some chilli powder. Without warning the teashop wallah picked up a large piece of glass that happened to be handy and smote Sitaram – a quiet-spoken Hindu whom Jungli and I both liked – across the face. Sitaram fell to the ground, blood spurting out of his head like a pump, and at first Jungli thought he was dead. The teashop wallah ran away in terror leaving Jungli, who could cope with such situations, to rip his turban into bandages to stop the blood. He took Sitaram to the clinic in the village on the hill where he had nine stitches, and gave him a glassful of ghee to drink in hot milk for relieving the pain.

Santji was livid. 'Beat him!' he ordered the dehra men, for Santji had his own laws and the police never came near us. So when the teashop wallah (rather foolishly I thought) returned next day to collect his belongings they set upon him with sticks and shoes. That time when he ran away he didn't come back for a month.

But Santji had changed his mind. 'Why did you beat him like that?' he demanded angrily. 'He had suffered enough.'

After that there was a bout of violence. There was the pitiable incident of the man who had built a small hut for himself close to the dehra and had taken a prostitute there to look after him. The dehra committee was outraged.

'We can't have that sort of thing going on here,' they decided unanimously, and they pulled down his hut. It was my turn to be furious. 'That's not fair!' I challenged Jungli when I heard about it. 'It was his hut and his land, which is more than Santji's dehra is: he can do what he likes in it.'

'Not here, he can't,' replied Jungli sardonically. His hut was right by the gates; everyone passed it, an exemplary pile of broken rubble, on the way to Number Nine.

Sometimes when we glanced out of our doorway we would see a stampede of white-clad dehra men brandishing sticks thundering across the scrub towards Number Nine in pursuit of an alleged transgressor. They took swipes at him as they ran, and when they caught him they pinned him down and beat him, stroke after stroke, for they knew no mercy. In each case it was said that the man had come to the dehra with alcohol in his belly, but half the time they must have just guessed. What about the opium in theirs? I seethed in helpless rage. And the ganja? Then Chhota Santji accused Jungli of being drunk on duty, and Jungli feared he would be next in line for the stick treatment.

'Surely they won't beat you!' I said, deeply shocked. It was months since Jungli had had a drink; he had recited the Sikh prayer and given it up.

'Why not?' he replied. 'While you were in Sri Lanka they beat the pathi who was having it off with the knitting machine wallah's wife. They said he told lies and they broke his arm. He was in plaster for two months.' And later they beat another of the pathis who had been wrongly accused of stealing a suitcase.

Jungli was serious and became very silent. My head was full of thoughts of what I would do, first to save and then to avenge him. I would go blazing into battle; I would kick them and scream at them and bash them over the head with my bucket, and I would get in front of him so they couldn't touch either of us. Then I would publicize the whole thing in the national press.

Jungli's instinct wasn't wrong; it rarely was. Chhota Santji and Kala Sap ordered Arjun Singh (who ran the langar) to beat him up. Arjun Singh told Jungli later how he had replied that he couldn't do it, at least not without Santji's sanction. And maybe Santji realized I would not sit passively while they beat my Jungli, and that being white I had the power to make trouble for them. Anyway they never touched him.

'I find your letter quite fascinating,' began a letter from an Australian friend in London, 'but don't know if I could stand saints.' For some time I'd been wondering whether I could stand them either.

My initial curiosity in the mystery surrounding Santji had not been long in working itself out, and for six months I had neither spoken to him nor attended any dehra function. I had observed him until my questions were answered. Was he a saint? Not according to the Guru's definition. Did he have spiritual power? Probably not, unless he kept it well hidden, and that was unlikely. Jungli as his head granthi had watched him for a year, and had never seen any evidence of it. But I still found it hard to gauge just how much of what people said about Santji they actually believed, how much they said out of fear of losing the roof over their heads, and how much they said because they were in on the charade themselves. The stories could have been invented to promote Santji's fame, twisted through frequent repetition, exaggerated for the sake of drama, guessed at when the tale was garbled, or misconstrued by error: how did one separate fact from fiction? Jungli was as gullible as anybody. Yet none but ourselves seemed to criticize the system, and our whisperings (still too audible to rule out eavesdroppers) conceivably abetted our unpopularity.

The healing matter was simple enough: people usually got better when they were ill (unless they died) and they got better faster if they thought they were going to. Jungli believed what power there was emanated from the Akhandpath readings.

'What about the secretary, though?' I asked him. The secretary was the one with terminal cancer.

'Who knows? We didn't see it. It could be a fabricated story to boost Santji's fame, like those about him raising people from the dead. Huh!' snorted Jungli.

'And the death dating?'

'That's not difficult. Anyone who repeats *path* a lot could do it.'

'And the exorcisms?'

'Exorcizing spirits isn't so hard either. I could probably do it too.'

The breaking point as far as Jungli was concerned had come when Santji returned from California in January. He hadn't been alone. Accompanying him was a pretty Panjabi girl who lived in California, the same girl who had been 'cured' of arthritis a year ago over seventeen Akhandpaths. She was ushered into Santji's inner sanctum before too many people caught sight of her, and when I arrived (she wanted to meet me so my presence had been summoned) was lying on his bed. Santji wasn't there.

'Huh!' Jungli exploded again when I told him, and there was bitterness in his voice. 'No-one is ever permitted to even sit on Santji's bed. It's his throne.'

But this girl couldn't move her legs: she was badly crippled. She stayed in that room with Santji for seven months and almost never came out; a canvas enclosure was erected so she could sit outside in privacy and get to the bathroom, and nobody was allowed to come anywhere near her. A man was posted by the door twenty-four hours a day to make sure they didn't.

Everybody knew though. Someone told Jatedar and Jatedar told Karam Chand and Karam Chand (who knew exactly what he was about) told Santji. Santji, in a fury, threatened that if anyone else so much as hinted at such a thing he would personally break every bone in their body. So no-one dared mention it after that. And when Jatedar wanted his job back he got a piece of Santji's mind instead.

Jungli cursed and swore. Hadn't Santji a wife and children in Panjab? Wasn't it strictly forbidden for a Sikh to associate with any woman other than his wife? And a man who called himself a saint too!

My own feeling was that you could allow a saint a certain latitude – the Gurus' definition was very tightly circumscribed – but that Santji overflowed the boundary like a tiny stream flooding a great plain. A Sikh saint should at least (I would have thought) observe the practice of Sikhism, have partially controlled the five vices of anger, lust, attachment, greed and ego, and be absorbed in the love of God enough to be charitable towards the people around him, a definition fulfilled by thousands of ordinary Panjabi villagers. Santji showed little interest in the outsiders who came to ask his blessing and he treated even his own dehra inhabitants unjustly: I often saw him angrily shouting at a group of quaking devotees. That he was conceited was plainly obvious: he loved show, he was fond of expensive Western clothes and he treated us all as inferior beings. His words and actions showed him to be revengeful, autocratic and unreliable. He smoked and, according to general opinion, had numerous casual affairs. People in the Ramnagri gurdwara said he practised black magic. Could such a man be a saint?

But Indians need saints, or there wouldn't be any. The Indian mind is channelled into submissiveness from early childhood and open to suggestion from stronger personalities. From respecting – even revering – the wishes, commands and beliefs of his parents as surrogate gods, the adult may turn his devotion towards the guru as surrogate parent. Living in a repressive society people subconsciously search for a higher authority who, in spite of all the opposing forces, has been able to find himself and can express what he has found. Someone who is able to take responsibility for their actions and discipline their weaknesses; someone on whom they can lean when in trouble. People drew comfort from the illusion of being under Santji's protection.

But in many ways he played a positive role, power or no power. He filled several thousand Indians' need for a saint-hero in their lives; his devotees claimed it was through Santji's blessing that their families were healthy, that endeavours were successful, and that they had a roof over their heads and enough to eat. At the dehra he provided food and shelter for over a hundred homeless people. He even employed a few. He gave clothes and the free service of a doctor to those who worked at the dehra, and provided a car to take the children to school in Chandinagar. He encouraged the feeding of the local poor, the sacred cow and the pariah dogs: five cows and six dogs regularly presented themselves at the langar at meal times.

In other ways he was destructive. His word, however crazy, was law. No-one could question anything he said or did, for it was his hand that fed them. What should have been a social system based on love and democracy was in fact the most autocratic and doctrinaire society I have ever laid eyes on. Not that it affected me physically: sometimes Jungli would tell me I had to do this or that, but I wouldn't if I didn't feel like it, and being a white goddess I got away with it. But the atmosphere rubbed off on all of us; it was impossible to ignore other people's troubles, or not share in their suffering.

Santji kept the dehra people down by threats, beatings and demotings. He withheld salaries. He kept people occupied every moment of the day, on the probable assumption that people with time and energy on their hands were liable to revolt. Thus everyone had to get up at three in the morning, sit cross-legged on the verandah with a sheet over their heads and repeat their mantra for an hour. Most people seemed to have the same mantra, and the gist of it was that Santji knew all about you, that he was your sole support throughout life and the medium through which to attain salvation. That fixed the fact more or less firmly in people's minds until three the next morning. Then there was boundary pacing to keep out evil spirits, and communal chanting until six; also compulsory. Jungli and I were the only dehra people not to attend, and every day we were both marked absent in the register (being 'married' to Jungli I was signed as Balwinder Kaur, his favourite name). After that people were busy with their families, getting the children ready for school and cleaning the hut, bit of hut or section of hall in which they lived. There were clothes to wash each day and then morning langar at eight (I told the time by a combination of the sun and the langar gong, and was amazed that the other hut people were unable to do likewise and were forever wanting to know the time). The morning meal was followed by dehra duty of some sort, to be performed most of the day – the hours depending on the type of work – until the drum called everyone to the verandah at three for communal chanting. Then came the second meal, followed immediately by sangat from four to six, arti at six (a Hindu ceremony frowned upon by true Sikhs, involving lighting ghee lamps in front of Santji's throne and the Pandit chanting special arti verses), last langar at eight and finally (a recent innovation), compulsory kirtan until eleven. Where was the time to sleep, to think, to relax, to be with one's family, to be oneself?

But that was exactly the point. Santji could exert the optimum power and influence when the minds of his disciples were devoid of independent thought, and were fixed upon him through their mantras, through the photographs most of his followers kept in their homes, and through constant confrontations. Their subconscious minds were thus laid open for manipulation.

If Santji wasn't a saint then he was a charlatan, which implied that the whole dehra organization could be summed up in a single word: business. And what business! Santji's UP sangat amounted to several thousand (amongst whom not one was a qualified professional, I discovered when I needed a sponsor to join a library). According to Kala Sap there were another four hundred and fifty devotees in California, and more affiliated to the four or five other dehras in India. All those to whom a mantra had been given were supposed to donate a tenth of their salaries to their respective dehra: Jungli received his pay with over a tenth already deducted and a 'Received with thanks' chit for it. No wonder the man was wealthy!

Santji's business was God, and with the proceeds he was creating an earthly empire. Besides the clutch of dehras Santji had his own trucks, cars and houses, and part ownership of at least one factory. His aspirations expanded alongside his material possessions. He was mounting a private army of a hundred men and there was to be a horse for each of them stabled at the main dehra. Santji himself would ride – like a maharaja – on an elephant. Already his soldiers had uniforms, and they appeared for the first time in July in their white homespun shirts and pyjamas with a white belt and special Santji buckle.

Santji's ambition was to reform Sikhism, as Guru Gobind Singh had done three hundred years before. He would change the onus of the discipline to suit the times, and maybe make his followers shave their heads (he hadn't quite made up his mind) and wear special clothes as a mark of his claim upon them. He had already instigated a new greeting in place of Sat Sri Akal, four times as long, which I refused to use.

In terms of financial success Santji's coming to UP and converting to Sikhism had been an excellent move. The proximity of Ramnagri meant a reliable source of income: several thousand of its inhabitants were Sikhs. City people had more available cash than villagers and the Sikhs were prosperous. Away from Panjab there was no threat of competition from other Sikh saints.

One evening in late July Santji issued an ultimatum to a complete assembly of the dehra people. Either they sign their lives over to the dehra or they leave. He gave everyone a day to think about it. Twenty-four hours later the victory drum again summoned them – about a hundred adults – to the verandah. I didn't go: I was still weak from malaria, but I probably wouldn't have gone anyway.

Santji explained the implications of signing the statement that would be issued to each member. You became the property of the dehra, and could no longer leave through your own volition. Everything you owned also became the property of the dehra: if you were told to leave you could take nothing with you, not even your bank balance; not even your wife and children. They too became the property of the dehra.

From now on you were to treat the dehra as your father and mother: your real parents would cease to have any meaning for you. As your guardian the dehra could do as it pleased with you, and you would have no recourse to common law. If you were given a hiding, if your legs were broken or if you were beaten to death, with justified cause or no, there was nothing anyone in the world could do to avenge you. Whatever new rules were issued you would have to obey. And if relatives or friends came to see you they would be directed first to the office where they would be searched and where they would have to deposit their money and belongings for the duration of their stay. Only then could they proceed to your quarters, where they could remain for a maximum of two hours. From then on they would be absorbed by the dehra and obliged to take part in its routine of activity.

On the benefit side the dehra would supply, free of charge, all your needs: food, shelter, clothes, schooling, medical facilities and marriage and death expenses. If you died it would care for your family for as long as it existed.

So Santji asked each in turn, 'Are you going to sign?' And they all said, 'I will sign': the office wallahs, the shop wallahs, the carpenters, the ragis, the tailors, the drivers, the electricity wallah, the langar wallahs, the pathis, the latrine sweepers, the shoe minders, the gate keepers, the waker-uppers, the sangat controllers, the night watchmen. The Pandit and Amma signed; the Muslims signed. Only three refused to sign: one of the original pathis (who changed his mind under pressure the next day), the knitting machine wallah, and Jungli. Santji appealed to Jungli, for he didn't want to lose his head granthi, and when Jungli still said no he made him a special offer. He could sign for himself alone, thus binding him but releasing me from the alternative – as I saw it – of lifelong serfdom at the mercy of Santji and the dehra men. But Jungli still said no, and Santji was offended.

The whole thing horrified me, not the fact that we would have to go – for refusal to sign meant the sack – but that ninety-eight per cent of the people had said yes! They were committing themselves to slavery, to a voluntary Belsen, and for life! What sort of people were they that had no sense of basic human rights? Didn't they know what wars were fought for? What kind of society was this that could suppress individual will so absolutely that people were actually happy to sign such a document? For there they were, God damn it, rejoicing! I could see them by the langar, beating drums and singing. Even dancing!

'What choice have they got?' demanded Jungli, instinctively rising in their defence. I thought. It was true: very few, to my knowledge, had anywhere else to go. It was that or the streets. But I know which I should have chosen. It was at such times I felt my difference.

After that episode, but before the new system came into force, life became stricter at the dehra. Leave was refused. Daily seva became compulsory, and a man would be sent to rout everyone out of their huts, usually at high noon, to carry earth on their heads in the sun. Jungli was blacklisted when he refused to comply, but he refused on principle. 'How can it be seva if it's compulsory?' he asked. 'Haven't I enough to do without carrying earth on my head half the day as well?' But the Big Ragi got his own back by inventing a sliding scale of fines for not attending boundary pacing at four in the morning: one rupee to be docked for the first day of absence, two for the second, three for the third and so on. In twenty-five days Jungli would lose his month's earnings, and in a further week those of the following month.

Other people were getting disillusioned too. Baldev Singh, the electricity wallah, left under a cloud. There were only four pathis left. Jungli was restless and knew he would have to go once the feudal system took root.

August passed quickly. My departure had become an unspoken understanding between us. Jungli seemed to accept at last that I could not stay, that I did not love him so totally that I could give him my future. I told him there could be others and he said yes, he knew, he had seen it in dreams.

Yet I still could not make that final move. Jungli accepted my leaving and yet he didn't; he accepted with his head though not with his heart. He put on a brave face in front of the hut people, to whom my departure was no big deal; they were always coming and going themselves, and they expected me back.

We filled our days with activity. Once recovered from malaria I went exploring in Ramnagri, walking around districts I had never been. We went shopping together and I bought Jungli a year's supply of clothes, a sop to my guilt. I returned to Rajasthan on a five-day pilgrimage to the Thar desert and the stepped wells of Bundi. We visited Vitu's family in Saharanpur, and would have gone to Kulu too but Jungli couldn't get leave. No more was he Santji's golden boy.

On my birthday Jungli gave me half a kilo of milk and told me to go and book my flight. I had been back in India a year and my ticket was due to expire. I needed that shove: the stamp of his acceptance.

The rains were over. God was in a spring-cleaning mood, making (through Santji as his mouthpiece) a number of alterations at the dehra. Within a week the entrance was moved and an enquiry booth constructed; the shop and tea stall were returned to their original positions; a new office was provided by making a door where there had formerly been a window and prior to that a door; and the six-month old brick and cement shop and tea stall and the Big Ragi's hut were pulled down to make way for a new row of mean-looking huts built in a continuous line along the back wall.

By 1983, Santji said, he would rule the world. Hadn't Guru Gobind Singh prophesied that he would return in another guise to establish a spiritual raj? He would start by overthrowing the government. The day was fixed, five men alerted and armed with sticks. There was the Big Ragi, Kali's man from the cow's house, that infamous teashop wallah and a couple of others: all practised fighters. They were to wait outside Parliament House in Delhi and when an important minister came out set upon him with their sticks.

'He's cracked!' I said to Jungli. 'What can five men with sticks do against a government? They'll all be arrested.' Which wouldn't have been a bad thing actually.

'He knows that,' said Jungli. 'His name will be in the papers and he'll be famous overnight.'

I looked in the papers next day, by which time I was deep in Rajasthan. But there was nothing.

The attack had been postponed: they'd got cold feet.

I left in early September. I tried to tell myself I wasn't really going, shut my mind to it, carried on performing my daily tasks right until the last moment as a buffer to my distress. Jungli lay on the charpoy, silent.

He came with me to the airport in Delhi. We camped on a narrow strip of grass in the middle of the taxi rank, our heads and legs sprawled across my baggage. There were sleeping people all around us: airport porters, taxi drivers, Panjabi villagers seeing relatives off to Toronto or Dubai. My plane left at dawn. One minute Jungli was beside me, helping to carry my bags. The next I was walking on alone.

Afterword

I WAS NUMB: no happiness; no sorrow. I changed planes at Kabul and slept most of the way to London. India already seemed like a dream, an interlude of suspended time. The English trees were large and soft; the deep green of autumn oaks. Where was the girl who less than twenty-four hours before had been squatting in front of a mean brick hut in the plains of Uttar Pradesh, scouring her pots with a handful of earth? She was dissolving into the past, a phantom of my imagination. I had lost her and I wanted her back.

Soon after I left the dehra Jungli got the sack. He packed our things into Jatedar's broken metal box and stashed them in the doctor's house – against my advice – for safe keeping. He didn't see them again because the doctor appropriated them for himself.

Back in Amritsar he received news that Pitaji was in hospital, seriously ill. Mataji, also unwell and unable to nurse him, was being cared for at home by the neighbours. Rajinder was slaving for Gurmit in Meerut and Balwant, as usual, was up to no good somewhere. So Jungli went to live in the hospital. He slept on the floor beside Pitaji's bed and tended him week after week while the doctors treated his symptoms and tried to discover their cause. They never did, but Pitaji recovered enough to be able to return to the village. Jungli went with him to look after the household and supervise the cultivation of the family land. For the first time Mataji needed him.

Meanwhile I was living in a seventeenth-century cottage in Herefordshire, with layer upon layer of damp flowery wallpaper obscuring its beams, a cold tap in the scullery, a leaky roof and an Elsan down the garden path. Its simplicity appealed to me. I wanted peace, and I believed I needed privacy and isolation. But in parting from Jungli I had lost my place in a community, and a belonging more tangible than any I had known in the country of my birth. I didn't know I had it till I lost it, and for a while I didn't realize I missed it. But yes, I missed it. The animal in me missed a certain challenge or danger, without which something deep inside that is alert and alive seems to sag and flop. I missed having to defend my territory and fight a bit for survival. I missed the unexpectedness, rawness and immediacy of life at the dehra. And I missed the close contact with the simple things and processes that made up my daily existence.

India had me trapped. Part of me remained there – not at the dehra or anywhere in particular, but in the abstract idea of India. It took six months and a small and beautiful island of green hills and deep blue sea in the West Indies to shatter the spell.

Jungli and I still wrote. I found it increasingly difficult, for less and less of what I was doing had any meaning or relevance to him. He wrote more often, sad sad letters that reawakened my feelings of self-reproach for leaving a man who had been physically and politically unable to accompany me. The letters told me nothing, for they were always about me. He believed I would come back and lived in that hope.

I cannot go back: I can only ever go on. It seemed to me that Jungli and I were no longer being vitalized by each other. His lack of reasoning power made it hard to communicate. His lack of enthusiasm disturbed me, his negative filling of days with sleep. And I was afraid of him. We could never have made each other happy, but my guilt still gnawed at my stomach. I knew with absolute certainty that Jungli would love me until his death.